PEDIATRIC SLEEP PROBLEMS

PEDIATRIC SLEEP PROBLEMS

A Clinician's Guide to Behavioral Interventions

LISA J. MELTZER and
VALERIE McLAUGHLIN CRABTREE

American Psychological Association • Washington, DC

Published by
American Psychological Association
750 First Street, NE
Washington, DC 20002
www.apa.org

To order
APA Order Department
P.O. Box 92984
Washington, DC 20090-2984
Tel: (800) 374-2721; Direct: (202) 336-5510
Fax: (202) 336-5502; TDD/TTY: (202) 336-6123
Online: www.apa.org/pubs/books
E-mail: order@apa.org

In the U.K., Europe, Africa, and the Middle East, copies may be ordered from
American Psychological Association
3 Henrietta Street
Covent Garden, London
WC2E 8LU England

Typeset in Meridien by Circle Graphics, Inc., Columbia, MD

Printer: Maple Press, York, PA
Cover Designer: Mercury Publishing Services, Inc., Rockville, MD

The opinions and statements published are the responsibility of the authors, and such opinions and statements do not necessarily represent the policies of the American Psychological Association.

Library of Congress Cataloging-in-Publication Data

Meltzer, Lisa J., author.
  Pediatric sleep problems : a clinician's guide to behavioral interventions / Lisa J. Meltzer and Valerie McLaughlin Crabtree. — First edition.
      p. ; cm.
  Includes bibliographical references and index.
  ISBN 978-1-4338-1983-4 — ISBN 1-4338-1983-X
  I. Crabtree, Valerie McLaughlin, author. II. American Psychological Association, issuing body. III. Title.
  [DNLM: 1. Sleep Disorders—psychology—Practice Guideline. 2. Adolescent. 3. Behavior Therapy—methods—Practice Guideline. 4. Child. 5. Infant. 6. Sleep Disorders—therapy—Practice Guideline. WM 188]
  RJ506.S55
  618.92'8498—dc23
                        2014043595

British Library Cataloguing-in-Publication Data
A CIP record is available from the British Library.

Printed in the United States of America
First Edition

http://dx.doi.org/10.1037/14645-000

To my family, whose support is unwavering and whose love is unconditional, and to Ari, the light of my life, who has given me many opportunities to practice my clinical sleep recommendations.
—Lisa J. Meltzer

To Keith, who has been the best support a wife could ever ask for, and to Noah and Eli, who love to tell their friends that they shouldn't have TVs in their bedroom because their mom says that isn't good for them.
—Valerie McLaughlin Crabtree

Contents

List of Handouts

Foreword

Behavioral sleep medicine has come a long way in the past 20 years, and a focus on pediatrics has come even farther. A quick search in PsycINFO of the terms *sleep* and *pediatric* finds that as of August 2014, there were 2,458 published articles. Of these, only 206 predate 1995. In contrast, 291 articles were published in 2013 alone.

The increase in publications reflects other major developments. In 2006, the American Academy of Sleep Medicine developed standards of practice guidelines for behavioral treatments of bedtime problems and night wakings. These were the first guidelines about any aspect of pediatric sleep across any medical or psychological organization—and they were about behavioral treatment! A defining moment, in any field, is when there is a critical mass and demand for a conference. The first pediatric sleep medicine conference occurred in 2005. This initial idea has now developed into a well-respected meeting that occurs every other year, with a companion meeting held in an international venue on opposite years by the International Pediatric Sleep Association. As the saying goes, we've come a long way, baby. The publication of this volume, *Pediatric Sleep Problems: A Clinician's Guide to Behavioral Interventions*, is a perfect next step in this journey.

I have been fortunate to have known both authors of the present volume for many years. Dr. Lisa Meltzer worked with me, completing her internship and postdoctoral fellowship at the Sleep Center at the Children's Hospital of Philadelphia. I have also had the great pleasure of collaborating with her over the years. She is a top-notch scientist and a leader in the field. She is currently chair of the Sleep Research Society's Trainee Education Advisory Committee and chairs the Best Practices course at the Pediatric Sleep

Medicine conference. Dr. Valerie Crabtree is also a highly respected academician and leader, whose accomplishments include serving as the secretary/treasurer of the Society of Behavioral Sleep Medicine and representing the psychologist voice on the program committee for the annual Sleep Conference, a meeting attended by more than 5,000 scientists and practitioners in sleep medicine. Both Dr. Meltzer and Dr. Crabtree are master clinicians in pediatric sleep who truly understand the needs of children and their families. In addition, they are two of the very first pediatric specialists certified in behavioral sleep medicine, of which to date there are still very few in the United States, and they have presented numerous clinical workshops and postgraduate courses to psychologists, physicians, nurses, and other health care providers. Their combined expertise and partnership in this project has resulted in an outstanding resource.

Pediatric Sleep Problems: A Clinician's Guide to Behavioral Interventions provides a much-needed resource for practitioners who are involved in treatment of youth of all ages. Drs. Meltzer and Crabtree have done an outstanding job of pulling together all of the tools that pediatric practitioners need to help families. This book presents information on a wide range of sleep issues, from bedtime problems and night wakings to other very common issues, such as sleepwalking, enuresis, and delayed sleep phase. The authors do so in a pragmatic, clinically focused manner, providing the practitioner with background information, assessment techniques, and a range of interventions that can be individually tailored to each child and his/her family. They provide practitioners with the nitty-gritty tools to implement empirically supported interventions. The material presented answers the question we all often ask ourselves after hearing an academic presentation or reading an empirical paper: "But what do you actually do?" Thus, a strength of this book is that it translates the research literature into everyday practice and helps practitioners tailor globally accepted interventions to individual treatment plans. Finally, the inclusion of additional resources and patient handouts completes the package.

This book is intended not only for psychologists and mental health practitioners but also for primary care physicians, pediatricians, nurses, social workers, and other pediatric practitioners. Behavioral interventions are not the sole domain of mental health practitioners; rather, all health care practitioners can use them. As anyone in primary care can attest, sleep concerns are one of the most common concerns raised by parents, especially those of young children.

Finally, it is important to understand that pediatric sleep is not the incredibly narrow specialty that everyone thinks of—it is exactly the opposite. Almost every medical and psychiatric issue has associated sleep issues. A 4-year-old with leukemia, a high school athlete with a concussion, a 5-year-old with autism spectrum disorder, and a 9-year-old with ADHD are all at risk for behaviorally based sleep problems. Add to that the incredibly cute 9-month-old with frequent night wakings and the 15-year-old who can't get up for school, and you have an eclectic array of individuals and families, all experiencing sleep issues. And fortunately, we have the tools and skills to help every single one of them.

Finally, my goal is to educate the world about sleep. As my colleagues and I have stated in an editorial piece, we want to give the gift of a good night's sleep to every child and every family. Please help us in doing so. Ask about sleep. Learn simple tools that families can use that result in a huge improvement in sleep for everyone. You will be surprised at what a difference you can make.

Jodi A. Mindell, PhD
Associate Director, Sleep Center,
Children's Hospital of Philadelphia
Professor and Director of Graduate Psychology,
Saint Joseph's University

Acknowledgments

We are very grateful for the support and encouragement of our mentors and colleagues who along the way have taught us about sleep and have supported us throughout this process. We thank Melissa Smith and Adrienne Mageors for their wonderful assistance with our handouts. We also very much appreciate the editorial assistance of Kristin Avis, Chasity Brimeyer, Sarah Honaker, Niki Jurbergs, Brooklee Lightsey, Lauren Pepa, and Jerlym Porter. At APA Books, we thank Beth Hatch for her review and assistance, and Susan Reynolds for her belief in us and support for this project from the very beginning. We are also incredibly grateful for the guidance and support of Dr. Jodi Mindell, who has provided mentorship throughout our careers, as well as support for this book from conception to completion. Finally, we are so appreciative of the children and families who have allowed us to work with them throughout the years, teaching us how to best help children and their families sleep better. We thank them all very much.

PEDIATRIC SLEEP PROBLEMS

Introduction

Have you ever heard any of the following in your clinical practice?

- "My child is a terrible sleeper."
- "She wakes up several times every single night."
- "Bedtime is a nightmare at our house, it will take at least 1 to 2 hours to get him down."
- "She is afraid of her room and afraid of sleeping, so we just let her sleep with us."
- "He is often late to school because he can't wake up, even with three alarm clocks and us throwing water on him."
- "She has her days and nights mixed up."

If the answer is yes, then this is the book for you. Sleep problems are common in children, with estimates of 25% to 40% of youth experiencing a sleep problem at some point during childhood or adolescence (Mindell & Owens, 2010; Owens, 2005). For children, parents, and families,

http://dx.doi.org/10.1037/14645-001
Pediatric Sleep Problems: A Clinician's Guide to Behavioral Interventions, by L. J. Meltzer and V. M. Crabtree

sleep problems pose a number of issues. Not only is the child not getting enough sleep, which can negatively impact growth, development, learning, and behavior, but parent sleep is also disrupted. Further, family stress is increased at bedtime, when everyone is tired (and parents often want their own quiet time after the kids are asleep), and in the morning, when it is a constant battle to get a child up and going. Thus, it is not surprising that so many families present to clinicians wanting to address these sleep problems.

The good news is that many sleep problems respond quickly to behavioral interventions—including (but not limited to) bedtime problems and night wakings in young children (Mindell, Kuhn, Lewin, Meltzer, & Sadeh, 2006), anxiety (Gordon, King, Gullone, Muris, & Ollendick, 2007a; Simard, Nielsen, Tremblay, Boivin, & Montplaisir, 2008) and enuresis in middle childhood (Glazener, Evans, & Peto, 2005), and insomnia and delayed sleep–wake phase in adolescents (de Bruin, Oort, Bögels, & Meijer, 2014; Schlarb, Liddle, & Hautzinger, 2011; Wyatt, 2011). Treating many behavioral sleep problems is incredibly rewarding, as patients often get better within a short period of time, and families are very appreciative of the treatment advice and support that is given. With a little practice, and the right tools, any clinician can provide behavioral interventions for common sleep problems. We wrote *Pediatric Sleep Problems: A Clinician's Guide to Behavioral Interventions* to provide clinicians the necessary information and tools to address the most commonly seen behavioral sleep problems from infancy through adolescence. Because we know how busy all clinicians are, we designed this guide to be a handy and accessible resource that can be used in all types of clinical practice.

Pediatric Sleep Problems

Although some sleep problems resolve spontaneously, many become chronic. When left untreated, these sleep problems can result in significant daytime impairments (Beebe, 2011; Owens et al., 2014). Insufficient or disrupted sleep in youth negatively impacts mood (including increasing or exacerbating symptoms of psychiatric disorders, e.g., depression and anxiety; Gregory & Sadeh, 2012), behavior (Gruber, Cassoff, Frenette, Wiebe, & Carrier, 2012), social development, academic functioning (e.g., attention, concentration, learning; Beebe, Rose, & Amin, 2010; Gruber, Michaelsen, et al., 2012; Sadeh, Gruber, & Raviv, 2003), and health (e.g., hypertension, weight gain; Beebe et al., 2013; Gangwisch et al., 2010; Hart et al., 2013). However, many common sleep problems are treatable with highly effective behavioral interventions.

In addition to the large number of typically developing children and adolescents with sleep problems, sleep disruption is frequently comorbid with psychiatric, neurodevelopmental, and medical disorders (Ivanenko, Crabtree, & Gozal, 2004; Konofal, Lecendreux, & Cortese, 2010; Lewandowski, Ward, & Palermo, 2011; Reynolds & Malow, 2011). Disrupted sleep is a hallmark feature of mood and anxiety disorders and may be predictive of severe mood disorders. Children with neurodevelopmental disorders, such as autism and attention-deficit/hyperactivity disorder, frequently have difficulties initiating and maintaining sleep, which often can disrupt the sleep of the entire family. In turn, difficulties with sleep can exacerbate challenging behaviors (e.g., inattention, self-regulation) in these populations. Finally, although children and adolescents with chronic medical conditions often have pain, nighttime care needs, and/or nighttime symptom exacerbation that disrupts their sleep, parents often are less strict with the basics of sleep (including a consistent nighttime routine and set bedtime); this can result in deficient or poor-quality sleep and may exacerbate daytime symptoms of their illnesses.

Although sleep problems are common, most health care providers, including psychologists, other mental health professionals, physicians, and nurses, receive very little (if any) training in sleep medicine, let alone pediatric behavioral sleep medicine (Lee et al., 2004; Mindell et al., 2013; Rosen & Zozula, 2000). Only 6% of clinical psychology training programs in the United States and Canada include a didactic course on sleep (Meltzer, Phillips, & Mindell, 2009). Physicians fare no better, with an average of only 4 hours of sleep medicine training (Rosen et al., 1998). Limited information is available for health care providers who want to learn more about pediatric sleep problems, with the available texts focused heavily on the medical side of sleep problems, and treatments for behavioral sleep problems often limited to only one or two chapters. Further, the information provided is heavy on the research and light on the practical application of interventions for behavioral sleep problems.

Drawing from the literature and our own clinical practices, we have presented numerous workshops and postgraduate courses to clinicians from a variety of backgrounds (i.e., physician, nurses, psychologists, social workers). After numerous requests for handouts, standardized treatment guides, and/or recommendations on how to handle the most common sleep issues that present in clinical practice, we decided to write this book for all types of pediatric providers. The purpose of this clinical guide is to provide clinicians with developmentally appropriate information that will enable them to treat commonly seen behavioral sleep problems. This book integrates the most up-to-date treatment approaches for sleep problems in infants, toddlers, children, and adolescents. With a concise format, the book provides clinicians a hands-on guide to behavioral treatments for pediatric sleep problems, with practical information, including

- the presentation, prevalence, and etiology of sleep problems;
- options for different treatment approaches, including considerations across development and for special populations;
- discussions of how and why treatments work;
- step-by-step instructions for implementing treatments;
- examples of what to say to families;
- ways to manage potential pitfalls; and
- treatment handouts for patients/families.

This clinical guide takes the empirically supported treatments in the literature and describes different approaches for how to implement these in your practice. This includes adapting the frontline treatments that clinicians are most likely to use in everyday practice and providing a tailored treatment plan for each individual patient.

It is important to note that this clinical guide is not a comprehensive review of every treatment that has been proposed and/or studied in the literature. Instead, it enables clinicians the flexibility of selecting from among the most common and effective interventions that can be used to address the same presenting problem. This guide is also not focused on the treatment of sleep disorders that primarily require medical interventions, including obstructive sleep apnea (OSA), narcolepsy, and periodic limb movements in sleep. Further, although a brief discussion about pharmacological or other medical interventions for behavioral sleep problems may be provided when appropriate, in general these treatment approaches are also beyond the scope of this book. That said, we believe clinicians will find this book to be a valuable resource for the treatment of behavioral sleep problems that commonly present in pediatric practice.

Overview of the Book

Clinicians have limited time and multiple competing demands. With this in mind, we have organized *Pediatric Sleep Problems: A Clinician's Guide to Behavioral Interventions* in three primary sections to facilitate learning opportunities about sleep and behavioral interventions, clinical basics, and detailed interventions for different presenting problems.

PART I: THE BASICS OF PEDIATRIC BEHAVIORAL SLEEP MEDICINE

Although it may be tempting for readers to simply jump to the treatment section, we strongly recommend starting with the basics of pediatric sleep medicine. This section was designed for all types of clinicians, including mental health providers who have received little (if any) training about typical sleep and sleep disorders; medical providers who have received little (if any) training in behavior theory and behavioral interventions; and all clinicians who have previously not used, or have had limited training in, pediatric behavioral sleep medicine.

Chapter 1 focuses on the basics of pediatric sleep, including the basic building blocks that are essential for all behavioral interventions. We begin the chapter with information about sleep and sleep regulation and then review typical sleep across development. This is followed by a discussion of healthy sleep habits and the critical features of a consistent nighttime routine and set bedtime.

Chapter 2 provides an overview of the most common pediatric sleep disorders, including those that primarily have a medical etiology (e.g., OSA, narcolepsy) and those that have a behavioral etiology (e.g., insomnia). For those new to the field of pediatric sleep, this chapter is essential to understand the different types of sleep disorders, as many children presenting for behavioral sleep issues may also have a comorbid medical sleep disorder (e.g., OSA).

Chapter 3 focuses on behaviorism. Before implementing many of the behavioral interventions outlined in this book, it is important to understand more about the theories behind these treatments. In particular, we review the concepts of behavioral theories in Chapter 3, including how these theories contribute to the development of behavioral sleep problems and how to apply these theories effectively when implementing a behavioral intervention. We review both classical conditioning and operant conditioning, and we provide information on how these theories are related to common pediatric sleep problems.

PART II: CLINICAL BASICS FOR PEDIATRIC BEHAVIORAL SLEEP MEDICINE

The chapters in this part focus on the clinical basics required for treatment implementation, including information on the clinical assessment of sleep and strategies for working with families to increase treatment success.

Chapter 4 provides a step-by-step guide for assessing patients for sleep problems, including detailed questions to ask, information about why it is important to ask these questions, and follow-up prompts for positive responses. Before treatment planning and implementation can begin, clinicians must first have a thorough understanding of the presenting problem. In addition to questions that screen for physiologically based sleep disorders (e.g., OSA), behavioral sleep questions ask about sleep schedules, sleep routines, and psychosocial factors that may be affecting sleep. We also review diagnostic and monitoring tools that may be used in conjunction with the clinical interview.

Chapter 5 considers how sleep problems and treatments impact families, as well as the need to design interventions with a successful goal-oriented approach. Strategies such as motivational interviewing are reviewed. We often joke that we have an almost 100% treatment success rate with certain pediatric behavioral sleep interventions—as long as the patients and families do what we ask. But the truth of the matter is that without patient and parent buy-in, there will be no treatment success. In addition, every patient and family is different, and thus it is essential to tailor interventions that draw on patient/family strengths.

PART III: PRESENTING PROBLEMS

We organized the chapters in Part III by presenting problem for quick and easy reference within a clinical practice. However, pediatric patients often present with more than one issue; thus, a multicomponent intervention is commonly needed. In addition, we present multiple treatment options for each presenting problem, further enabling a tailored intervention. The decision about which treatment to use should be based on a combination of clinician judgment and patient/parent buy-in.

Although some behavioral treatments are best used only in certain age groups, many of the interventions described in this guide can be used across development. That said, certain presenting problems are more common in younger children or in older children. Thus, Part III is loosely organized by age, beginning with sleep problems most commonly seen in young children, namely, sleep-onset associations, bedtime problems (due to stalling, protests, and "curtain calls"), and nighttime awakenings. This is followed by sleep problems most commonly seen in school-age children and adolescents (nighttime fears/anxiety, nightmares, insomnia, and delayed sleep–wake phase), with the last few chapters focused on sleep problems that can present at any age.

Each chapter in Part III starts with an overview of the presenting problem. For each intervention discussed, we present a brief overview of the empirical evidence for different interventions, goals for treatment, and an explanation of the concepts behind how the treatment works. This is followed by a step-by-step guide to implementation, as well as suggestions for how to manage potential pitfalls. When appropriate, modifications for different ages/developmental stages are provided, as well as considerations for special populations and/or contraindications for treatment use. Throughout each treatment chapter, readers will find examples of clinical cases, as well as example scripts for how to explain certain concepts and/or treatments to patients and families. Exhibits within each chapter include some tricks of the trade that we have repeatedly found to be useful in our own clinical practices. Although not empirically validated, these interventions are commonly used in conjunction with empirically supported treatments, providing a comprehensive treatment approach for patients and families.

Chapter 6 focuses on common complaints in infants and toddlers who are in a crib. This includes "my child has never slept through the night" and "he wakes up multiple times every night." Although nighttime awakenings can be seen across development, the treatments provided in Chapter 7 focus primarily on young children who have not learned to fall asleep independently and thus are unable to return to sleep following typical nighttime arousals without parental assistance (e.g., nursing, rocking). In this chapter, it is notable that many of the different treatment options are really variations on a theme (i.e., a child must learn to fall asleep independently). But the adaptation of these options enables the clinician to tailor the intervention for individual families, basing treatment decisions on a combination of the child's temperament and the parent's tolerance for crying.

Chapter 7 addresses the bedtime problems more commonly seen in older children who are no longer in cribs. The presenting complaint is typically a child who has difficulty falling asleep that is accompanied by a prolonged (1–2 hour) bedtime that is frustrating for both the parents and the child. For some families, these bedtime problems end only when parents remain with the child until she is asleep. Along with the different behavioral interventions outlined, instructions for working with parents on how to set limits at bedtime are reviewed.

Like Chapter 7, Chapter 8 focuses on the presenting complaint of a child who has difficulty falling asleep at bedtime. However, Chapter 8 focuses more on older children whose bedtime difficulties stem from fears, anxiety, and/or recurrent nightmares. Treatment approaches in this chapter include both cognitive and behavioral strategies to help the child gain mastery over his or her sleep.

For older children and adolescents, a common presenting problem is difficulty falling asleep, difficulty staying asleep, and/or waking early in the morning and being unable to return to sleep. These are symptoms of insomnia, which is the focus of Chapter 9. The primary treatment discussed in this chapter is cognitive–behavioral therapy for insomnia, with a description of the different components of this approach, namely, stimulus control therapy, sleep restriction therapy, and cognitive restructuring.

The primary complaint for adolescents with delayed sleep–wake phase is a prolonged sleep-onset latency, an inability to fall asleep before a certain time (e.g., 2:00 a.m.–4:00 a.m.), and difficulties waking in the morning for school. Although this may sound similar to insomnia, there are a number of differences in terms of etiology, sleep continuity, and daytime impairment. Thus, the treatments in Chapter 10 focus on realigning adolescents' internal clocks to better match their required daytime schedule.

Chapter 11 focuses on nonrapid eye movement disorders of arousal, namely, confusional arousals, sleep terrors, and sleepwalking. These partial arousal parasomnias often present with complaints about night-time awakenings accompanied with distress or purposeful behaviors, yet the child does not appear fully awake. Detailed instructions about safety and reassurance are presented, along with how and when to implement scheduled awakenings.

Chapter 12 addresses nocturnal enuresis, or nighttime bed-wetting, a relatively common disorder in school-age children, and one that persists for some adolescents. Behavioral treatment approaches outlined include urine alarms (also known as the bell and pad), full spectrum treatment, and scheduled awakenings.

For some children, positive airway pressure (PAP) therapy is required for the treatment of OSA. However, PAP adherence is poor across pediatric patients. The most common reasons for nonadherence include discomfort and a lack of patient/parent understanding or appreciation about the importance and benefits of using PAP daily. Therefore, Chapter 13 focuses on patient education and a multiple component behavioral intervention that includes differential reinforcement, desensitization, and distraction.

Finally, Appendix A provides additional information and resources for both clinicians and families, including details about websites and professional organizations related to the book's content. Appendix B comprises more than 30 handouts that can be used in your clinical practice. These handouts were designed to support the information provided to patients/parents during a clinical visit, including step-by-step instructions or guidance on how to implement many of the treatments described in Part III, a brief rationale for the intervention, and reminders to help families be successful. All of the handouts are also available for free online at http://pubs.apa.org/books/supp/meltzer/.

The Bottom Line

Children should spend up to 40% of their lives sleeping by the age of 18 years. However, for many children, sleep is not as simple as it seems. We wrote this book to help clinicians address the most commonly seen behavioral sleep issues in infants, children, and adolescents. It is designed to be a user-friendly resource for busy clinicians, with a brief description of how different sleep problems present, a basic explanation of how the treatments work, a step-by-step description of how to implement different treatments, and handouts that can be used in a clinical setting.

THE BASICS OF PEDIATRIC BEHAVIORAL SLEEP MEDICINE

I

Typical Sleep Across Development and Healthy Sleep Habits

1

To effectively identify a child or adolescent with a sleep disorder, providers must first be familiar with the basics of sleep, as well as the range of typical sleep in pediatric patients. With a firm understanding of healthy sleep habits, providers can more readily identify those children with problematic sleep.

In this chapter, we review the basics of sleep and development, the two-process model of sleep regulation, and the consequences of not obtaining sufficient sleep. This is followed by a discussion of healthy sleep patterns and developmental changes in sleep across infancy, childhood, and adolescence. We also review ways to promote healthy sleep habits, as well as the importance of a consistent bedtime and bedtime routine for children of all ages.

http://dx.doi.org/10.1037/14645-002
Pediatric Sleep Problems: A Clinician's Guide to Behavioral Interventions, by L. J. Meltzer and V. M. Crabtree

What Is Sleep?

Sleep is a reversible neurobehavioral state of reduced activity associated with a typical posture (i.e., lying down with closed eyes) that results in decreased responsiveness to stimuli (Cirelli & Tononi, 2008). There are a number of competing, yet complementary, theories that try to explain the purpose of sleep (Cirelli & Tononi, 2008; M. G. Frank, 2006; Mignot, 2008). The *adaptive* or *evolutional theory* suggests that inactivity at night is a protective mechanism from nocturnal predators; however, the counterargument suggests that it is safer to remain conscious to react to emergencies. The *energy conservation theory* posits that sleep reduces metabolic rate (e.g., lower body temperature and caloric demand), thereby lowering energy demands. The *restoration theory* proposes that sleep enables the body to repair and restore what is lost during wakefulness. Sleep deprivation in animals results in a loss of immune function and death, and in humans sleep is a time for restorative body functions (e.g., tissue repair, growth hormone release). Finally, the *plasticity theory* posits an essential role for sleep in brain development and has been supported by evidence showing that the location of slow-wave activity visible on electroencephalograms (EEG) is similar to that of brain maturation. For example, the visual cortex is rapidly maturing during early childhood, and slow-wave activity in the visual cortex is at its highest levels during this developmental period. In adolescence, slow-wave activity is most prominent in the frontal cortex, corresponding with the development of executive functioning. Further, the decrease in slow-wave activity during adolescence reflects the synaptic pruning that occurs during this stage of development (Kurth et al., 2012).

Sleep Architecture

There are two distinct stages of sleep: *rapid eye movement* (REM) sleep and *nonrapid eye movement* (NREM) sleep (Carskadon & Dement, 2010). Sleep stages can be determined only by overnight polysomnography, with standardized methods used to score the sleep stages. All humans cycle between REM and NREM sleep. In infants, these cycles last approximately 50 minutes. Throughout childhood the cycles lengthen, reaching maturity around middle childhood, with cycles lasting between 90 and 110 minutes. At the end of each sleep cycle, there is a typical arousal. These are usually very brief in duration, with a rapid return to sleep. On average, children have four to six arousals per night, with a decrease in the number of arousals with development, because of both the increased length of sleep cycles and shorter nocturnal sleep duration (Jenni & Carskadon, 2005).

REM sleep has unique characteristics that make it distinct from all other sleep stages. The features of REM sleep include a significant reduction in muscle tone and episodic bursts of rapid eye movements. Dreaming generally occurs in REM sleep. The first REM period is typically brief (approximately 5 minutes), occurring between 70 and 100 minutes after sleep onset. REM and NREM sleep stages alternate throughout the night, with REM periods increasing in length in the last third of the night. In newborns and young infants, REM sleep is called *active sleep*. Young infants enter sleep through active sleep (unlike older infants, children, and adolescents, who enter sleep through NREM), with active sleep composing approximately 50% of the night for young infants. Throughout development, the amount of REM sleep decreases, accounting for approximately 25% to 30% of the night in children and 20% to 25% of the night in adolescents (Jenni & Carskadon, 2005).

In infants, NREM sleep is called *quiet sleep*. After the first 6 months, NREM sleep is further divided into three distinct stages based on EEG patterns. Stage 1 (N1) sleep is the lightest sleep, occurring at the transition between sleep and wake. The first N1 period is typically brief (less than 5 minutes), and in total N1 accounts for only about 2% to 5% of the night. Stage 2 (N2) includes two characteristic EEG features: sleep spindles (frequent bursts of rhythmic EEG activity) and K-complexes (high-voltage, slow-wave spikes). N2 accounts for the greatest proportion of the night (45%–55%). Stage 3 (N3) is also known as *slow-wave sleep* or *deep sleep*. The distinguishing N3 EEG pattern includes continuous high-voltage, low-frequency activity. N3 sleep primarily occurs in the first third of the night and accounts for approximately 3% to 23% of nocturnal sleep. Early childhood is a time of predominant N3 sleep, with a rapid decrease in slow-wave sleep during adolescence (decline of approximately 50%). N1 sleep has the lowest arousal threshold, meaning it is easiest to wake a child from N1 sleep. N3 sleep has the highest arousal threshold, meaning it is most difficult to wake a child from N3 sleep (Mindell & Owens, 2010).

Several key facts about sleep architecture are important to remember when diagnosing and treating behavioral sleep problems in pediatric patients.

- Nocturnal arousals are normal. Although typically followed by a rapid return to sleep, a number of behavioral issues arise if children are unable to fall asleep independently at bedtime, requiring assistance to return to sleep following typical nocturnal arousals. Along the same lines, children who have significant nighttime fears or anxiety, or adolescents who have insomnia, may fully awaken following typical nocturnal arousals.

- Sleep cycles last between 50 and 110 minutes (depending on age). Many parents will complain that their child wakes "every hour on the hour." As explained in the previous point, this is in fact true with typical arousals occurring at the end of each sleep cycle. Thus, it is often helpful to reassure parents that their perception may be accurate but not necessarily problematic if the child is able to return to sleep relatively quickly and independently.

- Slow-wave sleep primarily occurs in the first third of the night. NREM disorders of arousals or partial arousal parasomnias (confusional arousals, sleep terrors, and sleepwalking) primarily occur with slow-wave sleep; thus, they are most commonly seen in the first part of the night.

- REM sleep increases over the night, with most in the last third of the night. Unlike NREM disorders of arousal, which occur in the first third of the night, nightmares (which occur during REM sleep) are most likely to be seen in the last third of the night. The timing of nightmares (vs. disorders of arousal) is one of the primary features used in a differential diagnosis.

- Recovery sleep following sleep loss can affect the frequency of parasomnias. If children have not obtained sufficient sleep the previous night (or over the previous several nights), when they do sleep more, they are likely to have what is called *recovery sleep*. With recovery sleep, the child is more likely to have more N3 the first night following sleep loss and to have more REM sleep the second night following sleep loss. As a result, children who have a history of partial arousal parasomnias may have an increase in symptoms the first night following sleep loss, whereas children with nightmares may be more likely to experience an increase in nightmares the second night following sleep loss.

- Sleepiness upon awakening depends on the duration of sleep and stage of sleep on awakening. Of course, if children have not obtained adequate sleep, they will be sleepy upon awakening. Amount of sleepiness also depends, however, on the stage of sleep on awakening. If a child awakens spontaneously, she likely is awakening from N1 sleep. If a parent awakens a child who is in REM sleep or N3 sleep, the child may be very difficult to awaken and feel very sleepy.

Two-Process Model of Sleep Regulation

Sleep is regulated by biological and behavioral factors that dynamically interact with one another. The biological two-process model of sleep regulation is used to describe the interaction between the sleep/

wake–dependent *Process S* (also known as *sleep homeostasis*) and the circadian timing of sleep and waking known as *Process C* (Achermann & Borbély, 2010; Borbély, 1982).

Process S (the pressure to sleep, or sleep need) has been shown to be very high in the first part of the night, decreasing with sleep. Process S is thus dependent on hours of wakefulness and hours of sleep. Pressure for sleep increases the longer a person is awake, whereas it rapidly decreases overnight (or with naps, in the case of younger children). The pressure or need for sleep changes across development. For example, sleep loss tolerance in newborns is low, thus they cannot maintain consolidated periods of wakefulness, resulting in brief episodes of sleep and wake that cycle around the 24-hour clock (Jenni, Deboer, & Achermann, 2006). As children get older, sleep loss tolerance increases, with the need for a daytime nap tapering off between the ages of 3 and 5 years. In addition, in middle childhood (6–11 years) and adolescence (12–18 years), there is a further increase in sleep loss tolerance, resulting in a later bedtime for many youth. It is important to note that individual differences are seen in Process S, whereby some children have less sleep pressure than others, resulting in an increased tendency toward difficulty falling asleep.

In Process C, the endogenous circadian pacemaker located in the suprachiasmatic nuclei creates a sleep–wake rhythm that is independent of sleep and wake duration. Newborns have no circadian rhythm (or internal clock) until approximately 12 weeks of age (Jenni & Carskadon, 2005). The lack of a circadian rhythm results in a polyphasic sleep pattern, with equal periods of sleep and wake across a 24-hour period. In middle childhood, the circadian phase preference (i.e., morning lark or night owl) begins to emerge. For adolescents, there is a correlation between pubertal stage and dim light melatonin onset (DLMO) time, commonly resulting in a delayed circadian phase (i.e., adolescents are unable to fall asleep early because their internal clock is set to fall asleep and wake up 1 to 2 hours later than in childhood; Carskadon, Acebo, Richardson, Tate, & Seifer, 1997). The circadian rhythm is regulated by a number of external cues (called *zeitgebers*, or time givers), with the light–dark cycle being the most prominent. Melatonin, a hormone that is secreted by the pineal gland, is triggered by dim light. Melatonin is the most essential hormone in regulating the sleep–wake cycle, and its release triggers the body to begin to feel sleepy, with release typically occurring 2 hours before sleep onset. Bright light, on the other hand, suppresses melatonin. Because people's circadian rhythm functions on a cycle longer than 24 hours, zeitgebers are crucial to maintain an effective circadian rhythm. Additional zeitgebers, such as meal times and social activities, are important in entraining circadian rhythm. Similar to individual differences in Process S, individuals vary in Process C, leading some to be more prone to circadian disruption and circadian rhythm sleep–wake disorders.

For most people, Process S and Process C work together to provide wakefulness during the day and consolidated sleep during the night. During the day, as homeostatic sleep pressure builds, the circadian rhythm helps maintain wakefulness. Overnight, as homeostatic sleep pressure rapidly decreases, the circadian rhythm helps maintain sleep. In the morning, the high level of sleepiness that results from the circadian rhythm is counterbalanced by a lack of homeostatic sleep pressure.

Understanding the two-process model is important for clinicians making differential diagnoses (e.g., delayed sleep–wake phase vs. insomnia). Further, these biological processes are sensitive to behaviors that children and adolescents may engage in during the day that interfere with sleep at night. Thus, after educating patients about the two-process model of sleep, clinicians may find it useful to provide patients and parents with additional information.

For example, it may be helpful to inform patients and parents that napping may interfere with sleep onset by alleviating sleep pressure. As described later in this chapter, naps are appropriate in younger children. However, for children and adolescents who regularly nap and present with difficulties falling asleep, naps may be disrupting their homeostatic sleep pressure. Essentially, the nap is killing off the sleep pressure, making it more difficult to fall asleep at bedtime.

It may also be helpful to inform patients and parents that significant sleep issues arise when sleep schedules differ on weeknights and weekend nights. When children and adolescents stay up late and sleep in on weekends, the result is *social jet lag* (Wittmann, Dinich, Merrow, & Roenneberg, 2006). The intersection between rapidly changing circadian timing and a reduced homeostatic sleep pressure will make sleep onset incredibly difficult on Sunday night and waking up even harder on Monday morning. The following is one example of how to explain social jet lag to patients/parents.

> Everyone has an internal clock; you've noticed yours when daylight saving time occurs in March and we spring forward an hour. For a couple of days, the wall clock will tell you it is time to go to sleep, but your internal clock is simply not ready to sleep yet. But with only a 1-hour time change, it only takes a couple of days to adjust.
>
> Now let's imagine you are going to travel across time zones, from New York to California, where it is 3 hours earlier than you are used to [show a map if needed]. On Friday afternoon, you travel west, and when you land it is only 8:00 p.m. and your friends want to go out to dinner. Although it is 11:00 p.m. on the East Coast, you manage to stay awake and have fun, going to bed at 12:00 a.m. West Coast time. This doesn't seem late, although it is already 3:00 a.m. on the East Coast. You sleep until maybe 9:00 a.m. West Coast time (which is 12:00 p.m. on the East Coast). Saturday night you go out again, going to bed around 12:00 a.m. West Coast time and waking at 9:00 a.m.

Then you travel back to the East Coast, where the clocks are 3 hours later. So when you try to go to bed at 11:00 p.m. Sunday night, your body doesn't feel sleepy because it is only 8:00 p.m. on the West Coast. Also, you've been awake for only 11 hours, which is not long enough to build up the necessary sleep pressure to fall asleep. So you don't get enough sleep Sunday night, and waking up on Monday morning is really hard! It takes several nights for your internal clock to get back on track, as well as for you to catch up on your sleep, and then guess what? It is Friday night and you start the cycle all over again. When you stay up late on the weekends, you are basically shifting your internal clock to West Coast time every week.

Consequences of Insufficient Sleep

It is common for children and adolescents to obtain insufficient sleep, meaning they do not get enough sleep to function optimally. One national survey in the United States found that most parents believe that their child is not getting enough sleep (Mindell, Meltzer, Carskadon, & Chervin, 2009; National Sleep Foundation, 2004). Specifically, 50% of parents reported that their infants were getting enough sleep, yet only 34% of parents reported so for toddlers, 32% for preschoolers, and 25% for school-age children were obtaining as much sleep as they needed. Another national survey in the United States reported that more than half of adolescents ages 13 through 18 were taking naps on school days to "make up" for not getting enough sleep at night (National Sleep Foundation, 2011). Overall, 60% of teenagers surveyed were getting less than 8 hours of sleep per night. Close to one half reported that they rarely or never get a good night's sleep on school nights; 60% said they often wake up feeling unrefreshed; and 20% reported excessive daytime sleepiness.

Insufficient nighttime sleep is related to many problems during the day. Thus, the significant proportion of children and adolescents who are chronically enduring insufficient nighttime sleep is concerning and problematic (Beebe, 2011; Owens et al., 2014). Children and adolescents who do not get enough sleep or have poor-quality sleep have been shown to have more difficulty regulating their behavior (Gruber, Cassoff, Frenette, Wiebe, & Carrier, 2012). As a result, sleepy children and adolescents may be far more likely to have temper tantrums or to be aggressive, inattentive, hyperactive, impulsive, and/or depressed and anxious (Gruber, Michaelsen, et al., 2012; O'Brien, 2009). Extending the amount of sleep that children and adolescents receive has been shown to result in improved behavior and mood, providing good support for using behavioral interventions to address children's sleep problems (Dewald-Kaufmann, Oort, & Meijer, 2013; Gruber, Casoff, et al., 2012).

In addition to poorer behavior and mood associated with insufficient sleep, children with insufficient or disrupted sleep are more likely to have trouble with learning and thinking. In particular, children with insufficient sleep are more likely to have problems with memory and executive functioning, both of which are essential to successful academic achievement (Beebe et al., 2010; Sadeh et al., 2003). Many studies have shown that children and adolescents with poor sleep are more likely to have poor grades and to have failed a grade in school (Asarnow, McGlinchey, & Harvey, 2014; de Carvalho et al., 2013). Allowing children to sleep longer at night has been shown to improve memory, attention, and school grades (Gruber, Casoff, et al., 2012; Sadeh et al., 2003).

Finally, sleep is important to health and immune functioning. Studies have shown that insufficient or disrupted sleep is a risk factor for hypertension, hypercholesterolemia, insulin resistance, and obesity (Bhushan et al., 2014; Flint et al., 2007; Gangwisch et al., 2010; Javaheri, Storfer-Isser, Rosen, & Redline, 2011; Schmid, Hallschmid, & Schultes, 2014). In addition, children who do not get enough sleep at night may be more susceptible to illnesses such as the common cold (Cohen, Doyle, Alper, Janicki-Deverts, & Turner, 2009). Taken together, to promote optimal development, health, and well-being, as well as to provide children with the greatest chance for effective home and school functioning, clinicians need to address insufficient sleep for children of all ages.

Typical Sleep Across Development

Sleep changes rapidly across development. With each developmental stage, children have different physiological sleep needs. In addition, the frequency and amount of different sleep stages changes with age (as previously described). Further, sleep patterns are affected by different intrinsic and extrinsic factors as children get older. Finally, the presentation and treatment of sleep problems also varies by age (Crabtree & Williams, 2009).

One of the most common, yet challenging, questions that parents ask is, How much sleep do children require? The National Sleep Foundation provides the following recommended ranges of sleep duration in a 24-hour period for each developmental stage:

- newborns (0–2 months): 12–18 hours;
- infants (3–11 months): 14–15 hours;

- toddlers (1–3 years): 12–14 hours;
- preschoolers (3–5 years): 11–13 hours;
- school-age children (6–11 years): 10–11 hours; and
- adolescents (12–18 years): 8.5–9.5 hours.

That said, multiple studies have shown that sleep looks more like a growth curve, with significant variability at each age (Galland, Taylor, Elder, & Herbison, 2012; Iglowstein, Jenni, Molinari, & Largo, 2003). Most children will fall within the recommended ranges outlined above, but some children may need more sleep and some may need less sleep.

When clinicians work with families, although it is important to consider the actual amount of sleep a child is getting, it is equally important to assess whether the child is getting the right amount of sleep for him. The following are signs that a child or adolescent is getting insufficient sleep.

- Needs to be awakened in the morning and is not able to get going within 15 minutes.
- On weekends or vacations, sleeps at least 2 hours per night more than on school nights.
- Falls asleep in school, during short daytime car rides (e.g., 10 or 15 minutes on the way to the library or grocery store), or at other inappropriate times (e.g., attending a sporting event, participating in an after-school activity).
- Behavior and/or mood is notably different following nights of increased sleep.

Following is a more detailed discussion of sleep needs for typically developing children.

INFANCY (0–12 MONTHS)

Infants show significant changes in their sleep patterns and structure across the first year of life. Within the first weeks of life, infants will spend approximately two thirds of their time asleep and have multiple periods of sleep and wake throughout a 24-hour period. These periods typically last 50 minutes each and repeat in cycles throughout the day and night. Over the course of infancy, a circadian rhythm develops in which infants begin to respond more to light/dark and environmental cues to indicate periods of wakefulness and sleep. As the circadian rhythm becomes more established, infants begin to sleep more at night and have more periods of wakefulness during the day, much to parents' relief. Although most 2-week-old infants will continuously sleep for 4 hours at the most, a 5-month-old infant may sleep up to 7 hours in one bout. Between 6 and 9 months of age, sleep consolidates, with most infants sleeping longer stretches at night, resulting in a total of 10 to 12 hours of nighttime sleep and two to three daytime naps (Anders,

Halpern, & Hua, 1992). By the age of 1 year, most infants will take two naps per day, with fewer and shorter nighttime awakenings (So, Adamson, & Horne, 2007). Variability in total sleep time is perhaps greater in infancy than at any other developmental period, with some infants sleeping 12 hours in a 24-hour period, whereas others sleep 18 hours in a 24-hour period. By the first birthday, the typical difference between infants in total sleep time narrows to between 14 and 15 hours in a 24-hour period (Iglowstein et al., 2003).

With rapid development comes rapid changes to sleep, as well as factors that influence (or interrupt) sleep. The most significant influence on newborn sleep is typically hunger, with the infant sleep–wake cycle driven by the need to eat frequently. Breast-fed infants commonly sleep shorter stretches, as breast milk digests faster than formula. Between 6 and 9 months, even the best sleeper tends to have disrupted sleep because of typical child development, including sitting up, rolling over, and pulling to standing. In addition, as growth hormone is released during sleep, teeth literally grow during sleep. Thus, teething pain can regularly disrupt infant sleep quality. Studies have also shown an association between sleep disruptions and motor development in infants, in particular learning to crawl and walk (Scher, 2005; Scher & Cohen, 2005). Sleep problems in this age group are primarily linked to difficulties initiating and maintaining sleep independently (e.g., without being nursed or rocked to sleep). Safe sleeping practices are also critical for infants (see Exhibit 1.1).

EXHIBIT 1.1

Safe Sleeping for Infants

The Back to Sleep campaign, which promoted placing infants on their backs for sleeping, was one of the most successful public health campaigns, reducing the rate of sudden infant death syndrome (SIDS) by approximately 50%. In 2011, the American Academy of Pediatrics revised and expanded its recommendations for a safe infant sleeping environment to prevent SIDS and other sleep-related infant deaths (Task Force on Sudden Infant Death Syndrome, 2011). These recommendations include

- placing an infant on her back to sleep;
- providing a firm sleep surface (preferably a crib) that does not include soft bedding (including bumpers);
- routine immunizations;
- breast feeding;
- room sharing, not bed sharing;
- pacifier use to facilitate initial sleep onset;
- avoidance of overheating; and
- avoidance of exposure to tobacco smoke, alcohol, and illicit drugs.

In 2012, the Back to Sleep campaign was renamed Safe to Sleep to highlight the importance of a safe sleeping environment in addition to back sleeping to prevent SIDS and other sleep-related causes of infant death.

TODDLER/PRESCHOOL PERIOD (1–5 YEARS)

Sleep across a 24-hour period is relatively stable for children in the pre-school period, with most toddlers (1–3 years) sleeping 12 to 14 hours in a 24-hour period, although preschoolers (4–5 years) sleep on average 11 to 13 hours in a 24-hour period. Getting more daytime sleep during naps, however, will typically result in less nighttime sleep, with children maintaining a relatively constant amount of sleep across the day and night. Thus, if a 3-year-old child takes a 2-hour nap each day, he is likely to then sleep 10 hours at night; whereas if a similar-age child takes only a 30-minute nap, he is more likely to sleep 11.5 hours during the night.

Daytime sleep declines substantially across the first 3 years of life. Although most 3-year-olds (~92%) take one nap per day, many children will stop napping between the ages of 4 and 5. However, approximately one of four children are still napping at the age of 5. Several factors influence the likelihood of preschool-age children to nap, including day care schedules, developmental expectations of parents, cultural differences, and individual differences in sleep needs/patterns. For example, African American children have been reported to continue napping until a much later age than Caucasian children, with the majority of African American children still napping at age 6, and 40% still napping at age 8 (Crosby, LeBourgeois, & Harsh, 2005).

Recent research has also shown the early influence of the two-process model of sleep in toddlers and preschoolers (LeBourgeois, Carskadon, et al., 2013; LeBourgeois, Wright, et al., 2013). In particular, DLMO appears to affect the timing of nighttime sleep onset for many young children. As a result, parents may attempt to put children to bed either too early or too late to be consistent with their circadian biology, which may result in bedtime struggles. In addition, napping may alleviate homeostatic sleep pressure, significantly interfering with the ability for young children to fall asleep at night. Together, these factors can contribute to prolonged bedtime battles.

Although toddlerhood and the preschool years are typically associated with fewer nighttime awakenings than infancy, most children in this age range continue to have at least 1 nighttime awakening per week in which they will alert their parents to being awake. How troublesome these nighttime awakenings are is highly dependent on the child's ability to return to sleep independently without requiring the parent's presence.

Preschool-age children experience a significant number of sleep issues. This is the peak age for obstructive sleep apnea, due to enlarged tonsils and adenoids (see Chapter 2, this volume, for more information). This is also the peak age for disorders of arousal or partial arousal parasomnias (i.e., sleep terrors, sleepwalking). Finally, increased independence often results in more bedtime struggles, whereas developing cognitive skills results in increased nighttime fears.

SCHOOL-AGE PERIOD (6–11 YEARS)

Most school-age children need 10 to 11 hours of sleep, but on average obtain approximately 8 to 10 hours per night. For most children, sleep occurs during the nighttime hours with naps a rare occurrence. As previously described, the circadian preference begins to emerge for many children in middle childhood. For those with night-owl tendencies (difficulties falling asleep early), bedtimes are often delayed. When paired with early rise times due to school schedules, the result is insufficient sleep. For example, children in sixth grade have been found to have bedtimes that are 45 minutes later, on average, than second graders, resulting in nearly an hour less sleep than their younger peers (National Sleep Foundation, 2004). Compared with younger children, older school-age children are also more likely to report feeling sleepy in the morning, and their parents are more likely to say that they are likely to fall asleep unintentionally (Sadeh, Raviv, & Gruber, 2000). This pattern of older children sleeping less than younger children tends to be apparent during the school week and absent on the weekends, when older children are more likely to sleep later in the morning. Thus, although many children sleep less as they age, this is more likely due to staying up later while needing to awaken early for school rather than a true decreased need for sleep in older children in comparison to younger children.

The most common sleep problems seen in school-age children are related to difficulties initiating sleep because of anxiety and nighttime fears. Nocturnal enuresis also continues to be an issue in approximately 10% of 6-year-olds, 5% of 10-year-olds, and 3% of 12-year-olds. This is often a very surprising fact for both children and their parents.

ADOLESCENTS (12–18 YEARS)

Adolescence is a period of significant change in sleep timing and sleep duration. These changes are due to the collision of biologically driven changes to sleep with academic, social, and extracurricular demands, as well as early school start times (Carskadon, 2011; M. Moore & Meltzer, 2008). Although many parents believe that adolescents stay up late to engage in social activities, changes to the timing of DLMO and the circadian rhythm also contribute to biologically driven later bedtimes and preferred wake times. In addition, later bedtimes can often result from homework, extracurricular or social activities, and/or part-time employment (Wolfson & Carskadon, 1998). When the resulting later bedtimes are paired with early rise times (due to early school start times), adolescents obtain on average only 7.5 hours of sleep during the week, despite the physiological need for 8.5 to 9.5 hours per night. In addition, less weekday sleep builds a sleep debt that will often result in much longer sleep periods on the weekend (Crowley, Acebo, & Carskadon, 2007), which can be highly disruptive to both the circadian rhythm and homeostatic sleep pressure (resulting in the previously described social jet lag). To reduce some of this sleep debt, some adolescents may benefit from a short (45 minutes or so) nap immediately after returning home from school. This should not be used, however, in adolescents who have difficulty falling asleep at bedtime after napping or for adolescents with insomnia.

For adolescents, the most common sleep problem is insufficient sleep. However, many adolescents also experience difficulties initiating and maintaining sleep that can be attributed to insomnia, a behavioral sleep issue in which the adolescent develops an inability to fall asleep or stay asleep because of heightened arousal around sleep and/or a delayed circadian phase, making it difficult for an adolescent to fall asleep at an early desired bedtime.

One issue of particular concern to adolescents is early school start times, which are common in the United States, with some starting as early as 7:00 a.m. This is clearly inconsistent with adolescents' naturally delayed circadian rhythm and has an even greater impact on teens with delayed sleep–wake phase. The Adolescent Sleep Working Group, Committee on Adolescence, and Council on School Health (2014) has called for all middle schools and high schools to start no earlier than 8:30 a.m. to enable students to obtain 8.5 to 9.5 hours of sleep. Although national movements (e.g., Start School Later) are working to change school start times, a number of social and political factors have prevented widespread adoption of these changes. First, as buses are used for all schools in one district, it is not possible for all schools to start later (and many parents do not want to put their 7-year-old at the bus stop at 6:30 a.m. in the dark but do not mind sending their 15-year-old out in the dark). Second, after school, older children may not require child care, whereas additional arrangements for child care are needed for younger children (or the older children have previously cared for the young children). Therefore, it is challenging to have school schedules in which younger children would return home from school before high school students. Third, it can be challenging to schedule after-school sports when one school gets out at 2:30 and another not until 4:00. Additionally, many schools rent out their sports fields in the evenings as a way to raise money. As a result, the schools need their own students to be finished practicing.

Despite the potential difficulties with moving school start times later, some districts have seen positive benefits. Across the country, school districts that have delayed high school start time to 8:30 a.m. or later have seen several notable benefits for the teens, including more sleep, improved grades, improved standardized test scores, better attendance and graduation rates, fewer tardies, less substance abuse, fewer symptoms of depression, and fewer motor vehicle accidents (up to 70% fewer in one state). Despite skeptics who say teens will just stay up later with later school start times, multiple studies have demonstrated that only wake times change, resulting in increased sleep duration for teens (Wahlstrom et al., 2014).

Healthy Sleep Habits

Of course, every infant, toddler, child, and adolescent (and adult, for that matter) should follow healthy sleep habits to promote overall mental and physical well-being. Establishing healthy sleep habits from a young age can help prevent many behavioral sleep problems that can emerge over time. As parents are helping their children establish healthy sleep habits, the child's sleep routine and sleep environment are important factors. As sleep habits can be ingrained, maintaining a consistent pre-bedtime routine and sleep promoting sleep environment are essential.

Clinicians should be mindful of the influence of culture and family values on the sleep environment of children. Because of safety issues (described in Exhibit 1.1), parents should not share a bed or other sleeping space with infants (although room sharing is encouraged until sometime between 6 weeks and 12 months of age). However, for families who make a conscious decision to cosleep with their children the entire night (also known as *proactive cosleeping* or *the family bed*), this can be maintained safely and effectively if done so in a consistent fashion. *Reactive cosleeping,* in which parents initially put the child in his own bed, intending for him to sleep the whole night there, but then bring the child to their bed (or allow their child to move to their bed during the night), tends to be problematic for families, especially when parents disagree about this choice, and/or restless sleeping children regularly disrupt parental sleep. Before successfully implementing any of the interventions in Part III, it is essential that healthy sleep habits be in place. If not, these should be the first steps for any behavioral sleep treatment. Handout 1 provides parents with detailed information on healthy sleep habits.

CONSISTENT SLEEP SCHEDULE, EVERY SINGLE NIGHT

Just as brushing and flossing is the cardinal rule of dental hygiene, the most important rule of healthy sleep habits is to maintain a similar bedtime and wake time 7 days a week. Ideally, bedtimes and wake times on the weekends and during school breaks should be no more than 1 hour later than during the school week. The maintenance of a consistent sleep schedule enables the circadian rhythm and sleep homeostasis to remain in balance, facilitating greater sleep quantity and quality. Inconsistent sleep schedules, on the other hand, can result in difficulty initiating sleep, bedtime battles, difficulty waking in the morning on school days, and daytime sleepiness during the school week.

CHOOSE AN AGE-APPROPRIATE BEDTIME

For most school-age children and adolescents, the bedtime will be dependent on the required wake-up time for school. This is also often the case for infants, toddlers, and preschoolers who attend day care or preschool. In these cases, understanding the sleep need is essential to determining the bedtime. For example, if a 6-year-old child must awaken at 7:00 a.m. to attend school, then she would likely require a bedtime between 8:00 and 9:00 p.m. For the most part, preadolescent children benefit from having a bedtime earlier than 9:00 p.m. (Mindell, Meltzer, et al., 2009). A 16-year-old who must awaken at 6:00 a.m. for school should have a bedtime at approximately 9:30 p.m. Some teens will have a delayed circadian rhythm (even if not a delayed sleep–wake phase disorder) and may require a bedtime between 10:00 and 11:00 p.m. if they are unable to fall asleep earlier. For infants and toddlers who do not have a required awakening time in the morning, the bedtime should be sufficiently early to avoid the forbidden zone when a child becomes overtired. For most infants and toddlers, this will mean a bedtime between 7:00 and 9:00 p.m., depending on the family's preference and scheduling.

IMPLEMENT A CONSISTENT BEDTIME ROUTINE

Before bed, parents should create a bedtime routine (usually no more than three to five steps) that is simple and easy to implement yet prepares the child for bed. Bedtime routines alone can be important zeitgebers in maintaining the circadian rhythm. Ideally, the end of the routine should occur in the child's bedroom (e.g., singing a song to the child in bed) to help him with the transition to bed. In infancy, parents should remove feeding from sleep onset. Rather, it is useful to encourage parents to feed the infant outside the child's room before starting the process of diaper changing, rocking, and so on, to disassociate feeding with sleep onset. Infants should be placed in bed drowsy yet not fully asleep to help them learn to fall asleep without the direct assistance of parents. Toddlers and preschoolers may respond well to a pre-bedtime routine that consists of a bath, brushing teeth, reading a favorite story, saying prayers, singing a song, or recalling one favorite event of the day. As children age, bedtime preparation can become increasingly independent. School-age children may begin reading stories aloud to their parents, and adolescents may choose to read independently for 10 to 15 minutes.

CREATE A CONSISTENT SLEEP ENVIRONMENT

To promote healthy sleep habits, clinicians should encourage parents to maintain a consistent sleep environment all night, every night. Because all children will have times when they naturally awaken during the night, parents should bear in mind that the sleep environment should be the same throughout the night as it was when the child fell asleep, helping her return to sleep independently. Much as adults will seek their pillow that has fallen off of the bed during a spontaneous awakening, children will seek the parent who had been lying with them at the beginning of the night (or rocking them to sleep, breast feeding them to sleep, etc.), and is no longer there. We often recommend that parents imagine what they would like their children's room to look like at 2:00 in the morning and make every effort to recreate that at bedtime—lighting (e.g., nightlight vs. no light), sound (silence, fan, white noise machine), presence/absence of parent, stuffed animals, and so on. If children are taught to fall asleep independently, they will be far more likely to return to sleep independently and not require their parents' help to do so.

HAVE TECHNOLOGY-FREE BEDTIME ROUTINES AND BEDROOMS

Electronic devices should be strongly discouraged at bedtime, and television viewing and/or video game playing should end at least 1 hour before bedtime to allow for a period of relaxation, reduced light exposure and reduced stimulation before sleep. In particular, light emitted from electronic devices may suppress melatonin secretion (Wood, Rea, Plitnick, & Figueiro, 2013), making it even more difficult for children and adolescents to fall asleep. For technology that is used in the evening, it is important to limit the light emitted from these devices (see Exhibit 1.2). For

---

EXHIBIT 1.2

Strategies to Reduce Light Exposure

Because bright light is known to suppress melatonin late in the day, it is important to limit light exposure as much as possible. Although this is important for every member of the family, this is especially true for older children and adolescents who engage in screen time (whether for homework or free time) after dinner. The following are ways to reduce the amount of late-day light exposure.

- Encourage the use of floor lamps or other smaller lights rather than bright overhead lights throughout the house.
- Change the brightness setting on computer screens, tablets, and other handheld devices to the lowest possible setting.
- Download an application (for both computers and handheld devices) that automatically dims the screen on the basis of the clock time of the device.
- When using any programs with bright white screens (e.g., word processing, electronic books), change the settings so there is a black background with white text.
- Add a removable blue light filter to any type of screen.
- Wear sunglasses or orange-tinted safety glasses.

---

all children and adolescents (and adults for that matter), it is important to remove technology from the bedroom. One suggestion is for parents to create a charging station in the kitchen for all tablets, cell phones, and other electronic devices for every member of the family. However, many adolescents use their cell phones as alarms, so provisions should be made for eliminating phone calls and text messaging at night. Phone carriers typically have a feature that enables parents to limit the times of day that calls or text messages may be placed or received, thereby enabling the adolescent to obtain uninterrupted sleep. Alternatively, families should invest in inexpensive alarm clocks to be used so that phones can be removed completely from the bedroom.

LIMIT CAFFEINE INTAKE

It is recommended that children and adolescents not consume any caffeine. That said, caffeinated beverages and products are becoming more and more accessible to youth, with the amount and timing of caffeine likely interfering with sleep. Children and their parents need to be educated about the half-life of caffeine (4–6 hours) so they can better understand the reasoning behind limiting caffeinated beverages in the afternoon and evening hours. In addition, children and their parents may need to be reminded about what products do and do not contain caffeine (e.g., many parents are surprised to learn that iced tea has caffeine).

Bottom Line

Sleep in infancy, childhood, and adolescence is a constantly changing developmental process. Although young infants sleep indiscriminately throughout the day and night, healthy developmental changes in sleep result in consolidated nighttime sleep, and over time no daytime napping. Insufficient or disrupted sleep can result in many daytime problems, including problems with overall health, learning, behavior, and mood. Healthy sleep habits, including an age-appropriate bedtime, a regular bedtime routine, and a consistent sleep schedule are the essential building blocks needed before implementing any intervention.

Common Pediatric Sleep Problems

2

Pediatric providers should be familiar with both medically based and behaviorally based sleep problems. Providers should know how to recognize signs of medical sleep disorders so that appropriate referrals can be made. Generally, medical sleep disorders should be treated first by the child's primary care physician or sleep physician before implementing interventions for behavioral sleep disturbances. In this chapter, we review the more common medical sleep disorders in children, as well as the typical behaviorally based sleep disturbances for which treatments are described later in the book.

Common Pediatric Medical Sleep Disorders

Although the focus of this book is on sleep problems that can be treated with behavioral and cognitive–behavioral interventions, it is also important for clinicians to understand

http://dx.doi.org/10.1037/14645-003
Pediatric Sleep Problems: A Clinician's Guide to Behavioral Interventions, by L. J. Meltzer and V. M. Crabtree

common sleep disorders outside the scope of this book. As described below, children who present with signs and symptoms of obstructive sleep apnea (OSA), restless-legs syndrome (RLS), periodic limb movement disorder (PLMD), or narcolepsy should be referred to a sleep specialist or physician for a thorough examination and sleep evaluation. Once the medical issues are addressed, the behavioral strategies included in this book can be highly effective in improving children's (and their parents') sleep.

OBSTRUCTIVE SLEEP APNEA

Although previously OSA had been seen as a disorder that occurred only in obese adults, in recent years it has become more widely recognized in children. OSA is defined as an obstruction of the upper airway during sleep; this may be either a partial obstruction that occurs over a prolonged period and/or a complete obstruction that occurs for a briefer period (American Academy of Sleep Medicine [AASM], 2014). These upper airway obstructions result in poor oxygenation and disrupted sleep. Signs and symptoms of OSA include the following:

- frequent, loud snoring;
- breathing pauses;
- gasping for air;
- sleeping in unusual positions (e.g., propped up or with the neck extended in an attempt to keep the upper airway open);
- excessive sweating during sleep; and
- sore throat, dry mouth, and/or headache in the morning.

Children may also have daytime sleepiness, although more commonly they experience behavior problems (e.g., hyperactivity) and/or learning difficulties.

Although up to 6% of children are reported by their parents to "always" snore, diagnostic studies reveal that between 1% and 4% of children have documented OSA (Lumeng & Chervin, 2008). The preschool and early school-age period is associated with increased risk of OSA due to enlarged tonsils and adenoids, with later childhood and adolescent OSA more commonly due to obesity. OSA tends to be more prevalent in boys and African American children, as well as children with craniofacial abnormalities that result in a narrowing of the upper airway (AASM, 2014).

Children and adolescents who present with signs and symptoms of OSA should be referred either to their primary care physician or a sleep physician for a physical examination and evaluation (Marcus et al., 2012). The gold standard for diagnosing OSA is an overnight polysomnography (PSG), which should be performed in an AASM-accredited sleep center that is experienced in conducting PSG in children (see the

Resources section for more information). Treatment typically consists of adenotonsillectomy for children with enlarged tonsils and adenoids, weight loss for obese youth, and/or positive airway pressure devices to maintain an open airway during sleep.

RESTLESS-LEGS SYNDROME AND PERIODIC LIMB MOVEMENT DISORDER

RLS (also known as Willis–Ekbom disease) and PLMD frequently co-occur. Both are associated with frequent/repetitive leg movements; however, RLS is a clinical diagnosis that includes the urge to move one's legs, occurring exclusively or primarily at bedtime and/or during the night. Further, this discomfort is alleviated with movement or rubbing (AASM, 2014). The following are signs and symptoms of RLS.

- Discomfort in the legs that is only improved with movement and an urge to move the legs when at rest, particularly at bedtime.
- Children and adolescents may use different terminology to describe the sensations associated with RLS. Descriptions may include feelings of
  - itching or burning,
  - creepy crawlies,
  - soda bubbles,
  - firecrackers popping, or
  - ants crawling in their legs (Picchietti et al., 2011).

Approximately 2% to 6% of children and adolescents are reported to have RLS (Picchietti et al., 2007, 2013), although these numbers may be an underestimate, as many children have difficulty identifying the uncomfortable sensations in their legs and/or parents may misinterpret complaints of discomfort as growing pains and/or the frequent movements as associated with hyperactivity. RLS is disruptive to sleep in that the child's urge to move his legs gets worse when at rest and in the evening and, as a result, often interferes with falling asleep or returning to sleep following typical nighttime arousals.

PLMD encompasses repetitive leg movements that occur during sleep and can only be diagnosed by overnight PSG. PLMD may be disruptive to sleep, as the frequent, repetitive leg movements may cause brief arousals and/or awakenings that interfere with maintaining sleep (AASM, 2014). Thus, the common clinical presentation of PLMD is a child who is excessively sleepy during the day despite a sufficient sleep opportunity. Clinical indicators of PLMD include a child who appears to be a very restless sleeper with the sheets and blankets off the bed or "tied in knots" in the morning. If parents witness their child sleeping, they will report seeing their child have frequent twitches, or quick movements in the toes, ankles, or entire leg.

RLS and PLMD commonly occur together, although this is not always the case (AASM, 2014). To further complicate the picture for many parents, there is a strong association between RLS, PLMD, and attention-deficit/hyperactivity disorder (ADHD; Picchietti et al., 1999; Picchietti, England, Walters, Willis, & Verrico, 1998). Children who have sleep disrupted by RLS and/or PLMD may exhibit more behaviors indicative of ADHD (e.g., inattention, hyperactivity) during the day. In addition, if frequent movements due to RLS are seen during the day, these may be misinterpreted as a fidgety or hyperactive child, resulting in a label of ADHD. Similarly, fidgeting at bedtime due to ADHD may be attributed to RLS.

Children and adolescents with suspected RLS and/or PLMD should be evaluated by their primary care physician and/or a sleep physician. For suspected PLMD, diagnostic evaluation will likely consist of a nocturnal PSG to document the repetitive nature of the limb movements and the level of sleep disruption that results. Although dopaminergic agents are typically used to treat these conditions in adults, low serum ferritin (<50 ng/mL) has been associated with RLS in children, and iron can be used for the treatment of both RLS and PLMD in children and adolescents (Durmer & Quraishi, 2011; Mohri et al., 2012).

NARCOLEPSY

The first sign of narcolepsy that is typically noted is excessive daytime sleepiness, even with a sufficient sleep opportunity at night. It is important for clinicians to keep in mind that the most likely explanation for excessive daytime sleepiness in children and adolescents is insufficient sleep. Narcolepsy should be considered only in cases when children have what appears to be sufficient sleep at night and continue to demonstrate excessive daytime sleepiness. Children and adolescents with narcolepsy may fall asleep unintentionally at school, even if they obtained a full night of sleep. This can lead to embarrassment, failing grades, and a perception that the student is unmotivated. *Cataplexy* (loss of muscle tone, particularly during times of strong emotions, e.g., laughter or fear) is pathognomonic for narcolepsy, meaning if one has cataplexy, one has narcolepsy. With the newest edition of the sleep disorders classification manual, the *International Classification of Sleep Disorders* (3rd ed.; *ICSD–3*; AASM, 2014), narcolepsy with cataplexy is now called *narcolepsy type 1*, and narcolepsy without cataplexy is called *narcolepsy type 2*. Other symptoms of narcolepsy include *hypnagogic hallucinations*, in which the dream state intrudes as the child is falling asleep, leading the child to believe that she is seeing and/or hearing things that are not present, and sleep paralysis, in which the child awakens and cannot move (AASM, 2014). Often, symptoms of narcolepsy can be more subtle than parents might expect. Children may be able to stay awake throughout school but may immediately fall asleep in the afternoon when they get home from school.

Patients with narcolepsy also may have microsleeps, in which they sleep for very short periods of time throughout the day. They and others around them may perceive these as lapses in attention rather than actual periods of sleep. In short, signs and symptoms of narcolepsy include the following:

- excessive daytime sleepiness, even with sufficient sleep opportunity;
- falling asleep in school;
- cataplexy;
- hypnagogic hallucinations; and
- sleep paralysis.

Narcolepsy occurs in approximately 25 to 50 per 100,000 people (Longstreth, Koepsell, Ton, Hendrickson, & van Belle, 2007). Although the disorder typically begins in adolescence, it is not usually identified until adulthood, often because of the subtle features that can be confused with attention lapses, poor motivation, or adolescent delayed sleep onset. If a child or adolescent presents with any of the symptoms of narcolepsy, a referral should be made to a sleep physician at an AASM-accredited sleep center. Evaluation should consist of a nocturnal PSG followed by a multiple sleep latency test, in which the child is presented with four to five opportunities to nap. Genetic studies may also be conducted to determine whether genes associated with narcolepsy type 1 are present.

Treatment typically will include psychostimulants to promote wakefulness during the day (Viorritto, Kureshi, & Owens, 2012). Other medications for treatment are also available, and the physician will determine the appropriateness of these specific medications on the basis of the age of the child and severity of symptoms. As an adjunct to medication, behavioral interventions may also be indicated in the treatment of narcolepsy. These may include scheduled naps, which are typically 15 minutes in length, one to two times per day. Clinicians may need to collaborate with the school to ensure that this is incorporated into an individualized education (Section 504 of the Rehabilitation Act of 1973) plan based on the child's health needs, and that the child is provided with a quiet, private room to nap in a way that does not interfere with learning time (e.g., during study hall). Caffeine should be avoided, and structured, consistent bedtimes and wake times should also be implemented to ensure that the child has adequate nighttime sleep to prevent sleep deprivation from exacerbating daytime sleepiness.

SLEEP-RELATED RHYTHMIC MOVEMENT DISORDER

Sleep-related rhythmic movement disorders are characterized by a repetitive body movement that the child engages in just before sleep or when feeling sleepy (AASM, 2014). In young children, these sleep-related movements typically consist of body rocking and/or head banging. Many children, and the majority of infants, engage in rhythmic movements to help them fall asleep, but a rhythmic movement sleep disorder is not diagnosed unless there are problems that result from the repetitive movements. These may include difficulty with sleep onset or maintenance, injury, or problems with daytime functioning. Sleep-related rhythmic movement disorders are far more common in infants and toddlers and typically subside by the age of 5 years old, when only 5% of children continue to engage in repetitive behaviors before sleep onset. Children with intellectual disability, autism spectrum disorders, or anxiety have higher rates of rhythmic movement disorders (AASM, 2014).

Safety is the primary concern when treating sleep-related rhythmic movement disorders. Most children do not cause serious self-injury. For these families, providing education and reassurance, along with simple suggestions, such as tightening screws on the crib or bedframe so that the noise does not disturb parents' sleep, is sufficient. For children who are likely to cause self-harm, however, safety measures must be taken, such as moving the mattress to the floor in children who engage in body rolling; or children with severe head banging that has resulted or may result in injury may benefit from a protective helmet. Although treatment of sleep-related rhythmic movement disorders is beyond the scope of this book, the typical treatment includes ensuring a consistent sleep schedule to allow for adequate sleep, having a consistent and soothing prebedtime routine, and habit-reversal training. In severe cases, sedating medications may be considered by the child's physician.

Common Pediatric Behavioral Sleep Problems

Because this book focuses on behavioral interventions to improve sleep in infants, children, and adolescents, a thorough understanding of how sleep can go wrong is important.

INSOMNIA

According to the *International Classification of Sleep Disorders* (2nd ed.; AASM, 2005), young children with difficulties falling asleep or staying asleep because of sleep-onset associations or limit-setting issues were considered to have behavioral insomnia of childhood. Older children and adolescents with more traditional insomnia, namely, difficulties initiating and maintaining sleep, were diagnosed with psychophysiological insomnia or primary insomnia (when using the *Diagnostic and Statistical Manual of Mental Disorders;* 4th ed.; American Psychiatric Association, 1994). With the *ICSD–3*, both adults and children who have difficulties with sleep onset or maintenance are diagnosed with either chronic insomnia disorder or short-term insomnia disorder (simply called *insomnia disorder* in the *Diagnostic and Statistical Manual of Mental Disorders;* 5th ed.; American Psychiatric Association, 2013), based on the duration of the sleep problems. Children and adolescents with insomnia will present with difficulty either falling asleep or staying asleep, resistance to going to bed when directed, and/or difficulty sleeping without parental presence or parental support (e.g., rocking, feeding, patting). To meet criteria for an insomnia diagnosis, the child must also have some daytime impairment associated with the sleep problem. These may include daytime fatigue or sleepiness; attention problems; irritability; behavior problems; and/or impairment in social, academic, or family functioning. The child must also have an adequate opportunity for sleep if an insomnia diagnosis is considered. Chronic insomnia disorder is diagnosed when the child has had difficulty sleeping at least 3 nights per week for 3 months or longer, and short-term insomnia disorder is diagnosed if he has had problems sleeping for less than 3 months (AASM, 2014).

Insomnia is the most common sleep disorder seen in children and occurs in 20% to 30% of young children (Mindell, Kuhn, Lewin, Meltzer, & Sadeh, 2006). Insomnia should not be diagnosed in infants younger than 6 months of age, as younger infants are not expected to maintain continuous nighttime sleep. Insomnia is found in 3% to 36% of adolescents and is more common in children and adolescents with chronic illness and/or developmental disorders. Although boys and girls are equally likely to have insomnia before puberty, after the onset of puberty, more females than males will present with insomnia (AASM, 2014). Strategies for assessing and managing insomnia are presented in this book in Chapters 6, 7, 8, and 9.

RECURRENT NIGHTMARES

Most people will have occasional nightmares, and young children in particular have fairly regular frightening dreams, with up to 75% of young children having occasional nightmares (AASM, 2014). To qualify for a diagnosis of nightmare disorder, however, the child or adolescent must have frequent nightmares that often include imagery of threats to their safety and security. When they awaken, they then immediately feel very alert and often remain very frightened. Children with nightmare disorder will then have daytime difficulties, including continuing to think about and fear the nightmare, and often will resist going to bed or staying in bed as a result of feeling fearful of reexperiencing nightmares (AASM, 2014). Many times, this has a very negative impact on the family as a whole, as parents are trying to reassure and manage the child's anxiety before bedtime, as well as cope with awakening during the night to care for the frightened child. Only those children who have significant impairment as a result of recurrent nightmares should be diagnosed with nightmare disorder and warrant treatment. For other children, nightmares are typically a transient experience that will spontaneously resolve.

Approximately 1% to 5% of prepubescent children experience recurrent nightmares, and they are seen much more commonly in children who have experienced trauma or severe stressors (Li et al., 2011). In fact, for patients with posttraumatic stress disorder, nightmares are one of the most common problems reported. Also, children who have generalized anxiety are far more likely to experience recurrent nightmares (AASM, 2014). Treatment of recurrent nightmares is described in Chapter 8.

CIRCADIAN RHYTHM SLEEP–WAKE DISORDERS

By far the most common circadian rhythm disorder in pediatrics is delayed sleep–wake phase disorder (DSP). The hallmark feature of DSP is a shifted sleep schedule that results in the patient's inability to fall asleep at a typical bedtime and awaken sufficiently early to attend school or meet social, academic, and occupational responsibilities. This delayed sleep onset and awakening must occur for at least 3 months for a clinician to diagnose DSP (AASM, 2014). For most patients, if they are allowed to choose their own sleep–wake schedule, they will choose much later bedtimes and wake times and will then achieve adequate quality sleep.

The vast majority of DSP cases begin in adolescents after the onset of puberty; between 7% and 16% of young adults are estimated to have DSP. Typically, adolescents who have DSP are described as always being night owls, but now their circadian rhythms have continued to delay in such a way that they are often unable to fall asleep for many hours after their ideal bedtime. Depression, academic failure, and substance abuse commonly co-occur with DSP (Wyatt, 2011). Treatment of DSP is presented in Chapter 10 of this volume.

PARASOMNIAS

Parasomnias are defined as unwanted behaviors that occur during the transition into or out of sleep or that occur while an individual is sleeping. Parasomnias are classified by the *ICSD–3* as nonrapid eye movement (NREM) parasomnias, rapid eye movement (REM) parasomnias, and *other parasomnias*. In this book, we focus on NREM parasomnias, specifically partial arousal parasomnias that typically occur during the transition from sleep to wake, and sleep enuresis, which is considered an other parasomnia, occurring during sleep (*ICSD–3;* AASM, 2014).

Disorders of Arousal

Partial arousal parasomnias are unwanted behaviors that occur during the transition to sleep, during sleep, or when arousing from sleep. The most commonly seen parasomnias in childhood include sleep talking, sleepwalking, sleep terrors, and confusional arousals, and occur when the child has an incomplete arousal from deep sleep. Thus in the *ICSD–3*, these NREM partial arousal parasomnias are now referred to as disorders of arousal (AASM, 2014). During an NREM parasomnia event, motor activity is similar to wakeful activity, and cognitive functioning is more similar to sleep. As a result, the child may appear to be intensely fearful or distressed (e.g., agitated, crying, sweating, and with pupils dilated) or engage in complex behaviors while having little to no memory of the events. For a child to be diagnosed with an NREM disorder of arousal, she must have reoccurring episodes of incomplete arousal, have limited or no response to parental efforts to redirect her, and have very little or no memory of the event (AASM, 2014). NREM disorders of arousal are distinguished from nightmares in that they typically occur during the first third of the night (when most NREM sleep is present) and are not associated with any specific memory of a dream. Children with NREM disorders of arousal are typically not as distressed by the event as the parents are, particularly because the child generally has no memory of the event. In contrast, when experiencing a nightmare, the child is very often highly distressed. Sleep terrors, sleep talking, and sleepwalking episodes generally are brief, but in the case of confusional arousals, they may last 30 to 45 minutes (Mason & Pack, 2007).

Both confusional arousals and sleepwalking are estimated to occur in approximately 17% to 40% of children and typically begin around the age of 2 years. Sleep terrors are present in approximately 1% to 7% of children, typically between the ages of 4 and 12, although up to 25% of very young children will have occasional sleep terrors. Most NREM disorders of arousal will resolve by the onset of puberty, although some adolescents will continue to experience episodes of sleepwalking (AASM, 2014). The most common trigger for these disorders is insufficient sleep, which may be exacerbated by illness, disruptions to schedules, changes to the sleep environment (e.g., vacation), or significant stress (Mason & Pack, 2007). As a result, ensuring that children receive adequate sleep can help prevent NREM disorders of arousal. Parents can typically be reassured that these episodes are benign; however, in children who engage in dangerous behavior or whose parasomnias occur so frequently that they are disruptive to the family, effective treatments are available and are described in Chapter 11.

Nocturnal Enuresis

Nocturnal enuresis (also referred to as *sleep enuresis*) is a parasomnia in which the child involuntarily urinates during sleep. Nocturnal enuresis is generally not diagnosed before the developmental age of 5, as urinating during sleep is considered part of typical development before this age. To qualify for a diagnosis, the child must urinate during sleep at least twice per week for at least 3 months. The disorder is further divided into primary enuresis, in which the child has never had a period of 6 months of consistent nighttime dryness, and secondary enuresis, in which the child has had a period of dryness for 6 months or longer but has resumed nighttime wetting (AASM, 2014). Typically, children with nocturnal enuresis cannot awaken to the sensation of a full bladder, resulting in the nighttime wetting episodes.

The associated features of primary versus secondary enuresis are distinct. In primary enuresis, the child is considered to have never developed the skill of awakening to the sensation of a full bladder and requires training to learn to awaken to this sensation. Secondary enuresis, on the other hand, is typically associated with either a comorbid medical condition (c.g., urinary tract infection or diabetes) or a precipitating significant stressor or traumatic event (e.g., abuse) and commonly co-occurs with chronic constipation and/or encopresis, as well as with OSA (AASM, 2014). Because secondary enuresis is very commonly associated with a significant precipitating medical or psychological condition, a thorough assessment of precipitating factors is essential.

Nocturnal enuresis may occur in 10% of 6-year-old children, and the incidence decreases with age. Boys are far more likely to experience enuresis than girls. Enuresis is also more common in children with ADHD (AASM, 2014) and sickle cell disease (Wolf, Kassim, Goodpaster, & DeBaun, 2014). Behavioral interventions are the treatment of choice for nocturnal enuresis and are described in Chapter 12.

Summary

Children may present with multiple sleep disorders, and a thorough assessment (as described in Chapter 4) of the nature and duration of symptoms, as well as associated features, should help the clinician identify the specific sleep problem or problems, as well as the most appropriate first steps toward treatment. Children with a medically based sleep disorder should be referred to their primary care physician or a sleep medicine specialist to be evaluated and treated before engaging in behavioral interventions.

Behaviorism and Essential Concepts for Pediatric Behavioral Sleep Medicine

3

P ediatric behavioral sleep medicine has its roots in behaviorism, a set of theories that help to explain how a behavior develops, how this behavior is reinforced, and what must be done for the behavior to change or cease. Thus, the focus of this chapter is to provide readers a basic review of behaviorism, as well as an introduction to the essential concepts in pediatric behavioral sleep medicine that are related to behaviorism. A sample of texts that provide a comprehensive review of behaviorism can be found in the Resources section.

The Role of Behaviorism in Behavioral Sleep Medicine

Behaviorism is a school of psychology dedicated to the study of objective behavior. A key feature of behaviorism is that behavior is not only observable but also can be developed

http://dx.doi.org/10.1037/14645-004
Pediatric Sleep Problems: A Clinician's Guide to Behavioral Interventions, by L. J. Meltzer and V. M. Crabtree

and changed with conditioning. The two major types of conditioning are *classical* and *operant*. Both are relevant for the treatment of pediatric behavioral sleep problems.

CLASSICAL CONDITIONING

Classical conditioning is one way to explain observable behavior change, where interactions with the environment are observed to shape behavior. Early studies of classical conditioning were conducted by Ivan Pavlov, who observed that when he paired a neutral stimulus (bell) with an environmental stimulus (food that causes the dog to salivate), a learned response (salivate when hearing a bell) occurred. In this example, the unconditioned stimulus (the sight or smell of the food) creates an unconditioned or automatic response (salivating). Pavlov then repeatedly paired a neutral stimulus (bell) that previously did not elicit the response (salivating) with the unconditioned stimulus (food). Over time, even in the absence of food, the dogs would salivate upon hearing the bell, demonstrating a conditioned response to the bell.

In classical conditioning, once a behavior has developed, it can be changed or unconditioned through extinction. *Extinction* occurs when the conditioned stimulus is repeatedly presented in the absence of the unconditioned stimulus. In the case of Pavlov, the conditioned response of salivating to the sound of the bell could be extinguished if the bell is repeatedly sounded without the presentation of food. Classical conditioning helps us to understand both the development and treatment of certain pediatric sleep problems.

Classical Conditioning and Enuresis

One of the first treatments in behavioral sleep medicine used classical conditioning for the treatment of enuresis. The bell-and-pad treatment was developed by Mowrer and published in 1938. From a behavior theory standpoint, the bell serves as an unconditioned stimulus, waking the child when a moisture sensor (the pad) becomes wet. Thus, pairing bladder distension (conditioned stimulus) with the sound of the bell (unconditioned stimulus) will result in waking to urinate (conditioned response). As described in Chapter 12 of this volume, more than 75 years later, variations of the bell and pad remain the most effective long-term treatment for enuresis.

Classical Conditioning and Sleep-Onset Associations

Night wakings, one of the most common presenting problems for young children, are most commonly due to negative sleep-onset associations.

Under the framework of classical conditioning, a *sleep-onset association* is a condition repeatedly paired with falling asleep, such that falling asleep becomes linked to that condition. Because nighttime arousals are typical (with all children waking two to six times per night), any sleep-onset association present at bedtime will also need to be present following typical nighttime arousals, helping the child return to sleep.

There are two types of sleep-onset associations. First, a *positive sleep-onset association* is a condition the child can create for himself (e.g., sucking his thumb, cuddling with a favorite stuffed animal or blanket). With a positive sleep-onset association, a child is able to put himself back to sleep following typical nighttime arousals. Infants who are able return to sleep independently (a developmental skill that occurs between 3 and 6 months of age for healthy, typically developing children) are often called *self-soothers.*

A *negative sleep-onset association* is a condition that requires someone or something else to facilitate sleep. This can include parental assistance (e.g., rocking an infant to sleep, lying with a school-age child), environmental stimuli (e.g., the sound of a vacuum cleaner), or a location other than the child's typical sleeping environment (e.g., pushed in the stroller, in the parents' bed). In the case of a negative sleep-onset association, the child pairs the skill of falling asleep with the external support. When seeking treatment, many parents do not complain about having to rock their child to sleep or lie with him until he is asleep at bedtime, but rather the concern is the need for this support every 2 hours following typical nighttime arousals (i.e., rocking the infant back to sleep every 2 hours, the child migrating to his parents' bed during the night). Infants with negative sleep-onset associations are sometimes called *signalers*, as they will cry following typical nighttime arousals because of their inability to return to sleep without assistance.

Because of the powerful role of sleep-onset associations in facilitating sleep onset and sleep maintenance, it is essential to identify negative sleep-onset associations (i.e., "that thing" that helps children fall asleep at bedtime or return to sleep following nighttime arousals). More information about evaluating for sleep-onset associations is provided in Chapter 4. Interventions to remove sleep-onset associations are described in Chapters 6 and 7. These include both rapid and gradual approaches to extinguish the association between sleep and a negative sleep-onset association (Honaker & Meltzer, 2014; Mindell et al., 2006; Morgenthaler, Owens, et al., 2006).

Classical Conditioning and Insomnia

Difficulties initiating and maintaining sleep are the hallmark features of insomnia. Whereas in younger children this is commonly due to a negative sleep-onset association, in older children and adolescents, insomnia looks more like that of adults. In other words, youth can develop a learned association between their bed and hyperarousal. What this looks like in practice is a patient may feel incredibly sleepy at bedtime, but as soon as she gets into bed, she becomes hyperaroused. Stimulus control therapy (SCT) is one of the primary components of treatment for insomnia (Bootzin, 1972; Morgenthaler, Kramer, et al., 2006). As described in Chapter 9, the goal of SCT is to extinguish this conditioned association by having the patient get out of bed if she is not asleep in 15 to 20 minutes, only returning to bed again when she feels sleepy. This helps weaken the association between lying in bed and not sleeping. Sometimes this process needs to be repeated multiple times in one night. When repeated every night for multiple nights, the association between sleep and bed is strengthened, and the patient's body is eventually retrained to fall asleep quickly once she is in bed.

OPERANT CONDITIONING

Operant conditioning is another way to explain observable behavioral change. However, unlike classical conditioning, behavior is shaped by consequences rather than antecedents. In other words, behaviors that are reinforced will increase in frequency, and behaviors that are punished will decrease in frequency. Operant conditioning is seen in everyday life. For example, when many parents potty train their young children, they will use a treat (a preferred sticker or piece of candy) to reward the child for using the potty. The treat then serves as positive reinforcement for using the potty, making the child more likely to sit on the potty again. In this case, the treat is an intentional reinforcer. However, accidental reinforcement also occurs commonly when reinforcers are provided following behaviors one does not want to increase. For example, most young children want attention from their parents more than anything else and will often do anything (including misbehave) to get their parent's attention. So when a child misbehaves and is subsequently yelled at by his mother, the child's misbehavior is being accidentally reinforced by the attention of his mother, so the unwanted behavior is likely to continue. However, if the mother provides differential attention, consistently ignoring the unwanted behavior but praises him for sharing toys and playing nicely with his sister, over time the unwanted behavior will decrease because it is no longer accessing attention, and the positive behaviors that access attention will increase.

There are two kinds of reinforcement that shape behavior. *Positive reinforcement* increases the likelihood a behavior will occur by adding something after the desired behavior (e.g., praise for the child who shares toys with his sister, stickers for the child who brushes her teeth). *Nega-*

tive reinforcement increases the likelihood a behavior will occur by stopping or removing a negative stimulus. For example, a child who does not want to eat his broccoli throws a tantrum at dinner until his parents remove the broccoli from his plate. Because his parents always give in to the tantrums by removing the broccoli, he will scream and fuss any time they put broccoli on his plate. Thus, his tantrums are being negatively reinforced as the stimulus (broccoli) is repeatedly removed.

In operant conditioning, behavior is changed with two primary reinforcement schedules. *Continuous reinforcement* is consistent and predictable, such that every instance of behavior contacts reinforcement. For example, a child is praised by her mother every time she hangs up her coat in the closet. *Intermittent reinforcement*, however, is unpredictable and does not occur after every instance of behavior, making it more difficult to extinguish a behavior. For example, at the grocery store a child begs for candy and his mother usually says no. But on a couple of occasions, the mother has given in and bought the candy. Now every time they go to the grocery store, the child will beg for candy in the hopes that this is one of the days his mother will say yes. The principles of operant conditioning are also commonly seen in behavioral treatments for pediatric sleep problems; we discuss these below.

Operant Conditioning and Bedtime Problems

Many parents struggle with limit setting around bedtime because they use an intermittent reinforcement schedule. For example, one night a parent may ignore multiple requests for attention at bedtime (e.g., another drink of water, one more bedtime book), but the next night the parent gives in and reinforces the child's behavior. This can result in bedtime stalling that is ultimately frustrating and exhausting for both the parent and child. However, when positive reinforcement for staying in bed is continuously provided (and no accidental reinforcement of out-of-bed behavior occurs), this bedtime stalling will decrease, as it no longer accesses reinforcement. In other words, if every night a child earns a token for every 10 minutes she stays in bed, for example, and in the morning she can exchange these tokens for a small prize, over time the child will be less likely to stall at bedtime in the hopes of earning more tokens. Another example is an infant who does not want to fall asleep alone, so she cries for 30 minutes until her mother rocks her to sleep. By rocking the child, the mother removes the stimulus of crying and achieves the goal of her baby falling asleep. For the infant, the stimulus of being alone is removed, and on subsequent nights the baby has simply learned to cry for prolonged periods of time to get rocked.

Operant Conditioning and Adherence to Positive Airway Pressure Therapy

As described in Chapter 13, positive airway pressure (PAP) therapy is used to treat obstructive sleep apnea for children who do not respond to or are not candidates for surgical interventions (e.g., removing tonsils and adenoids). Yet PAP therapy is not comfortable and poorly tolerated (a high stream of air pressure is blown into the child's nose and/or mouth to open his airway during sleep). It is common to see a child who becomes combative when a PAP mask is placed on his face, so the parents remove the mask immediately. Thus, the child learns that to remove the stimulus of the mask he needs to hit and bite, increasing the frequency of these unwanted and challenging behaviors in the future.

The Bottom Line

The etiology, maintenance, and treatment of behavioral sleep issues rely heavily on the concepts of both classical and operant conditioning. Whereas the treatment chapters in Part III of this volume also include some treatments based in cognitive theories (e.g., addressing dysfunctional thoughts and beliefs about sleep), this chapter has provided basic information on behavioral factors that influence pediatric sleep problems. The concepts of behaviorism are essential to fully appreciate the factors underlying most sleep pediatric sleep problems, as well as to choose the most effective treatment approach when working with a patient/family.

CLINICAL BASICS FOR PEDIATRIC BEHAVIORAL SLEEP MEDICINE | II

Clinical Assessment of Sleep

4

A s with any type of intervention, a thorough assessment of the problem is needed before treatment can begin (Babcock, 2011; Sadeh, 2011b). The details gleaned from clinical interviews, questionnaires, and even objective estimates of sleep (i.e., actigraphy) provide (a) guidance for choosing the best treatment approach, (b) information about the strengths of the patient and family, (c) potential barriers to implementing a treatment plan, and (d) baseline data that can later be reassessed to determine treatment success. This chapter provides specific information about different assessment methods, including the clinical interview and diagnostic and monitoring tools.

Clinical Interview

The clinical interview should be conducted with the child's primary caregiver(s), and should include direct questions for children and adolescents whenever possible. Children as young as

http://dx.doi.org/10.1037/14645-005
Pediatric Sleep Problems: A Clinician's Guide to Behavioral Interventions, by L. J. Meltzer and V. M. Crabtree

8 years of age can report on their sleep patterns, with studies showing that in middle childhood and adolescence parents are often not aware of difficulties with sleep initiation (i.e., falling asleep) or sleep maintenance (i.e., night awakenings). In addition, sleep quality is a subjective complaint. Although parents can report on the subsequent daytime consequences of a poor-quality or deficient night of sleep, older children and adolescents provide additional information about their sleep quality and/or whether they feel refreshed upon awakening (Meltzer et al., 2013; Owens, Spirito, McGuinn, & Nobile, 2000; Paavonen et al., 2000).

The clinical interview should focus primarily on the sleep history. However, sleep can be affected by a number of physical and psychosocial factors, and therefore the interview should also include a brief medical history, developmental history, family history, and social/environmental history (Mindell & Owens, 2010).

SLEEP HISTORY

The best place to begin the clinical interview is with a sleep history, starting with a question about why the family has come to see you. Once you have a basic understanding of the presenting problem, the sleep history then begins with questions about sleep patterns and sleep scheduling. This will be followed by questions related to other types of sleep disorders.

Sleep Patterns and Sleep Scheduling

When taking a sleep history, clinicians should capture not only what happens during sleep but also what happens in the hours leading up to sleep and what happens in the morning after waking up. For many families, the desire to emphasize the problems with a child's sleep often results in parents/patients reporting about last night and/or the worst night, then generalizing this to every night. Thus, it is important to follow up on vague responses (e.g., all the time, most nights, often) with more detailed questions (e.g., How many nights out of a 7-night week does that occur?).

To better understand behavioral sleep concerns, clinicians should try to identify issues related to sleep routines, sleep scheduling (i.e., bedtime and wake time), sleep initiation, sleep maintenance, and daytime sleepiness. One of the easiest ways to do this is to have a family describe a typical day, going around the clock, starting at dinnertime. The following are specific questions that can be asked, as well as what to look for in the patient's or family's response.

What time do you have dinner? By asking about the time of dinner, you can immediately sense whether the patient/family has a consistent schedule or evening routine. This information is important, as schedules and routines are essential for healthy sleep and a target point of intervention.

What happens after dinner? With this question, you walk a family step-by-step through their evening routine, including what type of activities they are engaging in (e.g., playtime, homework, television, computer, video games). These steps should lead all the way through the bedtime routine (e.g., bath, brush teeth, read a book), identifying the clock time the patient is in bed, as well as what time the patient attempts to fall asleep. Most families have a target bedtime, but for inconsistent families it is important to query how many nights per week the child is actually in bed at the target time.

Is this the same routine/schedule on weekends? What about over the summer or during school holidays? Variability in sleep schedules is another target point of intervention. Ideally, bedtimes and wake times should not differ by more than 1 to 2 hours from weekday to weekend.

Once the child is in bed, how long does it take for her to fall asleep? If you go to bed later, do you fall asleep faster? This second question can be asked directly of older children and adolescents. Sleep-onset latency (SOL) is how long it takes for a person to fall asleep. Prolonged SOL (greater than 30 minutes) is problematic and may signify several different sleep disorders depending on the child's age. These include bedtime problems, bedtime anxiety or nighttime fears, insomnia, or circadian rhythm sleep–wake disorder. For diagnosis and treatment planning, it is also important to understand where the child falls asleep (e.g., parents' arms being rocked, on the couch, in sibling's room), as well as who or what is present while the child falls asleep (e.g., bottle, parent lying next to child, television, cell phone, overhead lights on). The last question (*If you go to bed later, do you fall asleep faster?*) can assist with the differential diagnosis of insomnia versus circadian rhythm sleep–wake disorder. For example, a patient who falls asleep quickly every night during the summer when she goes to bed at 2:00 a.m. is more likely to have a circadian rhythm sleep–wake disorder, whereas a patient who takes 2 hours to fall asleep no matter what time she goes to bed is more likely to have insomnia.

Once the child is asleep, does he wake during the night? If yes, how often, at what time, how long until he returns to sleep, and how does the parent respond? Details about nighttime awakenings are necessary for differential diagnoses and treatment planning. For example, disorders of arousal typically occur in the first third of the night and are brief in duration, with the child having no memory of the event. Nightmares, on the other hand, occur in the last third of the night, with the child typically frightened and upset. Assessing parental response to night awakenings is essential to identify negative sleep-onset associations that may perpetuate night awakenings (e.g., rocking, parent lying with child). For older children and adolescents, night waking information again assists with differential diagnoses, in particular, insomnia and circadian rhythm sleep disorder. In other words, when patients who have difficulties falling asleep sleep great once asleep, this is more likely a circadian rhythm sleep–wake disorder, whereas patients who have difficulties falling asleep and multiple night awakenings are more likely to have insomnia.

What time does your child wake up on school days (weekends, summer)? How does she wake up (spontaneously, alarm clock, parent)? Is she difficult to wake (or does she take more than 15 minutes to get going)? Do you feel refreshed upon waking? This last question can be asked directly of older children and adolescents. Morning wake times and difficulties waking provide information about the patient's sleep quality and quantity. Although many children are not immediately happy upon waking, patients who have to be dragged out of bed in the morning likely have poor quality or insufficient sleep. Significant weekend oversleep (waking more than 2 hours later on weekends than weekdays) is also a sign that the patient is not getting enough sleep during the week. In addition, for school-age children and adolescents, gathering information about sleep schedules during the summer or over school holidays (when patients are not restrained by early school start times) can also help assess the child's actual sleep need. For example, an adolescent may sleep 10 hours almost every night in the summer, but only 7 to 8 hours per night during the school year. Thus, the primary cause of her daytime sleepiness and difficulty waking in the morning during the school year would be insufficient sleep.

Does your child nap during the day? If yes, when and for how long? As discussed in Chapter 1, naps are expected in younger children but can be a sign of deficient or disrupted sleep in middle childhood. For younger children, understanding where and how the child falls asleep for naps (similar to bedtime) is important for treatment planning.

Screening for Sleep Disorders

Although the focus of this book is on behavioral interventions for sleep problems, it is essential to screen for all sleep disorders, as the success of a behavioral treatment may be diminished in the presence of a comorbid sleep disorder that requires medical intervention (Mindell & Owens, 2010). Exhibit 4.1 identifies key questions to be included in this screening (questions in italics should be asked directly of the patient if age appropriate). When symptoms of sleep disorders are positively endorsed (e.g., frequent and loud snoring combined with daytime sleepiness), a referral to a sleep specialist may be warranted.

EXHIBIT 4.1

Sample Questions for the Screening of Sleep Disorders

Question	Follow-up questions if positive response
Obstructive sleep apnea (Chapter 2)	
Does your child snore?	How often? How loud?
Have you seen your child stop breathing during sleep, or do you feel the need to shake your child if he stops breathing?	
Does your child gasp or choke during sleep?	
Does your child complain of headaches upon waking in the morning (and not other times of the day?)	
Restless legs syndrome (Willis–Ekbom disease)/ periodic limb movements in sleep (Chapter 2)	
Does your child complain of pain or discomfort in her legs that occurs primarily at bedtime?	Is this made better by rubbing, stretching, or moving her legs?
Does anything bother you at bedtime, like your stomach, arms or legs?	
Does your child kick, twitch, or jerk during sleep?	How often?
Narcolepsy (Chapter 2)	
At bedtime or in the morning do you ever feel like you can't move your body if you had to? (Alternatively) do you ever feel like your brain is awake, but your body is still fully asleep?	
Do you ever see images or figures when you are falling asleep or waking up in the morning that you know are not really there?	
During the day, if you laugh or have a strong emotion like getting really angry do you get weak or feel like you are losing control over your muscles?	
Insomnia (Chapter 9)	
When you are trying to fall asleep, what are you doing?	
What kinds of things are you thinking about when you try to fall asleep?	*Do you worry that you are not sleeping?*
Have you ever NOT fallen asleep?	
Delayed sleep phase (Chapter 10)	
If you go to bed around 3:00 a.m., do you fall asleep faster?	
If you got to choose when to take the SATs (or another important exam), when would you be the most alert, morning, mid-day, or early evening?	
Disorders of arousal (Chapter 11)	
Does your child have sleep terrors or sleep walking?	How often? At what time of night? How do you respond? Does she respond to you if you check on her? Does she remember the event in the morning?

(continued)

EXHIBIT 4.1 (Continued)	
Question	**Follow-up questions if positive response**
Enuresis (Chapter 12)	
Does your child wet the bed?	How often? Has he ever been dry at night?
Excessive daytime sleepiness	
Does your child (do you) fall asleep in school?	
Does your child regularly fall asleep on short car rides (less than 10 minutes and not at naptime or bedtime)?	
Following a poor or short night of sleep, what do you notice different about your child (about yourself) the next day?	
Previous interventions	
What have you tried to make your child's (your) sleep better?	How long did you try that for? What happened?

Note. Questions in italics should be asked directly of the patient if age appropriate.

MEDICAL HISTORY

Both acute and chronic illnesses can be disruptive to sleep. Therefore, a brief medical history is needed to identify whether the child currently or previously has had chronic ear infections, gastroesophageal reflux, asthma, eczema, or other chronic illnesses. Similarly, medications can be alerting or sedating, so a complete list of medications, dose, and administration time is needed, including any current or previous medications used for sleep (including prescription, over-the-counter, herbal, or supplements). Finally, chronic or acute medical stressors (e.g., hospitalization, surgery) may contribute to the development of poor sleep habits or routines.

DEVELOPMENTAL AND PSYCHIATRIC HISTORY

Although the etiology of sleep problems in children with developmental disorders is yet to be clearly identified, it is well known that children with developmental disorders (e.g., autism spectrum disorder, attention-deficit/hyperactivity disorder, intellectual disability) have difficulties with sleep initiation, sleep maintenance, and/or early morning sleep termination. For children not diagnosed with a developmental disorder, an understanding of a child's development may assist with treatment planning (e.g., delays in speech, motor skills, or learning).

Sleep disturbance can be both a symptom and a functional outcome of many psychiatric disorders (e.g., depression, anxiety). Thus, it is important to screen for symptoms of, and/or a diagnosis for, a psychiatric disorder.

FAMILY HISTORY

Some sleep disorders have a strong genetic component (e.g., disorders of arousal, enuresis, insomnia, delayed sleep–wake phase); thus, a family history for any sleep disorder should be included. Developmental and mental health disorders in the family should also be screened for. In particular, a parent's depression or anxiety may have contributed to the development or maintenance of a negative sleep-onset association or poor sleep schedules, and/or may be an important factor in treatment success (e.g., a depressed or anxious parent may be less likely to follow treatment recommendations, especially if it involves the child crying or setting limits around bedtime).

SOCIAL AND ENVIRONMENTAL HISTORY

Finally, an understanding of the child's environment (social, familial, and academic) provides additional information needed for the differential diagnosis and treatment planning. Questions focus on where and with whom the child lives, academic performance, peer relationships, caffeine use, dietary intake, and significant life events (e.g., move, divorce, death, trauma).

For children with divorced parents, sleep routines and expectations may be inconsistent between houses. Children with school anxiety or poor peer relationships (e.g., children who are bullied) may have difficulties waking in the morning because school is aversive. Heavy caffeine use (>300 mg/day) or caffeine late in the day (within a few hours of bedtime) may delay sleep onset. Finally, a poor or limited diet may result in low ferritin (<50 ng/mL), which has been associated with restless and poor-quality sleep in children.

GOALS AND EXPECTATIONS

As we describe in more detail in Chapter 5, concluding the interview with questions about the patient's and family's goals and expectations for the appointment can tell a clinician where the family is in terms of readiness to change or the speed at which they want to change. Families who present expecting a pharmacological intervention may be unreceptive to behavioral recommendations. Parents who want to do infant sleep training with no crying would benefit from a very graduated extinction process, whereas parents who want the sleep issue fixed immediately would benefit from a more traditional extinction approach. Chapter 5 provides more details on tailoring treatment plans for each family, as well as tips for motivating families.

Diagnostic and Monitoring Tools

The sleep diary is the primary tool used for the subjective assessment of sleep. In addition, there are two objective measures of sleep: polysomnography (PSG) and actigraphy. Each type of assessment is described in detail in the following sections. In brief, the diary has clinical use as both a baseline and a posttreatment measure of sleep patterns. PSG is an overnight, multichannel study done primarily in a sleep laboratory (although home studies can be done) in a single night for the purpose of diagnosing underlying sleep disruptors (i.e., obstructive sleep apnea [OSA], periodic limb movement disorder [PLMD]). Actigraphy is a watch-sized device worn on the wrist (or ankle of young children) for multiple nights in the child's home providing an objective estimate of sleep–wake patterns for up to 2 weeks. It is important to keep in mind that these assessment approaches provide different information and are complementary but not interchangeable (e.g., PSG is limited by a single night in the lab and thus cannot provide information about irregular sleep schedules; actigraphy provides multinight data that show sleep onset and sleep offset times but cannot assess sleep-disordered breathing).

SLEEP DIARY

A daily sleep diary is completed by a parent or patient (if age appropriate). Although diaries differ in type, the basic information collected includes the following:

- time the child got into bed,
- lights out time or time the child attempted to fall asleep,
- sleep onset latency,
- frequency and duration of night awakenings,
- morning wake time,
- time the child got out of bed, and
- nap time.

Diaries may also include a place to subjectively rate the quality of sleep or provide additional notes/information. Two examples are provided in the handouts. Handout 2 provides a sleep log commonly used before the initial evaluation for all patients. This log is also beneficial for tracking the treatment of bedtime problems and night wakings in young children (Honaker & Meltzer, 2014). Handout 3 provides a sleep diary commonly used for the evaluation and treatment of insomnia (Carney et al., 2012), as it provides more specific details about bedtime, SOL, night waking duration, and wake time, allowing for the calculation of sleep efficiency.

Because many parents tend to report on either the previous night or the child's worst night of sleep during a clinical interview, the sleep diary provides complementary information to the parent report (as long as a 1- to 2-week prospective sleep diary is filled out before the evaluation). Sleep diaries can also be used to identify variability in a child's sleep schedule, patterns of sleep disruptions, as well as the monitoring of treatment progress.

NOCTURNAL POLYSOMNOGRAPHY

Nocturnal PSG is a multichannel (electroencephalography [EEG], electro-oculography, electromyography) measure of sleep staging (e.g., rapid eye movement [REM] sleep; delta, or slow-wave sleep). Additional channels are used to measure respiration, cardiac functioning, and limb movements during sleep. PSG is considered the gold standard for the diagnosis of OSA, as well as central sleep apnea and periodic limb movements in sleep (Marcus et al., 2012). An expanded EEG may also be included when there is a question about nocturnal seizures.

For pediatric behavioral sleep problems, the primary limitation of PSG is that it does not provide information about insomnia beyond that in a clinical interview; thus, PSG is not clinically indicated for the diagnosis of insomnia. Additional limitations of PSG are (a) a single night of data collection that does not provide information about a child's typical sleep patterns; (b) the first-night effect, in which the recorded night of sleep may not be representative of a true night of sleep because of the discomfort of the leads and the unfamiliar sleep environment; (c) cost; and (d) the limited number of accredited pediatric sleep laboratories in the United States (and around the world).

For children with insomnia who require an overnight PSG, the unfamiliar surroundings may even exacerbate a child's difficulty with sleep initiation or maintenance or, conversely, remove negative associations with the child's bed, facilitating more rapid sleep onset. Further, PSG may not be tolerated by young children or children with developmental disorders. However, if a PSG is needed for these populations, desensitization protocols can be effective in preparing the child for the study.

DAYTIME MULTIPLE SLEEP LATENCY TEST

The daytime multiple sleep latency test (MSLT) is used to screen for disorders of excessive daytime sleepiness, in particular, narcolepsy. The MSLT consists of four to five nap opportunities (each lasting 20 minutes) given every 2 hours. Using the multichannel PSG, data are collected on whether the child falls asleep, how quickly she falls asleep, and whether she has sleep-onset REM (Iber, Ancoli-Israel, Chesson, Quan, & American Academy of Sleep Medicine, 2007).

ACTIGRAPHY

An actigraph is a wristwatch-sized device that uses accelerometry to measure movement, operating on the premise that when people are awake, they move, and when they are asleep, there is an absence of movement. Thus actigraphy provides an estimate of sleep–wake patterns (Meltzer, Walsh, Traylor, & Westin, 2012; Sadeh, 2011a). Actigraphy provides information about a patient's sleep-onset time (when he fell asleep), sleep-offset time (when he woke up), and quality of sleep (e.g., frequent movements during sleep may indicate poor-quality sleep). If worn 24 hours a day, information can also be gleaned about daytime naps.

In a clinical setting, the strengths of actigraphy include a multiday assessment (3–14 days) of a child's sleep continuity (e.g., sleep-onset time, wake time, frequency and duration of night awakenings) in his natural sleep environment. Actigraphy is also considerably less expensive in terms of equipment and charges to patients. Finally, actigraphy can provide additional information about sleep patterns that are difficult to obtain from poor historians.

Actigraphy requires the concurrent use of a sleep diary to help identify artifact, as well as reported bedtimes and wake times. In particular, reported bedtime is essential to measure SOL. Because of this reliance on a subjective report of bedtime, SOL is not one of the stronger measures to be obtained from actigraphy. Studies have found actigraphy to have a good sensitivity to detect sleep compared with PSG (.88–.95) yet specificity to detect wake after sleep onset is much poorer (.17–.98, with the majority of studies <.60; Meltzer, Montgomery-Downs, Insana, & Walsh, 2012).

There are a number of limitations to actigraphy that need to be considered. First, although light and temperature channels in newer devices may provide some concurrent data useful for the scoring and interpretation of actigraphy, these devices primarily rely on a single channel of data—movement. In addition, artifact is common, and without a complementary sleep diary, inaccurate results may be identified. For example, motionless wakefulness may occur when an adolescent spends prolonged periods of time lying in bed watching TV before sleep onset. Alternatively, a young child who naps in the car may appear to be awake because of the motion of the car. Third, although the equipment costs less than PSG, the start-up cost for a single device is around $1,500 (including interface and software). Although a CPT billing code for actigraphy is available (95803), most insurance companies do not cover actigraphy, stating it is either experimental or not medically necessary. Finally, because of the costs of the device, it is critical to ensure that the family is reliable and will properly care for the actigraph, returning it in a timely manner without any damage.

PARENT OR SELF-REPORT QUESTIONNAIRES

There are a number of sleep-related questionnaires for infants, children, and adolescents. Some measures target specific sleep problems (e.g., sleep-disordered breathing), whereas others screen for a variety of sleep problems (e.g., bedtime problems, night wakings, daytime sleepiness). Most pediatric sleep questionnaires are to be completed by parents, with a small (but growing) number of self-report measures for older children and adolescents. Although a description of all pediatric sleep questionnaires is beyond the scope of this chapter, two review articles published in 2011 provide an overview of all measures that had been published at that time (Lewandowski, Toliver-Sokol, & Palermo, 2011; Spruyt & Gozal, 2011). Although questionnaires alone are not sufficient for diagnosis or treatment planning, these tools can provide supplemental information beyond the clinical interview. In addition, questionnaires may be a useful way to monitor treatment progress.

The Bottom Line

A good clinical interview is critical for the successful treatment of pediatric behavioral sleep problems. This interview should include not only detailed information about the child's sleep patterns, sleep habits, and sleep disturbances but also information about her health, development, and environment. The information collected in the clinical interview will help clinicians understand the presenting sleep problems, identify modifiable factors that are serving to maintain the problems, and consider which treatment approach will be most successful for each family. Because many of the common pediatric sleep problems have multiple intervention approaches, it is critical to understand where the patient/family is before tailoring these interventions for individual families.

Prospective sleep diaries are the primary assessment tool in pediatric behavioral sleep medicine, providing valuable information about a patient's sleep patterns, which can be used to monitor treatment progress. Overnight PSG is necessary for the diagnosis of OSA and PLMD but has limited use in the diagnosis and treatment of insomnia. Actigraphy may be beneficial in pediatric populations, providing more objective information about multinight sleep patterns within the child's natural sleep environment.

Working With Families to Increase Treatment Success

5

To ensure that children and adolescents have the greatest chance for success with behavioral sleep interventions, attention should be focused on strategies to enhance treatment effectiveness. As with any behavioral intervention, the clinician should assess the patient's and family's perception of the problem and willingness to change behavior before prescribing any intervention. Motivation and readiness for change should drive the intervention chosen (Prochaska & DiClemente, 1992). For adolescents and parents who are ambivalent about change, the use of motivational interviewing can be an effective clinical tool for enhancing motivation both to change behavior and to adhere to treatment recommendations.

http://dx.doi.org/10.1037/14645-006
Pediatric Sleep Problems: A Clinician's Guide to Behavioral Interventions, by L. J. Meltzer and V. M. Crabtree

Assessment Considerations

As described in Chapter 4, a comprehensive assessment of the sleep problem is essential to designing the most effective intervention. As part of this assessment, determining the patient's and family's perception of the magnitude of the sleep problem and their willingness to change behavior is critical. In addition to asking questions about the sleep problem itself, the clinician should also ask parents several questions about their motivation to change:

- How much of a problem is this for your family?
- What is your primary concern about your child's behavior, currently?
- What have you tried before to help this problem?
  - How helpful were those approaches?
  - What happened when you implemented them?
- What will happen if you make significant changes to your child's sleep routine?
  - With this child?
  - With your other children?
  - In your marriage/relationship?
  - To your frustration level?
  - To your sleep?
  - To your daytime fatigue?
- Who else can you rely upon to help you carry out this intervention?
- How likely are you to want to begin this intervention in the next week? Next month? Next 6 months?

Clinicians should also evaluate the readiness and motivation for change in older children and adolescents. Although it can be assumed that infants and toddlers are not motivated to change, older children and adolescents should be active participants in the intervention plan, and thus their motivation for change is crucial to determine. Clinicians should ask children and adolescents the following questions:

- How much of a problem is this for you?
- Do you want to improve your sleep?
- What would be better for you if your sleep were improved?
- What would be worse for you?
- What, if anything, worries you about making changes to your sleep?
- What have you tried before to help this sleep problem? How helpful were those strategies?
- How ready do you feel to start making changes to your sleep in the next week? Next month? Before the school year is out? Before next school year starts?

Determining the parents', children's, and adolescents' perceptions of how significant this problem is, as well as how ready they are to begin the intervention, will help guide intervention selection. In addition, this information will help the clinician prepare problem-solving strategies that will increase treatment adherence and success. Finding ways to circumvent problems and generate additional support before beginning the intervention should substantially reduce premature treatment discontinuation.

Recognizing the Impact on Parents

Carrying out a behavioral intervention to improve sleep can be burdensome, frustrating, and guilt inducing for parents. Most parents did not set out to create behavioral sleep disturbances in their children. The most common scenario is one in which children had difficulty initiating or maintaining sleep or had anxiety at bedtime, and parents had a strong wish (understandably) to have their child go to sleep. Parents are frequently bombarded with messages that children need enough sleep to grow, be healthy, and function optimally during the day (which is true). However, these messages often create a level of anxiety in parents that their children must get to sleep under any circumstance. Additionally, parents need their children to go to sleep. Parents have evening activities that must be carried out—dishes to be done, laundry to fold, bills to pay—before they go to bed. In addition, it is common for parents to want their children to be asleep so that they can have some down time before they themselves go to sleep.

All of these factors drive parents to use whatever tool they find is most helpful in ensuring that their children go to sleep. This can then lead to sleep-onset associations such as putting infants and toddlers to sleep by rocking, feeding, swinging, placing them in a bouncy seat on the dryer, or driving them in the car. It can also lead to parents lying down with their older children in their beds until they are asleep, rubbing their children's backs, singing them songs, holding their hands, and so on. These sleep-onset associations can be removed, but this can often result in children crying or having tantrums, which are frequently distressing to parents. In addition, even the most patient parents may find that when they are tired, remaining calm and consistent with children is challenging. This can result in bedtime battles, with children stalling and protesting. Interventions in Chapters 6 and 7 are included to assist these parents with making bedtime a more pleasant (and consistent) experience for everyone.

Difficulties with sleep maintenance can be equally, if not more, difficult for parents to manage. Listening to a child cry or argue at 9:00 p.m.

can be frustrating for a parent; listening to a child cry or argue at 3:00 a.m. can be almost impossible to manage. By that time of night, parents' frustration tolerance is at an ultimate low and rational thinking is typically gone. Any parent who has made an effort to return a child to his own bed multiple times throughout the night can easily identify with the strong desire to open up that comforter and invite the child into bed to have the speediest, least stressful, and most comfortable return to sleep.

As with any behavioral intervention, behavioral strategies to improve independent sleep will be met with resistance and refusal. Families that can carry out these interventions on their own do not present for treatment. Extinction bursts (an increase in crying, getting out of bed multiple times for mobile children, and/or arguing from verbal children) that occur just before the full extinction of the negative behavior are to be expected. It is important to inform parents about extinction bursts and to encourage them to continue with the behavior plan. This results in parents being far less likely to decide that the intervention is not effective and stop carrying it out. Certainly, stopping mid-intervention at the time of an extinction burst will create intermittent reinforcement, thereby strengthening the negative behavior. Parents should be cautioned against this so that they are fully prepared to push through the extinction burst.

Most, if not all, parents find extinction bursts frustrating and challenging, and it is essential to help parents identify at the outset of treatment which refusal behaviors their children are most likely to use and what impact this might have on the parent. Once this is identified, the clinician can help the parent best determine ways of coping with frustration. In two-parent homes, parents should be encouraged to take turns carrying out the intervention and/or listening to crying. When one parent is in charge of the intervention, the other parent may choose to use earplugs or headphones with music, go outside for a walk, or go to another part of the house where crying or arguing cannot be heard. In homes in which only one parent is present at night, the parent implementing the intervention may wish to enlist the support of friends or family in helping manage frustration. A family member may choose to come over in the evening and take turns carrying out the intervention or may agree to provide support by being available by phone to encourage the parent to continue with the intervention. Parents may also be encouraged to use relaxation strategies to help manage their own anxiety and frustration while their children are engaging in refusal/resistance. These can include deep breathing; imagery; progressive muscle relaxation; or simple strategies such as taking a bath, listening to calming music, or using distraction by watching a favorite television show.

A Tale of Two Children

CASE EXAMPLE: MARIA

Maria is a 3-year-old healthy girl who has had difficulty sleeping consistently through the night throughout her life. She resists her bedtime routine, runs around the house when her parents ask her to put on her pajamas, and takes at least an hour each night to get into her bed. Her mother then lies in her bed until she falls asleep each night. Once Maria is asleep, her mother leaves her room, and goes to bed in her own bedroom. Several times each night, Maria awakens, goes to her parents' room and requests that one of them go back to her room with her. Maria's mother and father take turns lying in her bed, and typically one will eventually fall asleep there for the remainder of the night.

Maria's mother is requesting help, as she is pregnant and expecting another baby in 3 months. She would like to have Maria sleeping independently before the baby's arrival. Maria's mother says that she is ready to begin an intervention immediately because she feels a great deal of pressure to not be awakening each night with a newborn and Maria. She also is becoming increasingly physically uncomfortable during her pregnancy lying in Maria's twin bed with her. She anticipates that she and Maria's father can alternate carrying out the intervention and asks to begin this week.

CASE EXAMPLE: ALEXIS

Alexis is also a healthy 3-year-old girl who resists bedtime, takes more than an hour each night to eventually get into bed, and cries for her mother to sleep with her at the beginning of each night. Alexis's mother, like Maria's, lies with her in her bed until she is asleep nightly. Alexis then awakens during the night and goes to her mother's bedroom. Sometimes Alexis's mother returns her to her room and lies in bed with her again. Other times Alexis climbs into her mother's bed without awakening her and sleeps there for the remainder of the night.

Alexis's mother is asking for help because she is exhausted from the nighttime awakenings and has been going to sleep later than she would like, as her nighttime chores are delayed by lying in bed with Alexis for prolonged periods of time. Alexis's father works a night shift, and her mother is solely responsible for bedtime and nighttime care. Alexis's mother says that she would like to change this pattern, but she does not have another adult to help her at night. She also is concerned that any intervention will be disruptive to the family, as Alexis shares a room with her 5-year-old sister.

Tailoring Interventions for Success

Although Maria and Alexis present with identical sleep patterns and needs for parental presence at night, and the goals of treatment are similar, the method for designing and implementing the interventions will differ dramatically. Maria's mother has substantial motivation for change and a clear time frame in mind for having a positive outcome from the intervention. She has another adult in the home with her to help implement the intervention and will have support when she becomes frustrated. Alexis's mother, although she has support from her husband with respect to the need for intervention, does not have another adult in the home at night to help her carry it out. She also will not have another adult to rely on if she becomes frustrated with Alexis's negative behavior as the intervention is carried out. She also has concerns that any resistant behavior, such as crying, leaving the bed, arguing, stalling, and so on, will disrupt Alexis's older sister's sleep. How should a clinician help Alexis's mother be successful in carrying out her intervention?

Before designing a specific intervention to improve Alexis's independent sleep onset, the clinician should spend time with Alexis's mother and ask how soon she would like to begin this intervention, what specific problems she anticipates arising, and who she can count on for support. Problem solving should take priority in this case. Whereas a clinician working with Maria's family can design a relatively intensive intervention and begin implementation immediately, Alexis's mother will require more time to identify barriers and solutions to those barriers. Perhaps they could start the intervention during a time when Alexis's father has vacation time planned, or perhaps a grandparent or other family member could spend several nights in the home to help her mother carry out the intervention. If Alexis's mother expresses confidence that she can manage the frustration and carry out the intervention alone but is more concerned about the impact of the intervention on Alexis's sister, time can be spent identifying alternative sleeping arrangements for her. Because the intervention should be focused on helping Alexis learn to sleep in her bed in her room, the best approach may be to place Alexis's sister in another room or have her stay with a grandparent or other relative during the time the intervention is being carried out. Perhaps a white noise machine could be placed in the room to mask the noise of Alexis crying or calling out. Another strategy may be to have Alexis's sister go to bed and go to sleep before putting Alexis to bed so that she is not prevented from falling asleep by Alexis's resistant behaviors. A number of strategies can be hypothesized, and Alexis's mother will be most able to identify what will work best for her family. More specific strategies and tricks of the trade are discussed in future chapters.

Motivation in Children

Although a parent may be highly motivated for change, children may be less interested in making changes to their sleep. Frequently, the sleep patterns that are established are comfortable for children, and they may be very resistant to implementing changes that may result in having less contact with their parents, having them feel alone, and increasing their anxiety. Because of this, adding positive reinforcement protocols can help substantially increase the effectiveness of the primary behavioral goal. Depending on the age and developmental level of the child, sticker charts with tangible rewards in the form of prize boxes can be very motivating. Verbal praise can also be highly meaningful to children. Parents should be reminded that placing focus on successive approximations to the desired behavior should not be overlooked. If a child gets out of bed four times during the night instead of six, as she did the previous night, parents should be strongly encouraged to praise the child the next morning for getting out of bed fewer times rather than chastising her for getting out of bed.

For older children and adolescents, positive reinforcement can also help increase motivation. Again, praise should be incorporated in parents' interactions with their children. Regardless of age, children and adolescents will respond well to positive interaction with their parents. Rather than sticker charts, other reinforcers that are motivating to the child should be used. For older children, reinforcers may include earned video game time, toys, books, or other items of interest. For adolescents, point systems can be designed to facilitate the purchase of gift cards, cell phone minutes, apps, or other items of their choosing. Involving the child or adolescent in the design of the plan and in the selection of reinforcers will help ensure that the items selected are of sufficient interest to increase motivation. Positive reinforcement is further described in several of the treatment chapters in Part III in relation to specific interventions.

Ambivalent Parents and Ambivalent Adolescents

One of the more difficult situations that clinicians encounter is that of ambivalence. When parents are ambivalent, they may be resistant to or inconsistent in their implementation of the behavioral intervention. When adolescents are ambivalent to change, they may be nonadherent to recommendations, thereby rendering the intervention essentially useless and perhaps counterproductive. In evaluating readiness for change, clinicians can provide direct instructions for carrying out the intervention for parents or adolescents who demonstrate that they are ready to begin. However, the clinician should carefully tailor the intervention to the specific needs of the adolescent and his family, problem solving potential solutions for anticipated barriers. For those patients and families who demonstrate ambivalence or are merely contemplating behavior change without being clearly ready for change, a more graduated approach is necessary (Prochaska & DiClemente, 1992).

Providing education about sleep needs, long-term consequences of insufficient sleep, and ways in which poor sleep habits can worsen and become more entrenched (information included in Chapters 1 and 2) is a critical first step for families who are not clearly motivated and not clearly ready to begin a behavioral intervention package. Once provided with appropriate education, families may be effectively served by a motivational interviewing (MI) approach to help facilitate readiness to begin a behavioral intervention. MI has been used quite effectively with several populations that can demonstrate significant ambivalence to change—including adolescents and adults with substance abuse; adults engaging in intimate partner violence; and adolescents and adults requiring behavior change to improve physical health, such as the need for diet change or weight loss to address hypertension (Ma, Zhou, Zhou, & Huang, 2014; Olson, Gaffney, Lee, & Starr, 2008; Schumacher et al., 2011; Walton et al., 2010).

Motivational Interviewing

MI is defined as

> a collaborative, goal-oriented style of communication with particular attention to the language of change, designed to strengthen personal motivation for and commitment to a specific goal by eliciting and exploring the person's own reasons for change within an atmosphere of acceptance and compassion. (Miller & Rollnick, 2013, p. 5)

The primary tenets of MI focus on the importance of partnering with the parent or patient to have a conversation about the change, collaborate, and evoke the adolescent's or parent's own motivation for change (rather than focusing on the clinician's ideas about the importance or rationale for changing). The focus of MI is on the autonomy of the individual. Therefore, the clinician should communicate the message that for the change to occur, it is up to the patient and/or parent, not the clinician (Naar-King & Suarez, 2010; Rollnick, Miller, & Butler, 2008).

To use MI, clinicians should focus on OARS, defined and described below.

- *Open-ended questions*, as described in the first section of this chapter, allow the parent and/or patient in her own words to describe the nature of the problem and the reasons they see for changing. It should also allow them to describe barriers to change and reasons change may be difficult or undesired.
- *Affirmations* help build rapport and focus on the strengths that the parent and/or adolescent bring to the table. Although a parent may be worried about a behavioral intervention making a sibling feel left out, a clinician may affirm the importance of the parent providing attention to all of her children and how this can guide the use of praise and attention for appropriate behavior in the child with the sleep disruption.
- *Reflections* are specifically used to focus on the negatives that the parent and/or adolescent identify for the current behavior as well as on potential positives if the behavior were to change. In an adolescent with delayed sleep onset who is having frequent tardies at school, this may take the form of reflecting the frustration and embarrassment the adolescent feels when walking into second period each day while also supporting the adolescent's statements that arriving at school on time may also help improve her grades in her first period class. Although the adolescent may also be describing a lack of self-efficacy that her sleep can change, the focus of the clinician should remain on the adolescent's own words regarding her desire for change.
- *Summaries* should highlight both the reasons against and for change, ending on the parent's and/or patient's reasons for change and moving in the direction of how the intervention can help support this. See the Resources section for more information on MI.

CASE EXAMPLE: CALEB

Caleb is a 14-year-old high school student who has had a 1-year history of problems falling asleep and awakening on time for school. This has resulted in frequent tardies and unexcused school absences. Caleb has had a significant decline in grades, from primarily *B*s to *C*s and *D*s, and is failing algebra, which is his first period class. His difficulty awakening in the morning and declining grades have resulted in such conflict with his mother that he now rarely speaks to her unless they are arguing. Caleb's mother is now concerned that he is depressed. She sees him as angry, irritable, and unmotivated. A thorough clinical interview reveals a significant sleep disturbance that the psychologist identifies as a delayed sleep–wake phase disorder. Caleb's mother understands the clinician's explanation of the diagnosis and is interested in pursuing interventions to advance his circadian rhythm in hopes that this will improve his mood and school attendance.

In an interview with the clinician, Caleb presents as alternately angry and defeated. He describes his frustration with his mother and his teachers and his perception that no one understands how sleepy he is and how hard it is to get up in the morning. He enjoys his time at night when the house is quiet and he is able to play on the computer without being "harassed" by his mother. At the same time, he describes his frustration that his grades have declined and notes that his peers are making comments about how often he is late or misses school. He also says that the more he misses school, the more behind he feels academically, and the harder it is to attend the following day. The clinician notes Caleb's ambivalence, with some secondary gain related to quiet time in the evening, as well as avoidance of school when he worries about his poor academic progress. These factors are coupled with what appears to be a desire to not be identified by his peers as truant and to reduce his conflict with his mother. Taking an MI approach, the clinician asks the following questions:

- How would you like to see your school life change?
- What would you like to be different about your interactions with your mom?
- How would changing your sleep affect those two issues?
- What would be the downside to changing your sleep? to being at school on time every day?
- What would be the upside to changing your sleep? to being at school on time each day?
- What about not staying the same/making no changes to your sleep? What would be good about keeping things the same?
- What would be the down side to staying the same?
- Let's think about when you were in seventh grade, before you had problems falling asleep and waking up in the morning. How were things then? How did you and your mom get along? How were your grades? How did you feel at school?
- What might happen if things don't change? How do you see the rest of this school year going? What about next school year? What about the rest of high school?
- What are your goals? In the next year? After high school? As an adult?
- How would staying the same affect those goals?
- How would changing affect those goals?

By using an MI approach, the clinician enables Caleb to express all elements of his ambivalence while focusing on change talk. After Caleb is provided with the opportunity to talk about his reasons for not changing the problem, the clinician ends the interview with reasons for changing Caleb's sleep schedule, using Caleb's own words to enhance and motivate Caleb toward making behavioral changes. Because Caleb identifies embarrassment about his tardies and truancy as well as frustration with his mother for "harassing" him, the clinician focuses treatment goals on improved peer and family relations, as well as future goals of graduating from high school to begin to create behavior changes.

Written Information

Finally, a lot happens during a clinical visit, from evaluation to education to intervention recommendations. If the child is present, often parents may be distracted by trying to entertain the child while listening to the clinician. In addition, written information prevents disagreements between two parents or between a parent and a child about what the clinician said. Thus, it is essential to provide written information and recommendations to patients to facilitate treatment success. When the steps are clearly written out, patients and families are more likely to follow through on treatment. This book supplies handouts that include education and step-by-step instructions for patients and families that correspond to each of the interventions described in Part III.

The Bottom Line

The behavioral interventions for the sleep problems described in this book are only as good as the family's willingness and ability to implement them. Even with the best-laid plans, a clinician cannot force a family to implement an intervention that they are either not ready to implement or that is not feasible for the family. At the outset of any intervention to improve sleep in children and adolescents, the clinician should assess all stakeholders' willingness to change. If any party is clearly not motivated and ready to change, MI can be used to evaluate where to begin the intervention. For those who are ready and motivated for change, families still require significant support in implementing interventions that can be challenging, particularly in the middle of the night with a sleep-deprived parent and child. Seeking family feedback about the feasibility of the intervention is crucial. In addition, it is essential to maintain a flexible approach to problem solving and addressing barriers. With a motivated family and a feasible intervention, everyone should see success!

PRESENTING PROBLEMS

Sleep-Onset Associations and Night Wakings in Young Children

6

One of the most common clinical complaints in pediatric behavioral sleep medicine is infants and toddlers who wake multiple times during the night, requiring parental assistance to return to sleep. The primary cause is negative sleep-onset associations that help the child fall asleep quickly at bedtime (e.g., rocking, feeding) but are then needed to help the child return to sleep following typical nighttime arousals. Although the majority of this chapter focuses on extinction methods to help young children learn to fall asleep and return to sleep independently, we also review other factors that contribute to nighttime awakenings, as well as other interventions that target nighttime awakenings not due to sleep-onset associations.

The focus of this chapter is sleep-onset associations and nighttime awakenings in young children (0–3 years, or those still in a crib). Once children transition to a bed, the extinction procedures that address sleep-onset associations are altered to consider the child's increased mobility, as well as common limit-setting issues seen in preschoolers and older

http://dx.doi.org/10.1037/14645-007
Pediatric Sleep Problems: A Clinician's Guide to Behavioral Interventions, by L. J. Meltzer and V. M. Crabtree

children (see Chapter 7, this volume). For children whose night wakings are due to fears, anxiety, and/or nightmares, interventions can be found in Chapter 8.

Assessment Considerations

Because night wakings in young children are so often closely tied to what goes on at bedtime, a detailed review of the bedtime routine, including how the child falls asleep, is essential. In addition, because there are multiple causes of nighttime awakenings, the detailed sleep history as described in Chapter 4 is important for identifying any potential factors contributing to the development of problematic nighttime awakenings. Once medical factors are ruled out and/or treated, the focus should then turn to behavioral factors that may perpetuate nighttime awakenings.

Medical Factors That May Contribute to Nighttime Awakenings

A number of medical factors may contribute to nighttime awakenings. Although behavioral interventions may be used concurrently with treatment of medical issues, if the medical concerns are not addressed or not well-controlled, the success of behavioral interventions will be greatly diminished. Although not an exhaustive list, the following are the most common medical causes of nighttime awakenings.

- *Teething.* Growth hormone is released during sleep, so teething pain in young children is often worse at night. Parents should check with their child's primary care provider for suggestions of pain relievers that are okay to give children.
- *Reflux.* Approximately one in four infants experiences reflux, and symptoms of reflux have been shown to be worse during sleep, contributing to frequent arousals. Most infants outgrow their reflux by 18 months of age. However, older children and adolescents can also develop gastroesophageal reflux disease, which again can disturb sleep because of discomfort.
- *Common acute illnesses.* Ear infections, upper respiratory infections, and diaper rash all make sleeping more difficult because of pain

and discomfort. A child who has always slept well and now has frequent nighttime awakenings following treatment for an acute illness may still have residual symptoms that need additional treatment (e.g., ear infection persists despite the child completing a course of antibiotics).

▪ *Food allergies and/or eczema.* Children with food allergies and/or eczema may have more nighttime awakenings due to discomfort such as stomach pain or itching.

▪ *Other chronic illnesses.* Many chronic illnesses and medications can disrupt sleep. For example, asthma and chronic pain in particular are well known to interfere with sleep quality, resulting in multiple nighttime awakenings due to symptoms (e.g., wheezing, pain). Other illnesses, including seizure disorders, Type 1 diabetes, and juvenile rheumatoid arthritis, may also interfere with sleep quantity and/or sleep quality.

Behavioral Factors That May Contribute to Nighttime Awakenings

For infants and toddlers, the three primary causes of nighttime awakenings are sleep-onset associations at bedtime, the need for feeding during the night, and the inability to distinguish night and day.

NEGATIVE SLEEP-ONSET ASSOCIATIONS

As discussed in Chapter 3, children who learn to fall asleep at bedtime with certain conditions present (e.g., mother nursing child to sleep, father swinging child in his arms) will require these same conditions to return to sleep following typical nighttime arousals. Whereas most parents do not mind helping their child fall asleep at bedtime, frequent nighttime awakenings that require parental assistance are quite bothersome and challenging for families to deal with.

Many parents are surprised to learn that what happens at bedtime is often the culprit for nighttime awakenings. Below is an example of how to explain this to parents.

Nighttime arousals are normal. Everyone, including adults and children, wake briefly at the end of every sleep cycle. This can occur approximately two to six times every night and sometimes even more in younger children. Usually, we roll over and go right back to sleep.

We also all have our favorite ways of falling asleep. Some people like having a hall light on, some people like a fan or white noise machine, and some people like having the TV on (which we do not recommend). I like sleeping on two pillows. When I put my head down on the two pillows, I fall asleep easily. In the middle of the night I wake up and find my two pillows on the floor. So I automatically think, "Oh, the pillows fell off the bed and that's what woke me up." But really, the pillows had fallen off my bed an hour ago and I slept right through it. Then when I had my normal arousal, I rolled over and couldn't go back to sleep since my pillows weren't there.

You have become your child's two pillows. Because you rock your child to sleep at bedtime [or lay with her or drive her around], when she has a normal arousal during the night, she cannot return to sleep in the middle of the night without your assistance. That is why we start by making changes at bedtime, to teach her the skill of falling asleep independently.

Both standard extinction and graduated extinction approaches described in this chapter are effective ways of removing negative sleep-onset associations at bedtime.

NEED FOR NOCTURNAL FEEDING

For infants in particular, it is important to provide parents with a realistic expectation of "sleeping through the night." Although one early study suggested that 50% of infants at the age of age of 6 months were sleeping through the night, defined as midnight to 5:00 a.m. (T. Moore & Ucko, 1957), most families seeking help with nighttime awakenings would not consider this to be sleeping through the night. But most healthy and typically developing 6-month-old infants should be able to sleep through the night with minimal, if any, feedings. Although it is not common, some children may still need one nocturnal feed after the age of 6 months because of developmental or health-related issues. Although not studied empirically, the dream feed (or focal feed) described later in this chapter provides a solution that is relatively easy to implement, acceptable to parents, and helpful for infants.

DISTINGUISHING BETWEEN NIGHT AND DAY

As adults, if we wake up during the night, we simply look at our clock to see whether it is time to get up. For young children who cannot tell time, there is often no clear way to distinguish between night and day. Although some parents may use darkness and light as cues to tell children when it is time for sleeping and time for waking up (i.e., you go to bed when its dark and don't get up until the sun gets up), this can backfire depending on the time of year and the location of the patient. For example, in the state of Washington, the sunrise in December is approximately 7:50 a.m. and the sunset is approximately 4:20 p.m., whereas in July the sun rises at approximately 5:30 a.m. and sets at approximately 9:00 p.m.

Other parents will set arbitrary rules about when it is okay for a child to get up (e.g., if he wakes before 6:00 a.m., we make him stay in his bed, but after 6:00 a.m. he can come to our bed). This can be confusing for a child who does not understand the difference between 2:00, 4:00, and 6:00 a.m., thus perpetuating nighttime awakenings as he wakes with each typical arousal wondering, "Is this the time I get to move to Mommy and Daddy's bed?" The good morning light intervention described later in this chapter, although not empirically validated, is clinically useful in helping children understand the difference between night and day, regardless of time of year or location.

Behavioral Interventions for Nighttime Awakenings

As previously described, nighttime arousals are typical. All children wake between two and six times per night at the end of each sleep cycle. Therefore, the circumstances that are present at bedtime (e.g., mom nursing, dad rocking) will also need to be present for night awakenings. Thus the first step of interventions focuses on teaching young children to fall asleep independently at bedtime, using standard or graduated extinction approaches.

THE EVIDENCE

A number of studies have examined the use of extinction-based procedures to teach young children to fall asleep and return to sleep independently (see Honaker & Meltzer, 2014; Meltzer & Mindell, 2014; and Mindell et al., 2006, for comprehensive reviews). In 2006, the American Academy of Sleep Medicine released a Practice Parameters Report that designated unmodified extinction as a "Standard" recommendation, and graduated extinction as a "Guideline" recommendation (Morgenthaler, Owens, et al., 2006). This means that unmodified extinction is a treatment that is generally accepted and well supported by the research literature, whereas graduated extinction is a treatment that is generally accepted but with fewer supporting studies in the literature. A more recent meta-analysis also reported that behavioral interventions result in significant improvements for sleep-onset latency, night waking frequency, and night waking duration in young children (Meltzer & Mindell, 2014).

In the following sections, we take these empirically supported treatments and provide step-by-step guidance for the busy provider on how to actually implement them in a clinical setting. Before starting any extinction-based intervention, practitioners should keep in mind that there are many different ways to modify these treatments for families. The ultimate decision on how to teach the child to fall asleep independently should be based on parental tolerance (i.e., how much crying they can handle) and child temperament (i.e., how upset the child becomes in response to intervention). Although both unmodified extinction and graduated extinction have been shown to be effective, the latter is better tolerated by parents (Reid, Walter, & O'Leary, 1999).

The decision on whether to use an intervention at bedtime only versus the entire night is also dependent on the child and the family. Some families may be more willing than others to tackle the entire night at one time. However, families seeking treatment for nighttime awakenings will likely need to have a more gradual approach that enables them to be successful at each step. Thus for these families, treatment should focus only on bedtime. For most infants, learning to self-soothe only at bedtime without parental assistance will generalize to nighttime awakenings within about 2 weeks (although for some, the generalization may occur faster). If the bedtime behavior does not generalize to nighttime awakenings within 2 to 3 weeks, these approaches can then be applied to the nighttime awakenings directly. Finally, these treatment approaches could be combined, with the use of standard extinction at bedtime only and a checking method version of graduated extinction for nighttime awakenings. *Note: It is critical before implementing the following interventions to ensure that the child has a consistent sleep schedule and bedtime routine.*

STANDARD EXTINCTION

Standard extinction is one of the fastest interventions to address nighttime awakenings, especially in young children, with treatment success typically occurring in about 3 to 5 days. The goal of this treatment is to completely remove the sleep-onset association both at bedtime and during the night so the child to learns to fall asleep independently at bedtime and return to sleep independently following typical nighttime arousals.

How It Works

Parents consistently ignore the child's cries and protests at bedtime and during the night until the child learns to fall asleep and return to sleep independently.

Contraindications and Considerations for Special Populations

Standard extinction should not be used on children younger than 6 months of age, as before this nocturnal feedings are still necessary in most cases. In addition, infants who have developmental issues or who have failure to thrive should also not begin this type of intervention until medically cleared by their primary care provider. Because this intervention often involves prolonged crying, it may not be appropriate for children with medical conditions that can be exacerbated by crying (e.g., severe reflux, reactive airway disease, seizure disorder) or for young children with a history of severe anxiety or trauma (e.g., abuse, neglect).

Although standard extinction is typically thought of as an intervention for only infants and young children, it has also been shown to be an effective treatment for children with autism spectrum disorder. Although it may take more than the standard 3 nights, children with autism spectrum disorder can learn to fall asleep independently with this treatment. However, families who are generally overwhelmed by managing daytime behavior issues may not have the resources or strength to be consistent in the implementation of this treatment.

In Practice

- After establishing a consistent bedtime and bedtime routine, the child is placed in the crib awake and the parents leave the room.
- Parents should ignore the child's protests until she is asleep. However, if there are concerns for safety or health issues, the parents should do a brief check of the child but not interact with her.
- Parents should also ignore the child's nighttime awakenings (after checking on the child for safety or health issues, if needed).
- After the first 3 to 4 nights, crying will decrease both at bedtime and during the night, to the point where the child then falls asleep and remains asleep without protest.

Handout 4 provides step-by-step instructions for parents on how to implement standard extinction.

Managing Potential Pitfalls

Inform parents about what to expect, in particular, that it will get worse before it gets better. First and foremost, the child may cry 45 minutes (or longer) at bedtime on the first night but will often cry even longer at bedtime on the second night (90 or more minutes). This is an *extinction burst*, in which the undesired behavior (crying) increases initially in the hope of reinforcement (e.g., parent rocking child to sleep). By the third night, crying duration typically decreases (around 20 minutes), with further decreases in crying over subsequent nights. Here is an example of how to explain extinction bursts to parents (note that this explanation can be adapted for any situation where parental consistency is a concern):

> To understand why your child's behavior will get worse before it gets better, think about a soda machine that you use every day to give you that can of caffeine you want. You put your money in and out comes your soda, goal achieved! But one day, you put your money in and nothing happens. So instead of pressing just once, you press the button over and over and over hoping to get what you want. But nothing happens, so you leave thinking that perhaps the machine is broken or needed to be refilled. The next day you return, and the same thing happens. No soda, so you press the button repeatedly, and when nothing happens, you get really mad, shake the machine, and you may even kick it. If nothing happens, you'll eventually give up and either find another machine or simply realize you don't really need that caffeine to get through the afternoon.
>
> So when your child's crying gets worse at night, she is upset because she is not getting what she wants to help her fall asleep. But if you remain consistent and don't go into her room, eventually she will stop crying and fall asleep. The second night, she will likely cry even more, as she is pressing your button to come in and help her. But if you remain consistent she will eventually stop crying and fall asleep. By the third or fourth night, she will cry for shorter periods of time, knowing that it will not get her what she wants.

Remind parents that this is only a short-term cost for a long-term gain. Parent buy-in is essential for this type of treatment to be successful. Many parents worry about causing long-term emotional damage to their child (e.g., child feels abandoned, worry about attachment) when prolonged crying is involved. However, they must be reassured that there are no studies supporting any negative outcomes to sleep training. In addition, parents should be informed that sleep problems will likely continue without treatment. Further, for many parents, it is helpful to learn that young children with untreated sleep problems have mothers with higher rates of depression. See Exhibit 6.1 for more information.

Warn parents that the child may vomit, and provide suggestions on how to respond. Although it rarely happens, this side effect of extinction is (understandably) quite distressing for parents. However, even infants can learn to vomit on demand, and if they are not prepared, parents may give up on the intervention, only further reinforcing the unwanted behavior (i.e., when "rescued" the baby learns that if she cries or vomits she will be rocked to sleep again). Parents should put a second set of sheets on the bed and lay out a second set of pajamas. That way, if the child does vomit, the parents can quickly change the sheets

---

EXHIBIT 6.1

"Won't Sleep Training Cause My Child to Feel Abandoned?"

Sleep training has become one of the most controversial topics in early childhood parenting. If you search the Internet or read popular parent blogs and websites, there is a perception that letting your child "cry it out" (as it is sometimes termed) is tantamount to abuse and neglect. This in fact is <u>not</u> true, and parents must be thoroughly educated on the reasons children cry at night during sleep training (i.e., he is tired and frustrated because he doesn't know how to fall asleep without assistance), as well as the pros and cons of sleep training. It is also important to note that there is no true no-cry solution. Although popular press parenting books all allow for different amounts of crying, they do involve at least some crying on the child's part. But if standard extinction is too hard for a family to handle, then a graduated extinction approach should be selected.

It is critical to inform skeptical parents that studies examining sleep training in young children have unequivocally demonstrated short-term benefits for the child and the parents, with absolutely no support for long-term negative consequences for the child, parent, or family unit (Hiscock, Bayer, Hampton, Ukoumunne, & Wake, 2008; Lam, Hiscock, & Wake, 2003; Price, Wake, Ukoumunne, & Hiscock, 2012). This is a very critical point to raise, as the media has wrongly interpreted studies of abused and neglected children (who were allowed to cry for prolonged periods of time not related to sleep onset) as evidence that sleep training is damaging to child development.

Rather, the literature has clearly and repeatedly shown that infant and toddler sleep training results in improved sleep for both the child and the parent, as well as lower rates of maternal depression and better family functioning. These benefits have been shown to be maintained for up to 4 years. As it is well known that children of depressed mothers are at greater risk for developing behavior problems, mood disorders, and have more health care utilization, it is critical to address sleep issues as soon as possible to improve the functioning of the entire family. In terms of parent–child attachment, which is the most common concern of parents not wanting to let their child cry, one study showed that 5 years after sleep training, no differences in attachment were found between children who had and those who had not received sleep training (Price et al., 2012).

---

and clean up the infant. But after a few moments of soothing, the baby should be placed back in the crib awake.

Encourage parents to work together (when there are two parents available). This is critical for success, as it is commonly seen that one parent cannot tolerate the infant's cries and thus rescues the baby after a short period of time. As previously stated, this only serves to reinforce the unwanted behavior of the infant crying at bedtime, perpetuating her inability to fall asleep independently. It can be helpful to identify the parent who will "give in" first before starting the intervention. This helps to prepare parents for how they will respond and work together. If one parent feels he/she is not able to follow through with the treatment, it may be useful to have him/her leave the house (e.g., go to the grocery store, go on a walk) during the treatment time to prevent sabotage or unwanted reinforcement of crying at bedtime.

Suggest ways to prevent disrupting sleep of other children in the home. Standard extinction may be disruptive to the bedtime routine and sleep onset of other children in the home. Problem solving with parents is critical to identify alternative sleeping arrangements if necessary (e.g., other child sleeps at the grandparents' house or in the basement for 3 nights) or other ways to distract the child (e.g., soft music or a white noise machine in the other child's room). In addition, it may be beneficial to put the other child to bed first and once she is asleep, initiate the standard extinction protocol with the patient.

Advise parents to discuss the treatment with neighbors who may complain about the crying. Depending on the living arrangement (e.g., apartment) parents may fear the neighbors will complain about the crying. Parents should warn neighbors about the sleep training plan and offer to provide them with ear plugs. A little gesture like this (and humor) may make neighbors more sympathetic. An early bedtime (e.g., 7:30 p.m.) can also assist with these complaints, as most neighbors are not trying to sleep at that time and can typically drown out the crying sounds with the television or music.

Consider scheduling dream feedings. If the child needs a feeding in between bedtime and wake time, it is helpful to implement a dream feed as described later in this chapter. The dream feed will prevent reinforcing the child's nighttime awakenings with a feeding, instead providing a feeding on the parents' schedule.

Identify the child's true wake time in the morning. A child falling asleep immediately after being fed in the morning suggests that she was not ready to wake for the day but rather was having her last nighttime arousal, which was then reinforced by feeding. Although many parents may not object to getting up at 5:00 a.m. to do this feeding, it may ultimately result in an increase in nighttime awakenings, as the child is unsure which arousal will result in a feeding. Thus, in addition to a dream feed, it is essential to identify the child's true wake time. When the parent gets her up for the day, the child should be changed and dressed, then taken to another room for the feeding to clearly disassociate waking with the feeding.

Suggest the use of a video monitor, if available. Families who can afford (or can borrow) a video monitor may benefit from this technology, as it enables them to monitor the child for safety without going in the room. In addition, video monitors can be useful for parents to see how children learn to self-soothe and put themselves to sleep at bedtime. Parents should be cautioned, however, to not stare at the monitor watching the child cry, as this can increase parents' distress.

Remind parents that consistency is essential for treatment success! Parents must be absolutely committed to completing at least 3 nights of standard extinction before they begin. Parents may follow the protocol and successfully tolerate the first night of crying but give in on the second night. As previously described, this will only serve to further reinforce that a child's prolonged crying will result in parental intervention. Although this is desirable for the child, this will further perpetuate his inability to fall asleep independently. Therefore, it is essential to inform parents that if they cannot follow through, it would be better to not begin standard extinction.

The Bottom Line

Standard extinction is a highly efficacious treatment, and in most cases will work in 3 to 4 nights. However, parental tolerance of this intervention is often very low because of the amount of crying involved. Most families who seek clinical treatment for nighttime awakenings either cannot handle this much crying or have previously attempted to, as some say, "cry it out" with little success. Parents who can successfully implement standard extinction rarely seek clinical treatment. That said, the option should always be provided to families, as some parents are at their wits' end and want to fix the problem immediately. For families who have previously not tried standard extinction because of concerns about the child feeling abandoned or causing long-term damage (see Exhibit 6.1), education about the benefits (and challenges) of standard extinction may persuade them to try this approach. In either scenario, however, clinical judgment about the parents' ability to follow through, as well as the use of problem solving to identify areas of concern that may interfere with treatment implementation, is critical to ensure success.

GRADUATED EXTINCTION

Although standard extinction is a well-validated and strongly recommended treatment approach, it is often not well tolerated by parents because of the amount of crying. In particular, for families seeking clinical care for nighttime awakenings, either the family is not willing to try standard extinction or they have previously tried it and failed after one or two nights. Thus, graduated extinction is one of the most common treatment approaches used in clinical practice for the treatment of nighttime awakenings. The goal of graduated extinction is for the child to learn to fall asleep independently only at bedtime, without a negative sleep-onset association. Although crying is involved with all sleep training, graduated extinction allows for greater interaction between the parent and child, often resulting in less crying than standard extinction.

Once a child learns to fall asleep independently at bedtime, this behavior will most likely generalize to nighttime awakenings. Graduated extinction is better tolerated by parents because a child crying at bedtime is easier to tolerate than multiple crying episodes through the night, which disrupt the parents' sleep.

The two primary options for graduated extinction are with and without parental presence. The basics of both approaches are outlined below, with Exhibit 6.2 highlighting variations to graduated extinction, as well as how to more gradually remove negative sleep-onset associations, such as nursing/feeding or rocking the child to sleep.

How It Works

Graduated extinction without parental presence uses a consistent checking schedule, in which the parent will check on the child at set intervals to provide reassurance (for both the parent and the child), while enabling the child to learn to self-soothe and fall asleep independently. Graduated extinction with parental presence has the parent remain with the child until she is asleep, gradually removing the parent's presence until the child learns to self-soothe and fall asleep independently. For both approaches, once the child learns to fall asleep independently, that behavior will generalize to nighttime awakenings in about 2 weeks, with the interval between sleep onset and the first waking increasing in length until the child no longer signals the parent following a typical nighttime arousal.

Contraindications

Similar to standard extinction, graduated extinction should not be used on children younger than 6 months of age. In addition, infants with developmental issues or failure to thrive should also not begin this type of intervention until they are medically cleared by their primary care provider. Because this intervention often involves prolonged crying at bedtime, it may not be appropriate for children with medical conditions that can be exacerbated by crying (e.g., severe reflux, reactive airway disease, seizure disorder) or for young children with a history of severe anxiety or trauma (e.g., abuse, neglect).

In Practice—Graduated Extinction Without Parental Presence

- After establishing a consistent bedtime and bedtime routine, the child is placed in the crib awake and the parents leave the room.
- Parents check on the child at set intervals. For some parents, the starting point is checking on the child every 1 minute, with the

EXHIBIT 6.2

Hierarchy of Sleep-Onset Associations and How to Change Them

Although the literature has examined very specific approaches to graduated extinction, the following variations are based on our clinical experience and can be modified based on the needs of each family. It is not necessary to follow every single step (e.g., some families may be able to skip from Step 1 to Step 6).

1. If parents are nursing or bottle feeding the infant to sleep, move the feeding earlier in the routine. Typically the feeding should occur before the bath or putting the infant into pajamas, and then rock the child to sleep.
   - It is important to assure parents that the child does not need to be topped off before bed.
   - If at all possible, when nursing is involved, it is best if another adult rocks the child to sleep. The scent of a lactating mother can increase distress in infants who will want to nurse themselves to sleep.
2. If parents are rocking the infant to sleep, decrease the duration of rocking each night so the infant is placed in the crib drowsy but awake. With the decrease in time being rocked, it is likely the child will be less drowsy each night when placed in the crib. This is okay, as the goal is to place the infant the crib calm and relaxed, yet awake, in order for him to fall asleep without assistance.
3. Parent present and interactive with child but not holding, rocking, or feeding him to sleep. The first step for this treatment allows the parent to remain present until the infant is asleep, rubbing the baby's head or providing soothing verbal reassurances. However, for some children, the presence of a parent who is not rocking or holding them will increase distress. In this case parents should skip to Step 6.
4. Infant in crib awake with parent in room but not physically interacting with child, instead providing only verbal reassurances.
5. Infant in crib awake with parent in room but not interacting with child.
6. Infant in crib awake and alone, falling asleep independently.

To get from Step 5 to Step 6, there are three options:

A. Leave the room and check on the infant as needed (e.g., every minute or every 5 minutes). Parents should be encouraged to increase the time between checks each night. The longer parents can stay out of the room, the easier it will be for the child to learn to fall asleep.
B. Move a little farther away from the crib every few nights. This can be accomplished in two ways: (a) Moving a couple of feet away from the crib toward the door every few nights or (b) moving half the distance to the door for a few nights, then to the doorway for a few nights, then to the hallway for a few nights.
C. Stay for a few minutes then take a short break (i.e., 1 minute). Each night, the break should get a little bit longer (e.g., add a minute each night), with the goal of the child learning to fall asleep when the parent isn't in the room.
   - The duration of the break and the frequency and duration that the time interval increases should be based on how the child reacts to being alone and how well the parent tolerates the child's distress.
   - Again, the longer the parent can stay out of the room, the better; however, small steps with success are better than big steps with failure!

duration between checks increasing each night (2 minutes on the second night, 3 minutes on the third night). Alternatively, parents can increase the duration of breaks over the course of the night (first break is 1 minute, second break is 2 minutes, third break is 5 minutes, etc.).

- The frequency of checks should be determined on the basis of the parent's tolerance for crying and the child's temperament. For example, some anxious parents may be unable to stay out of the room more than 1 minute before needing to check on the child to provide verbal reassurances. However, the parent's coming in increases some infants' distress, which is counterproductive for self-soothing and sleep initiation. In this case, parents should be encouraged to check less frequently.

- Parents should be instructed that these checks are brief and boring, and are more for the parent than the child. Parents can give a repeated message ("I love you, it's sleeping time") but should leave the room without picking the child up. In some cases, parents may pick up a crying child and return the child to the crib drowsy, as described below.

Handout 5 provides step-by-step instructions for parents on how to use graduated extinction without parental presence.

In Practice—Graduated Extinction With Parental Presence

- After establishing a consistent bedtime and bedtime routine, the child is placed in the crib awake and the parent remains with the child until he is asleep.

- For the first few nights, the parents may provide verbal reassurance (e.g., "I love you, it's sleeping time") and minimal physical interaction (e.g., rubbing the child's head).

- After 3 to 5 nights of establishing the child's ability to fall asleep in the crib, the parents gradually remove their presence.

See Exhibit 6.2 for a detailed description of options on how to remove parental presence and Handout 6 for step-by-step instructions for parents on how to use graduated extinction with parental presence.

Managing Potential Pitfalls

The following strategies for managing potential pitfalls are described in the Standard Extinction section and also apply to graduated extinction. (Please see the previous section for detailed explanations and suggestions.)

- Inform parents about what to expect, in particular, that it will get worse before it gets better.

- Remind parents that this is only a short-term cost for a long-term gain.
- Warn parents that the child may vomit and provide suggestions on how to respond.
- Encourage parents to work together (when there are two parents available).
- Suggest ways to prevent the sleep of other children in the home from becoming disrupted.
- Advise parents to discuss the treatment with neighbors who may complain about the crying.
- Consider scheduling dream feedings.
- Identify the child's true wake time in the morning.
- Suggest the use of a video monitor if available. In addition to the benefits described in the standard extinction section, a video monitor enables parents using graduated extinction to respond more slowly to night wakings, as they can often watch a child have an arousal, but then put himself back to sleep.
- Remind parents that consistency is essential for treatment success!

In addition, the following strategies are helpful for graduated extinction.

Inform parents that because graduated extinction is initially used only at bedtime, nighttime awakenings will continue. Parents will need to be reminded that the child needs to first learn how to fall asleep independently at bedtime, but until this new behavior generalizes to nighttime awakenings, these wakings will continue.

Identify a consistent response to nighttime awakenings. Parents' inconsistent response (e.g., most of the time dad rocks the child, but by 3:00 a.m. they give up and mom nurses him) will serve to maintain the night wakings. Thus, parents need to select a response that they can agree upon and follow through with for every single night waking. For example, every time the child wakes, he is rocked back to sleep by the father. Alternatively, every time he wakes, the mother nurses him back to sleep.

Discuss with parents the potential consequences of picking the child up to provide brief comfort. In general, parents should be discouraged from picking the child up at bedtime to provide comfort, as there is a high likelihood he will fall asleep in the parent's arms. This only reinforces that if the child cries enough, the parent will "rescue" him. However, in certain cases the child may become so distressed (past the point of no return) that picking him up briefly may be necessary to calm him enough to help facilitate sleep onset. That said, the child must be returned to the crib awake. Clinical judgment should be used when providing this option to parents to ensure that they know when it is okay to pick the child up, as well as when the child must be returned to the crib. Parents should also be provided with the pros and cons of picking the child up, even for brief periods.

The Bottom Line

Although similar to standard extinction, graduated extinction has been shown to be better accepted and tolerated by parents, enabling them to interact with the child at bedtime while the child still learns to fall asleep independently. For graduated extinction without parental presence, when parents are given permission to provide frequent checks, they will often check less frequently than you have recommended. However, it is important to keep in mind that although equally as effective as standard extinction, graduated extinction takes longer to implement. In addition, as the skill of returning to sleep independently may not occur until approximately two weeks after the child learns to fall asleep at bedtime independently, the parents need to expect that nighttime awakenings will continue for the near future. It is often useful to remind parents that they have been dealing with this issue for a long time, and thus they will be able to make it a few more weeks to see success in changing the child's ability to fall asleep independently.

DREAM FEED (OR FOCAL FEED)

The purpose of the dream feed is to provide a nighttime feeding at a time close to when the parent is going to sleep but after the baby has already been asleep for a while. Parents often report how frustrating it is to be awakened only 30 to 60 minutes after falling asleep because of the infant's need to feed. Thus, the dream feed is a preventative measure for this and can create a longer stretch of sleep during the night for both the baby and the parent. Dream feeds can be introduced as early as 2 months but can be used with older infants as well, especially for those children whose parents believe a nocturnal feed is required or there is a medical concern about the child needing additional calories during the night because of growth or other health issues. By having the parent choose the time of the dream feed, the child will get the feeding she needs and the parents can be assured that it is okay to ignore (or provide a nonfeeding response) any other nighttime awakenings.

How It Works

Parents select a time to gently rouse the child for a feeding and then provide no additional feedings for the duration of the night.

In Practice

- Work with the parent to select a time for the dream feed. This is usually around the time the parent goes to bed or about 2 to 3 hours after the child has fallen asleep at bedtime.

- The parent gently rouses the child and provides the feeding (nursing or bottle). Then the child is placed back in the crib (it is okay if she is asleep at this point).
- For all additional nighttime awakenings, parents provide a consistent response that does not include feeding (e.g., rocking back to sleep, rubbing child's back, or checking on child for safety and then allowing her to return to sleep without assistance).

Handout 7 provides step-by-step instructions for parents on how to use the dream feed.

Managing Potential Pitfalls

Assist parents in identifying a consistent response to all nighttime awakenings. It is important to work with the parents to determine what their response will be for all nighttime awakenings. The parents must be in agreement to be successful. For example, if it becomes clear that one parent will eventually bring the child into the bed, then the parents should be encouraged to bring the child into the bed at the first awakening and not wait until the second or third waking.

Encourage the involvement of a second parent/caregiver when possible. For nursing mothers in particular, if there is a second parent in the home, success will be increased if the nonnursing parent attends to the child for all additional nighttime awakenings. Otherwise, the child may become frustrated when the nursing mother is present but not nursing her, prolonging nighttime awakenings.

Instruct families to start the day without immediately feeding the child. When the child wakes for the final time, she should be dressed and removed from her room before another feed (e.g., take her downstairs to the couch before feeding). This will help to extinguish other nighttime awakenings where the child is anticipating being fed.

Ask parents if the child is feeding for nutrition or comfort during the night. Often a discussion with the parents about whether they think the child is feeding for nutrition or comfort will provide additional motivation. Many parents can readily identify that the child is not actually hungry, as she only feeds for a couple of minutes before returning to sleep. In this case, a dream feed is likely not necessary, but it may be helpful to review the role of sleep-onset associations.

The Bottom Line

To address nighttime awakenings in children who require a nocturnal feed, the dream feed can be an effective intervention. As described in the previous sections, it is also important to ensure that the child is able to put herself to sleep independently at bedtime. Finally, reinforcing to parents that in most instances, multiple nighttime feeds in children older than 6 months are more likely for comfort rather than nutrition can also contribute to success.

Case Example: Billy

Billy is an 8-month-old boy whose parents complain that he wakes up almost every hour during the night. He will return to sleep only if mom nurses him or dad rocks him. By 4:00 a.m., both parents are exhausted and Billy ends up in their bed for the remainder of the night. At bedtime, Billy gets a bath, lotion, and in his pajamas. Then he is taken into the parents' room, where mom nurses him. If that does not put him to sleep, dad will then walk around the house until Billy is asleep.

Billy's mother said she can't handle any crying, but Billy's father wanted things to change quickly. We discussed the option of having mom stay with her parents for 3 nights while dad used standard extinction. However, mom was not comfortable with that, as she had a history of childhood trauma. Despite multiple reassurances, she was concerned that Billy would be traumatized by the sleep training. So, we decided to begin by moving nursing before Billy's bath. At bedtime, dad would rock Billy until drowsy but put him in the crib awake and leave the room. The parents decided they could wait at least 3 minutes before checking on Billy. Because Billy had a history of reflux and poor weight gain, mom felt it was necessary for him to have at least one night feed. Therefore, before she went to bed at 10:00 p.m., mom would do a dream feed, and for all remaining nighttime awakenings dad would rock Billy back to sleep, consistently returning Billy to his crib each time.

The first night, Billy cried at bedtime for 40 minutes and had two night awakenings; the second night, he cried for 1 hour and 10 minutes at bedtime and had one night awakening; and the third night, he cried for 20 minutes at bedtime and did not wake until 5:30 a.m. At that point, mom got him up, changed and dressed him, and then nursed him in a different room to start his day. The family continued with the dream feed after that, and although they heard Billy cry for a few minutes each night at bedtime, he would then settle and put himself to sleep.

GOOD MORNING LIGHT

As previously described, in some cases nighttime awakenings are perpetuated by inconsistent parental responses during the night and/or first thing in the morning. For example, the parents may decide it is okay to bring a child to bed after 1:00 a.m. to get him back to sleep, but not before 1:00 a.m. But because the child is unable to tell time, he is more likely to wake after typical nighttime arousals wondering, "Is this the time I get to move?" To help a young child learn to understand the difference between night and day, it is important to provide a visual cue for when it is okay to wake up.

How It Works

The changing of the Good Morning Light (from on to off or from off to on) is paired with a specific event (i.e., a parent coming to get the child to start the day). In essence, it serves as an alarm clock for children who wonder with each nighttime awakening, "Is it time to wake up?"

In Practice

- Using a sleep diary for at least 1 week, determine the child's average bedtime and wake time.
- Plug a nightlight into a timer (e.g., the kind that would be used for holiday or vacation lights). The timer should be set so that the light turns on about 30 minutes before the child's typical bedtime. Thus, during the bedtime routine the parent can reinforce that the light is on, so it is almost sleeping time.
- For each night waking, the parent should immediately respond with the brief and boring message: "The light is on, it is still sleeping time."
- The light should be set to turn off at the earliest time the child may wake up to start the day. Any waking before this time (even 15 minutes before the light changes) should be treated as a nighttime awakening.
- Once the light turns off, the parent should immediately go into the child's room and make a big deal about the fact that the light is off and it is time to get up (e.g., "Hooray! The light is off, so it is time to get up!").
- Once the association is made between the light and sleep (i.e., consistent response for at least 1 week), if a later wake time is desired, the timer can be set to go on about 15 minutes later every 5 to 7 nights.
- The Good Morning Light can also be used for naptime.
- For children who do not sleep with a nightlight on during the night, the light can be turned on during the day and set to turn off 30 minutes before bed and on at the designated wake time. In this case, the message should be, "Your light is off, it is still sleeping time."

Handout 8 provides step-by-step instructions for parents on the use of a Good Morning Light.

Managing Potential Pitfalls

Ensure that the child is old enough to understand. Although parents may introduce the Good Morning Light sooner, children may not understand it until they are between 16 and 18 months of age.

Review the importance of providing a consistent response. If a parent responds to the child (e.g., bringing him to the parents' bed) before the changing of the light in the morning, the child may become confused. In addition, the parent's responding serves as an intermittent reinforcement, ultimately delaying success.

Remind parents that it is possible that the child will wake before the light changes. Once the association is made, children may wake on occasion 15 to 30 minutes before the light goes off; thus, parents should be informed that the child will learn to self-entertain until the light changes (as long as the parents are consistent in their response). However, if the child is consistently waking at least 30 minutes before the light changes, the parents will need to move the time that the light changes to better align with the child's natural waking time.

Warn parents to not change the wake time too quickly. The use of sleep diary data helps to identify the child's naturally occurring wake time. However, some parents may want a rapid change to the child's wake time and thus adjust the time too quickly (e.g., 5:00 a.m. the first night, 5:30 a.m. the second night, 6:00 a.m. the third night). This will likely lead to prolonged crying and frustration on the child's part, which may interfere with the parents' ability to be consistent and, ultimately, with treatment success. Additional education about a reasonable wake time may also be needed (e.g., a child who regularly wakes at 5:00 a.m. may not learn to sleep until 7:00 a.m. simply because that is more convenient for the parent).

Ensure that the child can see the light change. The light that is used should be one that the child can clearly see from his bed. In some cases, this may be a small table lamp instead of a nightlight. In addition, if a child's bedroom becomes light in the morning (i.e., in the summer months) and the nightlight being used is one that uses a light sensor (e.g., turns on when the room is dark and off when the room is light), the light may go off before the designated time.

Prevent the child from playing with the timer. Although in general children should be discouraged from playing with anything plugged into an outlet, some children may discover the timer and move the dial or change the clock/timer feature. In these cases, the timer and light should be placed in a location that is not accessible to the child (e.g., use of a small table lamp that sits on top of a dresser, with the plug behind the dresser).

The Bottom Line

The Good Morning Light provides a consistent visual cue that teaches young children and those who cannot tell time when it is sleeping time and when it is time to get out of bed. This is an especially useful intervention for children who wake frequently in the hope that they will get a parental response (e.g., nursing or taken to the parents bed), as well as for children who tend to wake very early (e.g., 4:30 a.m.) but would likely self-entertain until it is time to get up.

Case Example: Emma

Emma is an 18-month-old girl who has reportedly slept through the night once in her entire life, and that was 6 nights before her clinic visit. According to the 2-week sleep diary, Emma has nighttime awakenings between one and four times per night. These occur as early as 11:00 p.m. (on one night), with most wakings between 1:00 a.m. and 4:00 a.m. Handwritten notes identify that on more than half the nights, mom nurses Emma between 11:00 p.m. and 1:00 a.m.

Mom reports that she nurses Emma at bedtime, but she is "pretty sure" Emma is awake when she places her in the crib and leaves the room, after which Emma falls asleep independently. If Emma wakes before 1:00 a.m., mom will nurse her back to sleep. After 1:00 a.m., she is brought into her parents' bed for the duration of the night. Emma wakes to start her day between 6:00 and 7:00 a.m. and is nursed upon waking.

For Emma's mother, several changes were made. Despite mother's assurances, it was important to ensure that Emma was not sometimes falling asleep at bedtime nursing. Thus, mom was instructed to move nursing earlier in the bedtime routine, before Emma's bath. In addition, the morning nursing was delayed until after Emma was up and dressed in the morning, and nursing was done in the family room. To help Emma distinguish between nighttime and morning, a Good Morning Light was introduced. The light was scheduled to go on at 7:00 p.m. (30 minutes before her bedtime) and to go off at 6:00 a.m. (the earliest that she would typically wake).

After 2 weeks, Emma was consistently falling asleep independently in her crib, and her nighttime awakenings had ceased. She also never woke before 6:15 a.m., so her parents adjusted the timer on her Good Morning Light to this later time. Concurrently, mom introduced the Good Morning Light at naptime and reported that Emma was now sleeping longer during the day as well.

Summary and
Take-Home Points

Although parents may present complaining of nighttime awakenings in young children, behavioral treatments focus primarily on teaching the child to fall asleep independently at bedtime. These behavioral interventions are highly effective in teaching children to fall asleep independently at bedtime, which in turn helps them to return to sleep following typical nighttime arousals. Specific points to remember are summarized below.

- Any possible medical factors contributing to nighttime awakenings need to be identified and treated.
- There are multiple approaches to teaching children to fall asleep independently at bedtime. Choosing the right one requires clinical judgment and partnering with parents to have treatment success. It is essential to consider both the child's temperament and the parent's tolerance for crying when making this decision.
- According to behavior principles, when changing a child's behavior (e.g., teaching her to fall asleep independently), unwanted behaviors (e.g., crying) will likely get worse before they get better. Parents must be prepared for this and other challenges that occur with sleep training.
- When using a graduated extinction approach (i.e., sleep training only at bedtime), once a child learns to fall asleep independently at bedtime, the skill will generalize to nighttime awakenings, although this may take at least 2 weeks.
- Although a negative sleep-onset association at bedtime is usually the culprit for the maintenance of nighttime awakenings, it is also important to consider how the child differentiates between night and day, as well as what happens when a child wakes in the morning to start the day (e.g., nursed immediately, brought to the parents' bed).

Bedtime Stalling, Protests, and Curtain Calls | 7

Bedtime problems come in many forms, with stalling, protesting, and outright refusal most common in toddlers (who are no longer in a crib), preschoolers, and school-age children. The typical presentation is when a parent complains that bedtime takes 1 to 2 hours (or longer) and is accompanied by one or more of the following: (a) the child stalling at bedtime and refusing to participate in the bedtime routine (e.g., child will not put on pajamas, spends 20 minutes in the bathroom looking in the mirror but does not brush teeth); (b) multiple curtain calls once the child is in bed, including repeated requests for attention, trips to the potty, another drink, and so on; (c) tantrums in which the child "throws a fit" when he is placed in bed or the parent leaves the room; and/or (d) arguments where the parent ends up yelling at the child, something they may not otherwise do during the day.

For some children, these prolonged bedtime issues end with the child falling asleep independently and sleeping through the night. However, for other children, the battle ends only when the parent lies with the child to get him to

http://dx.doi.org/10.1037/14645-008
Pediatric Sleep Problems: A Clinician's Guide to Behavioral Interventions, by L. J. Meltzer and V. M. Crabtree

fall asleep, resulting in a negative sleep-onset association. In these cases, the child may then migrate to the parents' bed in the middle of the night following a typical nighttime arousal. Alternatively, at the end of the battle, the parents will simply allow the child to fall asleep in their bed, where he will remain for the duration of the night (because if the parent moves him back to his own bed after falling asleep, the child again simply migrates to the parents' bed in the middle of the night).

For even the most patient, well-organized, and structured parent, bedtime problems can be exasperating because everyone is tired, thus emotions are running high while patience and logic are almost nonexistent. For families without a consistent bedtime and bedtime routine, or in cases in which parents are inconsistent in their responses to child behavior (both during the day and at night), bedtime problems are even more challenging.

Common Behavioral Causes for Bedtime Problems

BEDTIME STALLING AND REFUSAL— YOUNGER CHILDREN

For toddlers and preschoolers, bedtime stalling and refusal is a typical part of development, which emerges with increased independence. As a result, children in these age groups begin to understand that parents are not going to bed when they do; they may not want to stop playing; typical fears may develop with increased imagination (e.g., monsters in the closet); and many toddlers are transferred from a crib to a bed, making it easier to "escape" at bedtime (see Exhibit 7.1 for more information about transitioning children from cribs to beds). Bedtime stalling or refusal can occur before the bedtime routine (e.g., "one more TV show"), during the routine (e.g., "one more snack"), or once the child is in bed (e.g., "one more story"). When parents are inconsistent in their response (sometimes saying no, other times giving into requests), it creates intermittent reinforcement, which only increases the likelihood of stalling on subsequent nights.

CIRCADIAN AND HOMEOSTATIC FACTORS

In addition to the previously described behavioral factors that contribute to bedtime issues, for some children, bedtime protests are simply a sign of being overtired. However, bedtime stalling and refusal may also be a response to the fact that they are not yet ready to sleep, because of circadian and homeostatic factors (LeBourgeois, Carskadon, et al., 2013;

EXHIBIT 7.1

Transitioning Children From Cribs to Beds

In general, we recommend that children remain in a crib until the age of 3 years (unless it is no longer safe, as described below). The main reason for this is that many children will take advantage of their newfound freedom to get out of bed and "torment" parents by waking them up repeatedly during the night, or else they will "wreak havoc" on the house, playing with toys and leaving a path of toy (and sometimes food) destruction in their wake. By the developmental age of 3, most children will understand "stay in bed," as well as any consequences associated with getting out of bed, whereas younger children may not have the same level of understanding.

The simplest way to successfully transition from a crib to a bed is to set up the new bed in the child's room near the crib. The child should be told if he gets out of bed, then he will have to sleep the rest of the night in the crib. Of course, the parents must follow through on this threat, regardless of the child's protests. After getting up only once or twice and then returned to the crib, it is unlikely the child will get out of his bed again. The crib should remain in the child's room for about two weeks to provide an immediate reminder that he should stay in bed. If a Good Morning Light (see Chapter 6, this volume) has not already been introduced, this is a good time to use it to help the child learn when it is okay to get out of his bed. If the crib is one that transitions to a toddler bed, the side that is removed should be placed in sight (but in a safe place) so that the child is reminded that the bed can easily be turned back into a crib if needed.

The following are three common reasons parents decide to move their child from a crib to a bed, and how to respond to these concerns.

1. **"He hates his crib, which is why he cries at bedtime."** This is a common claim that parents make. Subsequently, parents will get the child out of the crib and rock him to sleep, lie with him on a separate mattress in his room, or bring him to the parents' bed. In these cases, parents should be educated about how children enjoy small spaces. For example:

   > "Have you ever noticed where small children like to play? They like small spaces like under the desk or in a large box. That is because these spaces provide a child-sized perspective of the world and are just the "right size." The crib is the same thing. Children do not mind the small space, and in fact it keeps them safe at night. The reason your child cries at bedtime is not because he hates the crib but because he is unable to fall asleep without you present, and every time he cries at bedtime you reward him by helping him fall asleep."

   At this point, it would be important to teach the child to fall asleep independently in the crib, using one of the approaches described in Chapter 6 (this volume).

2. **Arrival of a new baby.** Parents may decide to move a child out of his crib because the family is expecting a second baby. Thus they will move him into a toddler bed 1 or 2 months before the baby arrives to have the crib ready. The problem with this approach is that, as previously described, the child may not be old enough to understand the importance of staying in his own bed, thus creating new problems for the family. In most cases, newborns do not sleep in the crib, so it is helpful to encourage parents to keep the baby in a bassinet or portable crib as long as possible, and by the time the baby needs the crib, the older child should be ready for his bed. Alternatively, the parents should be encouraged to buy or borrow a second crib.

(continued)

EXHIBIT 7.1 (*Continued*)

3. **Fearless, jumping toddlers.** For some families, the decision to move a child out of a crib is an appropriate safety response. Although not common, there are acrobatic and adventurous children who at a very young age learn to climb out of their cribs. This can be more challenging to deal with than the previous two situations. The first option is to ensure that the crib mattress is on its lowest setting. Some parents are not aware that most cribs can be adjusted to make it more difficult to climb out. Another option is to remove any vaulting objects, such as crib bumpers or stuffed animals, that help the child scale the crib. If both of these have already been done, likely the only other choice is to remove the child from the crib for his own safety. For these families, if the child is not old enough to benefit from the strategies in this chapter, it is important for clinicians to work closely with parents to identify the best strategies to ensure that the child stays in his room, including using the Good Morning Light (see Chapter 6), putting up a gate in the doorway, and/or closing the door and removing any toys or other objects that could be damaged. It is important to remind parents that you are not trying to cage or lock their child up, but rather you want to create a safe sleeping space for the child that does not involve multiple disruptions to the parents' and child's sleep.

LeBourgeois, Wright, et al., 2013). For example, a child who "never" falls asleep before 9:00 p.m. likely has a delayed internal clock and will not be able to suddenly fall asleep at 7:30 p.m. simply because that is the time the parents want to end the bedtime routine. In this case, bedtime fading can be used to gradually adjust the child's internal clock, ultimately facilitating an earlier sleep onset.

It can be difficult to distinguish between protests due to simply being tired versus those due to a later internal clock. However, it is important for parents to monitor sleep patterns, tracking the start time of the bedtime issues, the duration of the stalling/protests, the attempted bedtime, and the final sleep-onset time. Inconsistent sleep-onset times preceded by less than 30 minutes of protests are most likely due to a child being overtired. A consistently late sleep-onset time (regardless of protest duration) likely signals a circadian delay.

Between the ages of 3 and 5 years, napping may also interfere with bedtime, as a child's homeostatic sleep pressure is relieved during the day, making sleep onset at bedtime more difficult. Napping can also complicate bedtime during the transition from one nap to no naps, especially if a child naps only on some days but not others. Thus, bedtimes may need to be slightly later on days when a child naps and earlier when a child does not nap. See Exhibit 7.2 for more information about when it is appropriate to stop a child's naps.

BEDTIME PROBLEMS THAT END WITH PARENTAL PRESENCE

As mentioned, it is common for a prolonged bedtime routine to end with the parent present, creating a negative sleep-onset association.

EXHIBIT 7.2

Naps in Young Children

At the age of 3 years, more than 90% of children are still taking a daily nap. By the age of 5 years, approximately one in four children are still taking a daily nap. A number of factors determine whether and how long a child naps, including day care schedules and individual need for sleep. However, during this period, bedtime problems may arise secondary to the child napping. In other words, if a child naps during the day, she has alleviated some of her sleep pressure, making it more difficult for her to fall asleep at her once consistent and early 7:30 p.m. bedtime.

Along with the other interventions in this chapter, it is important to discuss with parents the pros and cons of napping. For example, when a child skips her nap, she may become "unbearable" in the late afternoon, with increased meltdowns and tantrums. But she will typically be asleep on these days by 7:30 p.m. Alternatively, when the same child is allowed to nap, she is happy and engaging after school and during dinner but rarely falls asleep before 9:30 p.m. In both cases, the child wakes spontaneously in the morning around 7:00 a.m., so she is getting sufficient sleep. Thus, the decision about keeping or skipping the nap becomes a personal one for the family, who has to prioritize the importance of having an early bedtime (e.g., parent must get work done after the child falls asleep) with having more quality time with the child in the evening (but sacrificing adult time to do chores or even simply to relax and watch television without the child present). Finally, it is important to educate parents about the end of napping, as this transition can take weeks or months for some children who will nap some days and not others.

Subsequently, following typical nocturnal arousals, the child may migrate to the parents' bed or require the parent to return to the child's room to facilitate the child's return to sleep. Although parents have the option to consistently walk the child back to his own bed and leave following every nighttime awakening, this is exhausting for the parents and ultimately does not address the root problem—the negative sleep-onset association at bedtime. Thus, we describe several alternative approaches to address the issue of bedtime problems that include a negative sleep-onset association. Unlike the interventions described for young children in Chapter 6, the variations of graduated extinction treatment approaches in this chapter are designed for children who are in their bed (and thus can get out of bed at bedtime, often prolonging the bedtime routine).

Assessment Considerations

To determine where to begin the intervention, it is important to first understand the current routine and bedtime. If neither is consistent, that is where treatment should begin. Otherwise, a detailed, step-by-step history of what happens between dinnertime and the child's falling asleep will be essential to identify the key places for intervention. Information is needed about how parents respond to nighttime awakenings (if present), the child's wake time (and how he wakes up and knows that it is morning), and any daytime napping. In addition, before instructing families on limit-setting approaches, it is helpful to have a clear understanding of how they manage behavior problems throughout the day. Finally, if the bedtime problems are not related to limit-setting issues but rather are more anxiety based, the treatments in Chapter 8 may need to be used first, or concurrently with the interventions in this chapter.

Behavioral Interventions for Bedtime Problems

A number of factors may have initially contributed to bedtime problems (e.g., a colicky baby that resulted in "bad sleep habits"; family stress; a parent's guilt about working during the day, resulting in "giving in" to the child at night), but ultimately, a parent's inability to consistently set limits around bedtime serves to perpetuate bedtime problems. Again, even a parent who is consistent with limits throughout the day may struggle at bedtime as everyone becomes more tired. The following interventions build on parents' strengths, giving them tools to deal with this difficult time of day while also teaching them appropriate ways to set limits at bedtime. See Exhibit 7.3 for some basic limit-setting strategies to provide to parents.

Although a consistent bedtime routine and a regular sleep schedule are essential first steps for any behavioral sleep intervention, they are absolutely critical for behavioral interventions for bedtime problems. In milder cases, when paired with a consistent bedtime, a short, simple bedtime routine that is the same every night, moves in one direction, and ends in the child's room may be sufficient to address the bedtime issues. Without a bedtime routine, however, the following interventions cannot be implemented.

In addition, similar to treatments in the other chapters, the treatment for bedtime problems is often multicomponent, using more than one of the following interventions. It is important to identify the components that will help each individual family reach success at bedtime, along with spending time problem solving any concerns that may arise before and during treatment implementation.

BEDTIME CHART/PICTURE SCHEDULE

Everyone is tired at bedtime, making consistency difficult for parents and reasoning difficult for children. Thus, to create a more consistent

EXHIBIT 7.3

Helping Parents Set Limits

Setting limits is incredibly challenging for many parents. When a child behaves differently for someone other than the parent (e.g., goes to bed easily for the babysitter but not the parent), limit setting is often the culprit. Parents need to be gently reminded that their job is to set the limits; the child's job is to push or test the limits. This is how children learn self-control, boundaries, and rules. When parent behavior or expectations are inconsistent, children may become confused and anxious, responding with behavior problems. There are several key factors to setting limits:

1. **Consistency, consistency, consistency.** When parents are inconsistent with limits and rules, children will protest when the rules change. For example, if bedtime is inconsistently enforced, the child will protest every night in hopes that tonight she gets to stay up later.
2. **Follow through.** Part of consistency is following through with set limits. Although rewards are preferred over punishments (see Point 8, below), parents need to follow through with any promise (i.e., "If you do this, I will give you . . .") or threat (i.e., "If you don't do this, I will take away . . ."). Otherwise, parents lose credibility, decreasing the likelihood that children will respond to a parent's promises or threats in the future.
3. **When setting new limits, behavior problems may increase before they improve.** For children who have not previously had consistent limits, protests or negative behaviors may initially increase following the implementation of new rules/limits. This is done in an effort to get the parent to give in. However, if a parent is consistent, over time the child learns that he or she will no longer "win," and protests will decrease.
4. **Use verbal transition cues.** Many children have difficulty with transitioning from one activity to another (i.e., going from playtime to bedtime). Thus, it is important to provide verbal cues (i.e., 15 minutes until bedtime, 5 minutes until bedtime) to prepare the child to transition.
5. **Set (and blame) the timer.** When preparing for a transition, have the child set a timer for the remaining time (e.g., 15 minutes). When the timer goes off, the child cannot argue, as she set the timer. In addition, the parent is not the one telling the child it is now time to begin the bedtime routine.
6. **Use forced choices.** Children like to have a sense of control over their environment, so it is helpful to provide them with forced choices (e.g., Do you want to use the blue or green toothbrush?). Not only does this prevent parents from asking questions they don't want the answer to (i.e., Do you want to brush your teeth?), it forces the child to follow through with the behavior because she made the choice.
7. **Catch them being good.** Children will do just about anything for parental attention, including protesting at bedtime. Parents should be taught to provide differential attention to child behavior. In other words, when the child engages in a desired behavior (i.e., putting on her pajamas), she should be praised. When the child engages in a negative behavior (i.e., demanding another snack), she should be ignored.
8. **Rewards go further than punishments.** Similar to the previous point, avoid using punishments, as this is not an effective way to change child behavior. For example, taking away a child's favorite toy as punishment increases the child's distress, which is directly incompatible with easily falling asleep. In addition, once the favorite toy is gone, parents have no additional leverage to obtain desired behavior. When explaining the preference for using rewards, many parents will protest "I don't bribe my child." In this case, an example of consistent reinforcement should be used. For example,

> "I really love my job and working with families; however, if I didn't get a paycheck every 2 weeks, I would eventually stop coming to work. Of course, we would love our children to do everything they are supposed to do simply because they are good children. But the truth of the matter is that children will respond faster if they are rewarded for desired behaviors, and over time, these new behaviors will become part of their daily routine and will no longer need to be rewarded."

bedtime routine that everyone in the family follows every night, a picture chart/book can be used to identify the steps of the bedtime routine, keep everyone on track, and provide parents with a way to set limits on bedtime stalling.

How It Works

As previously described, a consistent bedtime routine is essential for any sleep intervention. The Bedtime Chart provides a picture schedule that can be understood even by young children, providing a consistent, predictable bedtime routine. In addition, if there is more than one caregiver, the Bedtime Chart ensures a consistent bedtime routine no matter who is in charge on a particular night.

The Evidence

Although a bedtime routine is a common part of many treatment studies, only one study has examined the benefit of a consistent bedtime routine as a stand-alone intervention (Mindell, Telofski, Wiegand, & Kurtz, 2009), with a shorter sleep-onset latency (SOL) and both a decrease in the frequency and duration of nighttime awakenings. Thus, we recommend including a bedtime routine and chart with other elements of interventions described in this chapter.

Considerations for Special Populations

The Bedtime Chart or picture book may be especially helpful for children with autism spectrum disorder or attention-deficit/hyperactivity disorder (ADHD) or for those who generally have difficulties with transitions. Tangible objects (e.g., toothbrush, doll's pajamas, toy, bed) may further assist some children in understanding what the next step is in the routine. These objects can be permanently affixed to a poster board or attached with Velcro to a cardboard strip, with each item removed when the task is completed. Clear visual timers (e.g., sand timers) can be especially helpful for these children. For children with chronic illnesses, medications and/or medical treatments that are part of the routine should be included with the chart. Providing an extra reminder to parents and children, this may also help with medical nonadherence.

In Practice

- Create a bedtime routine. First, a routine needs to be established that is short and sweet, moves in one direction (e.g., from the kitchen to the bathroom to the child's room), and ends in the child's sleep environment. (See Chapter 1, this volume, for more information.)

- Create a picture chart or picture book. Using a digital camera, children can help parents take pictures that represent each step of the routine (e.g., picture of a yogurt for snack, picture of a glass for the last drink, picture of a toothbrush, picture of the toilet, picture of the pajamas, picture of two books, and picture of the child's bed). These can be printed and put on a poster board or individual pages of heavy paper. Alternatively, pictures can be cut out of magazines or downloaded from the Internet.
- Follow the chart every night. Parents should be encouraged to have the chart in an easily accessible location so that the child can help identify what comes next in the routine.
- Reward each step of the routine. A sticker or check mark can be placed next to each step on the chart or in the book to reinforce successful completion of each step. A timer may be useful to encourage the child to complete each step in a timely manner.
- Blame the chart. When the child asks for something that is not on the chart, a parent should reply, "I'm sorry, but *the chart says* no more books and that it is now time for sleep." This prevents any negotiating on the child's part, and it enables the parent to sympathize with the child while maintaining the consistent routine.

Handout 9 provides step-by-step instructions for parents on how to create and use a Bedtime Chart.

Managing Potential Pitfalls

Remind parents to expect protests. When implementing the Bedtime Chart, especially if there has not previously been a consistent routine, parents can expect the child to protest at each step of the routine. However, the parents must be encouraged to maintain a consistent response and follow the routine every time. When extinguishing a behavior such as protests, parents should expect that initially the protests will increase (as the child hopes to get what he wants). If the parents are consistent, however, protests will decrease over time. See Chapter 6, this volume, for an example of how to explain these extinction bursts to parents.

The Bottom Line

A Bedtime Chart is an intervention that may not resolve all issues when used alone (e.g., the child may require a multicomponent intervention that also addresses the sleep-onset association of parental presence at bedtime). However, the Bedtime Chart is a simple intervention that can be recommended to all patients to reduce bedtime stalling and protests, as well as implement consistency during the most challenging time of day for families.

BEDTIME FADING

As previously mentioned, some children protest and stall at bedtime because they are simply unable to fall asleep early because of a delayed internal clock. The goal of bedtime fading is to align a child's natural circadian rhythm (i.e., the time he regularly falls asleep) with the desired bedtime/sleep-onset time, reducing bedtime protests, stalling, and refusal.

How It Works

By moving the child's bedtime to match his naturally occurring sleep-onset time, the child learns to fall asleep faster at bedtime, thus associating bedtime with sleep onset. Over time, the bedtime is slowly moved earlier until the desired bedtime is reached.

The Evidence

Bedtime fading has been examined in both typically developing children and children with special needs, although some of the published reports have been case studies or small samples (e.g., Ashbaugh & Peck, 1998; Piazza & Fisher, 1991). Early reports used only bedtime fading (as described in the following section), whereas later studies paired bedtime fading with response cost (where the child is removed from the bed if not asleep within a specified amount of time). In general, bedtime fading has been shown to increase sleep duration, decrease nighttime awakenings, and decrease cosleeping (Ashbaugh & Peck, 1998; Piazza & Fisher, 1991; Piazza, Fisher, & Sherer, 1997).

Contraindications and Considerations for Special Populations

Children should be carefully screened for any potential cause of difficulties initiating sleep (e.g., restless legs syndrome, bedtime fears) that may be the primary reason for prolonged SOL. Faded bedtime was originally described in the literature for children with developmental disorders. Thus, there should be no significant concerns when using faded bedtime for children with autism spectrum disorder or ADHD. In fact, some believe that melatonin regulation is different for these children, making early sleep initiation more challenging. However, parents who have to manage difficult behaviors all day often do not want to hear that they should allow their child to stay up later. Again, careful education is the key to helping parents understand the logic behind a faded bedtime. During the extra time before bed, children can be encouraged to have quiet playtime in their room (when possible), as additional wind-down time is often needed. For children with chronic illnesses whose sleep schedule may be erratic because of their medical needs, faded bedtime may help facilitate sleep onset with a consistent bedtime.

In Practice

- Using a sleep diary, monitor the child's sleep-onset time for 1 to 2 weeks.
- Delay the start of the child's bedtime routine until 30 to 45 minutes before the child's current sleep-onset time (e.g., start routine at 8:45 p.m. for a child who falls asleep around 9:30 p.m.).
- After 5 to 7 nights, or when the child is falling asleep consistently and easily in less than 30 minutes, move the bedtime up by 15 minutes.
- Continue to move bedtime earlier by 15 minutes every week (as long as the child is falling asleep quickly and easily) until desired (and age appropriate) bedtime is reached (e.g., 8:00 p.m.).
- Maintain a consistent sleep schedule every night (even on weekends). Allowing children to stay up late on Friday and Saturday nights may seem to parents like the right thing to do ("It's the weekend, after all"); however, it is important to remind parents that this will likely backfire, as the child may become overtired or will catch a second wind, which may make sleep onset increasingly difficult. Ironically, for young children and school-age children in particular, going to bed later does not typically translate to waking up later. Some of the most difficult children to wake on school days will hop out of bed even earlier on weekends to play or watch cartoons.
- Set a consistent wake time that is maintained every day (even on weekends). This last point is really critical. Although it is more likely for younger children to wake spontaneously and not sleep in, if parents allow a child to oversleep on weekends, it will interfere with his ability to fall asleep at bedtime.

Handout 10 provides step-by-step instructions for parents on using bedtime fading.

Managing Potential Pitfalls

Explain to parents the importance of delaying bedtime. Parents are often skeptical when a clinician recommends moving bedtime later. This comes from the belief that the child should go to bed early and fall asleep quickly. However, parents should be provided education about the circadian rhythm and how the child is currently not able to fall asleep before a certain time. Thus, moving the bedtime later will result in a shorter SOL and a reduced bedtime battle but not a decrease in the child's sleep duration.

Warn parents to not move bedtime up too quickly. Once a child has initial success with falling asleep quickly, the parents may decide it is time for him to fall asleep at the desired bedtime (1–2 hours earlier). By parents' suddenly moving bedtime earlier, the child will likely be unable to fall asleep, resulting in a return to the bedtime challenges. Again, providing parents and patients (when age appropriate) with education about how the circadian rhythm impacts sleep onset is essential.

Remind parents about the importance of a consistent sleep schedule on both weekdays and weekends. Although described in the In Practice section, this concept is so essential for treatment success that it is important to remind parents that young children rarely sleep in on the weekends. Therefore, it is critical for parents to maintain the same bedtime on weekdays and weekends. The importance of a consistent bedtime has already been stated multiple times, but it is especially critical when doing bedtime fading. Otherwise, any improvements made in terms of the child falling asleep at an earlier time will be erased each weekend when he is allowed to stay up late.

The Bottom Line

Many parents who present with complaints of bedtime difficulties and delayed sleep onset are quite surprised to hear that they should have their child go to bed later. However, with careful education about how the circadian rhythm works, as well as reassurances that the child is not getting any less sleep (because she never falls asleep early anyway), most parents are willing to implement this treatment, with great success.

Variations of Graduated Extinction for Older Children

Because bedtime problems in older children often end with the parent being present when the child finally falls asleep (e.g., lying next to the child, allowing the child into the parents' bed), graduated extinction approaches are also used to teach these children to fall asleep independently at bedtime. However, unlike with younger children who are in cribs, the ability of the child to get out of bed may require further modifications, including a gradual withdrawal of parental presence, increased duration of parental absence, or a frequent checking method.

In addition, success with these interventions is often increased when paired with a reinforcement system.

THE EVIDENCE

Graduated extinction procedures have been shown to be highly effective in reducing bedtime problems in young children (for a comprehensive review, see Honaker & Meltzer, 2014; Meltzer & Mindell, 2014; and Mindell et al., 2006). However, most of these studies have focused primarily on young children in cribs and not necessarily on those children who are in beds. The following sections provide step-by-step guidance on how to modify graduated extinction approaches for older children, on the basis of both limited descriptions in the literature (e.g., Blunden, 2011; Kuhn, 2011) and on our own clinical experience.

REMOVING PARENTAL PRESENCE

There are three primary approaches for removing parental presence at bedtime for older children: (a) gradual withdrawal of parental presence, (b) increased duration of parental absence, and (c) the frequent checking method. However, the goal is the same for all three: having the child fall asleep independently while the parent is not in the room. The decision about which approach to use should be made with parents, who will most likely know how they and their child will respond with the least amount of protests. For example, some children will learn to fall asleep if the parent remains present, whereas other children will be okay staying in bed alone with the parent frequently checking on them. In addition, for children motivated by rewards, a positive reinforcement system may be used to increase treatment adherence and success.

How It Works

By allowing parents to be present initially and/or to check frequently on their child, often the stress at bedtime is greatly reduced. Further, as the amount of parental presence is gradually reduced for each approach, the child is able to relax (even when a parent is not present) and to eventually fall asleep independently.

Contraindications and Considerations for Special Populations

Children with severe separation anxiety that occurs throughout the day (not only at bedtime) should address this concern before removing parental presence at bedtime.

In Practice—Gradual Withdrawal of Parental Presence

▪ After establishing a consistent bedtime and bedtime routine, the child is placed in the bed, and the parent remains with the child until he is asleep. Parents' interactions with the child should be minimal (e.g., "It is time to sleep now, I love you"), and they should not engage in discussions or answer repeated questions.
▪ After 3 to 5 nights of establishing the child's ability to fall asleep in his own bed with the parent present, the parent sits farther away from the child (e.g., moves 3 feet every 3–5 nights; or moves half the distance between the bed and the door, moves to the doorway, and then moves to the hallway).

Handout 11 provides step-by-step instructions for gradually withdrawing the parent's presence (Moving Parents Out).

Managing Potential Pitfalls—Gradual Withdrawal of Parental Presence

Remind parents to not interact with child. For many children, having the parent there may increase demands for attention; children may ask questions or try to have a conversation with the parent. If this happens, the parent should simply give a predetermined response over and over (e.g., "It is time to sleep now, I love you"). If the parent is unable to do so or if the presence of the parent increases SOL, then an alternative approach should be used.

Identify a consistent response to nighttime awakenings. For children who seek out parents in the middle of the night or migrate to the parents' bed, a consistent response to these wakings needs to be determined before starting treatment. Options include simply letting the child into the parents' bed with the first waking or consistently walking the child back to his bed every time and remaining present until he returns to sleep. Parents who do not notice their child migrating into their bed but want him to remain in his own bed should be encouraged to close their door and hang some type of bell (e.g., jingle bell, cowbell) on their door to alert them as to when the child comes in.

In Practice—Increased Duration of Parental Absence

▪ Using a sleep diary for 1 week, identify how long it takes the child to fall asleep with a parent present (assuming, of course, a consistent bedtime and bedtime routine are already in place).
▪ The parent should then stay with the child for half the time it typically takes the child to fall asleep (e.g., 10 minutes if SOL is 20 minutes).

- After the designated amount of time (e.g., 10 minutes), the parent takes a short break (1 minute for the first few nights) using some type of excuse (e.g., "I have to brush my teeth").
- After the short break, the parent returns, provides a lot of verbal praise for the child remaining quietly in bed, and then stays with the child until he is asleep. Alternatively, the parent can provide the child a small token (e.g., poker chip, ticket, marble in a jar) to reward him for remaining quietly in bed. The child can then exchange the token for a small reward the next day (e.g., small treat, special game with parent, 5 minutes of screen time).
- Each night the break gets a little bit longer (e.g., add 1 minute to the break each night) until the child falls asleep independently without the parent in the room.

Handout 12 provides step-by-step instructions for parents on how to take these breaks.

Managing Potential Pitfalls—Increased Duration of Parental Absence

Address prolonged SOL (child regularly takes more than 30 minutes to fall asleep at bedtime). In this case, it would be beneficial to first implement or concurrently implement the faded bedtime.

Remind parents to always return from their break. As the break gets increasingly longer, parents may become engaged in other activities (e.g., paying bills, doing work, watching television) and forget to return to the child's room. If this happens, the child may not trust that the parent is going to return, resulting in an increase in curtain calls and bedtime protests. Parents should be encouraged to set a timer to ensure that they remember to return.

Consider providing a small token or sticker once the child has fallen asleep. Occasionally, children will believe that their parent never returned from the break if the child fell asleep while the parent was out of the room. In these cases, the parent can leave a small sticker as a sign to the child that he did return.

Provide parents with a consistent response to use if the child gets out of bed before the parent returning. In this case, the parent should shorten the time of the initial break (down to even a few seconds if needed). This increases the child's likelihood of successfully staying alone. However, if the child does come out of his room, the parent should calmly walk him back. It is important at this point that verbal response be minimal (e.g., "Back to bed, it is time for sleeping"). This will help increase the value of the positive verbal praise provided when the child remains in bed.

In Practice—Positive Reinforcement With Frequent Checks

▪ The parent provides the child with positive reinforcement for completing each step of the bedtime routine in a timely fashion (see Exhibit 7.3 for tips on setting limits).

▪ Once the child is in bed, the parent returns for a Second Goodnight or additional goodnights at agreed-upon intervals (e.g., every 5 minutes). If the child is still lying quietly when the parent returns, he is verbally praised and earns some type of token (e.g., poker chip, ticket, marble in a jar).

▪ If the child calls out or gets out of bed, the parent returns him to bed with minimal interaction (i.e., ignoring child's request and behavior) and removes a token.

▪ Over time, the time between checks should be increased.

▪ Once a certain number of tokens are earned, they may be traded for previously agreed-upon prizes that the child desires (e.g., each token earns 1 extra minute of screen time; filling the jar to a pre-set line with marbles earns a small gift card).

▪ Over time, the number of tokens needed to earn a prize should be increased for future prizes.

Handout 13 provides detailed step-by-step instructions for parents on how to use the Second Goodnight.

Managing Potential Pitfalls—Positive Reinforcement With Frequent Checks

Assist parents with finding a reward that is motivating to the child. For some children, parent attention (even just the act of walking a child back to bed) is more motivating than any tangible reward. Thus, the clinician should work with the parents and child to determine what will be motivating for the child (and acceptable to the parents). In addition, parents should understand that initially the rewards may need to be frequently modified to maintain the child's interest.

Emphasize the importance of providing positive reinforcement and that this is not bribery. As described in Exhibit 7.3, parents are often resistant to using positive reinforcement, as they equate this to bribery. The difference between bribery and rewarding should be explained, namely, that a *bribe* is something given ahead of time in hopes of getting something in return (e.g., paying off a judge to give your competitor a bad score), whereas a *reward* is something you earn for doing something good (e.g., winning a trophy or medal for giving the best performance). Parents should be reminded that as adults, we receive external reinforcement on a regular basis in the form of a paycheck. Reassurance should be provided that over time, the frequency of external reinforcement will be faded

EXHIBIT 7.4

The Sleep Fairy

Limit setting can be difficult for many parents, but the use of a rewards system rather than punishment can go a long way in changing behaviors. One "quick and dirty trick" to increase motivation for falling asleep that works with preschool and younger school-aged children is the Sleep Fairy. In short, the Sleep Fairy delivers a prize under the child's pillow once she is asleep. Using schedules of reinforcement, the sleep fairy initially comes every night for 2 weeks (continuous reinforcement) to facilitate the child going to bed with minimal protests and falling asleep independently. Then a more intermittent schedule is used to keep the child guessing and maintain the newly learned behavior of going to bed and falling asleep.

Here is an example of how to explain the Sleep Fairy to parents in the presence of the patient.

> The Sleep Fairy comes to visit children at night after they fall asleep and leaves a small prize like a sticker under their pillow. She comes every night for a couple of weeks, and then we don't know when she is coming to visit because she has a lot of houses to stop at!

Older children who understand the concept of the Tooth Fairy can also be told that the Sleep Fairy is friends with the Tooth Fairy, as this will help solidify their understanding of what will happen once they fall asleep. In a published case series, the Sleep Fairy approach was shown to reduce disruptive bedtime behaviors in four children (Burke, Kuhn, & Peterson, 2004). A detailed explanation of the Sleep Fairy for parents can be found in Handout 14.

and no longer necessary. Parents should also be encouraged to weigh the cost–benefit ratio, as the benefit of the child going to bed and falling asleep without protests, stalling, or battles will likely outweigh the cost of the reinforcements used. Finally, parents should be reminded that instead of food or expensive toys, positive parental attention/interaction (e.g., special time with one parent, family game time, movie night) is a highly desired reward for many children.

Provide child with a final token once he or she is asleep. Some children are very excited about earning tokens and thus will wait for their parents to return. This may have the reverse effect of prolonging SOL. If SOL increases, parents should provide an extra token once the child is asleep to further encourage the child to fall asleep. One way to provide this final token (and additional incentive for falling asleep) is the Sleep Fairy. Exhibit 7.4 provides more information about this technique, and Handout 14 provides detailed instructions for parents.

The Bottom Line

Variations of graduated extinction are useful interventions to reduce bedtime problems when the child has learned to fall asleep with a parent present. The decision about which variation to use should be made with the family, as parents will clearly be able to tell you how they think their child will respond to this (e.g., whether he will stay in bed or whether he will destroy his room while waiting for his parent to return). The use of a reinforcement system may improve the child's motivation to remain in bed quietly if the parent is not in the room. Over time, as children learn to fall asleep faster and easier, fewer rewards will be needed. That said, a token reward system can be used for any desired behavior (e.g., homework, practicing the violin) throughout the day to increase motivation and compliance.

Case Example: Lilia

Lilia is a 3-year-old girl whose parents complain that bedtime has become a "nightmare," with Lilia refusing to go to bed. Up until 22 months of age, Lilia was described as a "good sleeper," but once they moved her to a bed, her sleep deteriorated. The bedtime routine begins around 7:30 p.m. but will last for up to 2 hours. Lilia will ask for another snack, book, trip to the potty, drink of water, and anything else she can think of to get attention. Most recently, she has been coming out of her room to ask her parents "an important question" or because "I have something I have to tell you." If she does not get what she wants, she will throw a temper tantrum until the parents give in (which they regularly do). If they leave her alone at bedtime, she will get out of her bed repeatedly and come to find her parents to tell them they also have to go to bed. Between 9:00 and 9:30 p.m., the parents will finally go in and lie next to Lilia until she falls asleep (which takes up to 45 minutes). If they get up and try to leave before she is asleep, she will again tantrum. Dad (who is 6'4") even stated that "she won't let me leave the room." Once asleep, Lilia has two to three night awakenings. If the waking is before 4:00 a.m., a parent will give her 4 ounces of milk and stay with her until she returns to sleep. If the waking is after 4:00 a.m., they will simply let Lilia into their bed.

For Lilia's parents, the first part of the treatment discussion focused heavily on limit setting. A lengthy discussion focused on the fact that it was important for Lilia's parents to remember that they are the parents and they are in charge—not Lilia. With this in mind, the Bedtime Chart was used to help the parents regain some control at bedtime by having a set routine that Lilia could not challenge. However, the chart also allowed for Lilia to feel as if she was in charge by telling her parents what the next step of the routine would be. With help from her parents, Lilia took pictures of each step of the routine and created a picture book. Based on the sleep diary, Lilia never fell asleep before 9:30 p.m., so Lilia's bedtime was moved later, starting the routine at 8:45 p.m. and lights out at 9:30 p.m. At bedtime, one parent stayed with Lilia for 5 minutes, then would take a break lasting only 1 minute per night, returning until Lilia fell asleep. After a few nights, the time the parents were out of the room gradually increased each night. In addition, for nighttime awakenings Lilia's parents were to have minimal interaction with her but were to remain with her each time until she returned to sleep. A Good Morning Light was put in place to help Lilia understand when it was okay to come into her parents' bed.

The first few nights, Lilia fought each step of the routine, but the parents remained consistent in referring to the chart and her protests began to decrease. Over the course of a few weeks, Lilia's bedtime was also faded until she was in bed at 8:00 p.m. and asleep by 8:30 p.m. most nights. After about two weeks of Lilia falling asleep independently, the frequency of her nighttime awakenings also decreased, and she learned to not come into her parents' bedroom until the light changed.

BEDTIME PASS

The Bedtime Pass is an approach that gives older children additional control over the bedtime routine by allowing them to choose whether to seek parental attention. As with the other interventions in this chapter, the goal of the Bedtime Pass is to reduce the frequency of curtain calls and increase the child's ability to initiate sleep independently.

How It Works

The Bedtime Pass allows the child a valid opportunity to get out of bed if she desires but extinguishes unnecessary curtain calls by ignoring subsequent bedtime resistance.

The Evidence

Several studies have demonstrated the effectiveness of the Bedtime Pass in both younger and school-age children, reducing the frequency of events defined as "bedtime resistance," as well as the average time to quiet (Freeman, 2006; Friman et al., 1999; B. A. Moore, Friman, Fruzzetti, & MacAleese, 2007).

In Practice

- Determine the initial number of Bedtime Passes to begin with (i.e., one to three passes). Although one is the traditional number, some families may believe that their child needs more than one opportunity for parental attention at bedtime.
- Have the child and parents create the Bedtime Pass. This can be a decorated index card, ticket, or poker chip.

- When the child is placed in the bed, she is given the Bedtime Pass (e.g., under her pillow, on the nightstand) and reminded that if she calls out to her parents or gets out of bed, she will have to give up the pass. However, if she does not call out or get out of bed, she can exchange the pass for a small prize in the morning.
- If the child calls out or gets up, the parent should attend to the child's request (i.e., hug, drink) and then return the child to bed. After the pass or passes have been given up, the child should be returned to her bed with minimal interaction, ignoring any additional requests.
- If the child still has the pass in the morning, it can be exchanged for a small immediate prize (e.g., sticker, small toy). Alternatively, the child can save the passes and exchange them for larger rewards (e.g., three passes earns special time with one parent, five passes earns an extra 30 minutes of screen time on the weekend).
- If more than one pass is used initially, over time the number of passes should be decreased. For example, the child may get three passes for the first few days, two passes for the next few days, and then only one pass after that.

Handout 15 provides step-by-step instructions for parents on how to use the Bedtime Pass.

Managing Potential Pitfalls

Remind parents to not provide any reinforcing attention once the pass has been exchanged. As with previously described interventions, when parents are inconsistent with their response to the child calling out or getting out of bed, it further reinforces the child's escape from bed. Reminding parents about the importance of consistency and ignoring unwanted behaviors is essential.

Rewards are not motivating. As described in the previous section (Managing Potential Pitfalls—Positive Reinforcement With Frequent Checks), it is important to assist parents with finding a reward that is motivating to the child and acceptable to the parents.

Identify whether the child is experiencing anxiety at bedtime. For children who are anxious, the Bedtime Pass may need to be combined with other behavioral interventions like Worry Time and/or cognitive restructuring (see Chapter 8, this volume).

Monitor the child's SOL to ensure she is falling asleep. Some children may hold their passes at bedtime and simply lay quietly without signaling for the parents. Although this reduces the bedtime battles, it may not have the added benefit of the child falling asleep faster. Thus, this approach may need to be paired with a faded bedtime.

The Bottom Line

For bedtime resistance in older children, the Bedtime Pass can be a quick and highly effective way to help the child go to bed and fall asleep without parental presence. This system also boosts children's confidence by giving them control over the situation (choosing whether to use or keep the pass). However, for some children the pass may not be sufficient, and once the pass has been sacrificed, parents may not be able to maintain a neutral response when returning the child to bed. Thus, when clinically appropriate, the patient and the family should be involved with the decision about whether to use the Bedtime Pass or positive reinforcement with frequent checks.

Case Example: Justin

Justin is an 8-year-old boy who presents with difficulties sleeping, which his parents reported have been present "since birth." Currently, Justin fights going to bed and can take up to 2 hours to fall asleep at bedtime. At 7:00 p.m. when his parents tell him it is time to go to bed, he will ask to watch one more TV show. About half the nights his parents agree because they want to finish cleaning up from dinner. After that, Justin will fight every step of the bedtime routine, crying, whining, and running away from his parents when he is supposed to put on his pajamas or brush his teeth. Justin's mother tries to negotiate with him, whereas Justin's father has "no patience" for this and threatens to take away his toys. This only makes Justin more upset. Once in bed, Justin will come out of his room multiple times asking for another snack or drink or to read another chapter in his book. Justin rarely falls asleep before 10:00 p.m., and this will often be in his parents' bed, and once he is asleep they will transfer him back to his own bed. Mom wakes Justin at 7:30 a.m. and describes him as difficult to wake, taking approximately 30 minutes to rise. On weekends, because Justin does not have school, his parents let him go to bed at 9:00 p.m. Although he still protests, it is not to the same extent as during the week, and he is typically asleep by 10:00 p.m. Justin wakes spontaneously at 8:00 a.m. on weekends.

Justin's bedtime problems were addressed with a combination of interventions. The first steps were implementing a consistent bedtime routine, introducing bedtime fading, and teaching Justin to fall asleep independently. On the basis of the sleep diary data, it was determined that Justin's typical sleep-onset time was around 10:00 p.m. Thus, his bedtime routine was set to begin at 9:30 p.m. and to include a snack, getting ready for bed, and reading one chapter from his favorite book. For each step, a timer would be used, and if Justin finished the activity in the set time, he would earn a marble in his jar. Lights out would be 10:00 p.m., with one parent present until he fell asleep. After 1 week,

Justin's parents used positive reinforcement with frequent checks, giving Justin a second goodnight every 5 minutes. When they returned, if Justin had not called out or gotten out of bed, he would earn another marble. After the first week, his parents began to increase duration between checks by 1 minute each night. The final step was to advance Justin's bedtime by 15 minutes every 3 to 5 nights, as long as he was still falling asleep within 20 to 30 minutes. Eventually, he was able to go to bed at 9:00 p.m. every night and fall asleep fairly quickly, continuing to have a 7:30 a.m. wake-up time for school.

Summary and Take-Home Points

Bedtime problems are common in toddlers, preschoolers, and school-age children and are frustrating and exhausting for the entire family. A prolonged bedtime battle may or may not also include a negative sleep-onset association (i.e., parental presence at bedtime), which then results in an additional complaint of nighttime awakenings. A number of behavioral interventions can be used to make the bedtime routine and bedtime calmer and easier for both children and their parents. However, the most important key to success is parents learning to be consistent and set limits. Other specific points to remember are outlined below.

- Consistent routines and transition cues are essential at any age and throughout the day, but they are especially critical at bedtime, when everyone is tired.
- Even in younger children, circadian and homeostatic sleep factors need to be considered. In particular, afternoon naps may interfere with a child's ability to fall asleep at bedtime, resulting in bedtime problems. Similarly, a child may have a naturally delayed circadian rhythm, and an early bedtime may be the primary cause of the prolonged bedtime battle.
- The use of consistent positive reinforcement and rewards will lead not only to behavior change but also to less stressful and more positive bedtimes for the entire family.

Nighttime Fears, Anxiety, and Recurrent Nightmares

8

B edtime problems are one of the most common presenting problems in pediatric sleep. Although younger children may not want to go to bed because they want to stay up and play or spend time with parents, a significant number of preschool children, school-age children, and adolescents also present with bedtime problems and difficulties falling asleep because of bedtime fears and worries that can delay sleep onset. In younger children, development of imagination may result in fears of monsters or witches. In school-age children and adolescents, however, fear and anxiety are more often related to school performance, peer interactions, and/or news events (e.g., kidnapping, natural disasters). Finally, although nightmares are considered a rapid eye movement (REM) parasomnia, treatment for recurrent nightmares is addressed within this chapter because of their co-occurrence in children with anxiety. For children who experience recurrent nightmares, going to bed can be very distressing with the prospect of having a nightmare that evening.

http://dx.doi.org/10.1037/14645-009
Pediatric Sleep Problems: A Clinician's Guide to Behavioral Interventions, by L. J. Meltzer and V. M. Crabtree

An understanding that bedtime refusal, curtain calls, or excessive crying out from bed are based in fear can be very helpful in understanding the most appropriate strategy for addressing these behaviors. Whereas in Chapter 7 we described strategies for addressing bedtime stalling based more on the child's desire to avoid going to bed, in this chapter we focus more on strategies for assisting children and adolescents in managing their fear and anxiety at bedtime. These strategies can increase a child's self-efficacy and not only are effective in managing bedtime problems but also may be generalized to other feared objects or events during the day. When a child's anxiety pervades throughout the day and night, anxiety management strategies are clearly necessary to address the symptoms around the clock. It is important to note that because anxiety management can be very difficult at bedtime when children are tired and anxiety may be at its highest, anxiety management strategies should be practiced during the day before being implemented at bedtime. Insufficient sleep can impact mood and behavior regulation. A focus on anxiety reduction at bedtime that results in sufficient sleep, therefore, can help the child better control thoughts and emotions during the day. Before implementing an anxiety-reduction intervention, however, a thorough assessment of the pervasiveness of the child's fears and anxiety is crucial.

Assessment Considerations

Most children with nighttime fears will not have a history of clinically significant anxiety or trauma. If the fears and anxieties are ubiquitous and interfering with developmentally appropriate activities, however, the global anxiety should also be addressed by a mental health professional. The following questions can be used to help identify the pervasiveness of the child's anxiety:

- Does your child worry more than other children her age?
- Is the anxiety only at bedtime or throughout the day?
- Are the fears/anxieties interfering with separation from parents, day care/school attendance, and/or social activities?

In addition, when trauma is suspected or reported by the child or parent, the following questions can be used to gather more information:

- Has the child had any recent significant changes (i.e., death in the family, parental separation/divorce)?
- Has the child been physically, sexually, and/or emotionally abused?
- Has the child been the victim of a violent event?
- Has the child witnessed violence?

If the child's nighttime fears are related to a history of trauma, he should be treated by a mental health professional with expertise in treatment of childhood trauma. However, the child may still require a specific intervention for the nighttime fears, either concurrently with the trauma-focused intervention or after the trauma exposure has been treated.

In addition, some children will present with fears that are, in fact, based in reality. Again, here are some questions that can help probe the child's fears:

- Are the fears related to actual potential events (e.g., robberies, natural disasters) versus imaginary creatures (monsters, dragons)?
- Does the child live in an environment where she could potentially be exposed to real feared events (e.g., urban neighborhood with high rates of gun violence)?

If the child lives in an environment with a high likelihood of the feared events, treatment should focus on assisting the parent in providing the child with reassurance as to safety measures that are taken rather than focusing on reducing irrational fears.

Bedtime Problems Related to Fear

NIGHTTIME FEARS

Nighttime fears are one of the most common nighttime experiences of young children. As part of typical development, young children often have difficulty distinguishing fantasy from reality. As a result, feared objects (e.g., monsters, dragons, television characters) that may seem obviously imaginary to adults seem very real to children. As children are expected to go into a darkened room alone to sleep, these fears may become so frightening that the child begins to have curtain calls and/or begins having bedtime refusal behaviors that she has not demonstrated previously.

Nighttime fears are most common in the preschool-age period (3–5 years of age) as children begin to engage in more fantasy. Children in this age group most frequently report fear of the dark, nightmares, and fear of being separated from their parents. Most children will eventually outgrow their nighttime fears, particularly as they begin to better distinguish reality from fantasy. Unfortunately, for some, the fears they experience are so intense or their reactions are so strong that they cause significant family disruption or sleep loss for both the child and her parents; these are the children that will need interventions to address their nighttime fears.

NIGHTTIME ANXIETY

Most school-age children have occasional worries that may worsen at bedtime. These are typically related to upcoming events, social interactions (e.g., arguments with friends), or tests at school. Children in the middle childhood years who have significant nighttime anxiety, however, are more likely to have excessive worries that pervade throughout the daytime and evening hours that may be more based in reality (even if they are irrational fears). Instead of fearing that a monster may grab them, children in this age group are more likely to fear that their house will be burglarized, that there will be a fire, that their parents may die, and so on. For those with generalized anxiety, worries that are present throughout the day become intensified at night when the child is expected to lie quietly in bed with no distractions from his anxiety. This frequently will result in a child engaging in bedtime battles, lying in bed awake and ruminating, and/or doing other activities in bed (e.g., playing on an electronic device) in an attempt to distract himself from excessive worries.

Cognitive–Behavioral Interventions for Nighttime Fears, Anxiety, and Recurrent Nightmares

Interventions to reduce nighttime anxiety and improve compliance with bedtime focus on three key areas: exposure, anxiety reduction, and positive reinforcement of "brave" behaviors and compliance with the bedtime routine. In addition to these components, recurrent nightmares are also treated with imagery rehearsal therapy (IRT), a multifaceted intervention that helps children gain mastery over their nightmares.

As with all pediatric behavioral sleep interventions, a consistent bedtime and bedtime routine is the first step for any intervention. In addition, the selection of a specific treatment will depend on the presenting issue, the developmental stage of the child, and the ability of the parent and child to be consistent with recommendations. Finally, it is likely that a multicomponent intervention will be needed, incorporating more than one of the treatment strategies described below.

THE EVIDENCE

Several studies aimed at reducing children's nighttime fears have demonstrated that a cognitive–behavioral approach can be highly effective in reducing those fears as well as in generalizing to less global fear. In a review of 29 studies, Gordon, King, Gullone, Muris, and Ollendick (2007b) concluded that the most important elements of a treatment package for nighttime fears include systematic desensitization, cognitive self-instruction (e.g., repeated brave statements), and positive reinforcement. The authors also recommended clearly incorporating parents into the treatment package, as the parents are present in the home at bedtime and can serve as in vivo therapists (Gordon et al., 2007b). It is important to keep in mind that although positive reinforcement can be an important adjunct to cognitive–behavioral interventions, use of positive reinforcement alone has not been shown to maintain the same degree of treatment improvements over time as is seen with more self-management strategies, such as desensitization and cognitive self-instruction (Pincus, Weiner, & Friedman, 2012). Cognitive components of the interventions, such as Worry Time, have also had demonstrated effect on reduction of anxiety and improved overall well-being (Borkovec, Wilkinson, Folensbee, & Lerman, 1983; Jellesma, Verkuil, & Brosschot, 2009).

EXPOSURE WITH RESPONSE PREVENTION

Even the most rational child can become fearful at bedtime. The combination of a developing imagination with decreased emotion regulation at bedtime can exacerbate a simple fear into a major bedtime problem. Although a parent's innate response is to comfort a fearful child, this can result in reinforcing the child's fear by providing extra attention at bedtime. Exposure strategies focus on providing the child with an opportunity to experience the feared stimulus (frequently, a dark room alone) without experiencing negative consequences (the actual feared object) or allowing the child to escape (which reinforces the fear). These strategies serve as a backbone of anxiety management interventions but can easily be combined with positive reinforcement and cognitive strategies described later in this chapter.

How It Works

Through both classical conditioning and shaping, the child is repeatedly and gradually exposed to the feared stimulus (without being permitted to escape/avoid it) while pairing the child's fear with neutral or positive stimuli. As the child learns that the anxiety-provoking stimulus is not harmful, confidence is built in his ability to manage the anxiety.

Contraindications and Considerations for Special Populations

Exposure should not be the first line of treatment for children with severe separation anxiety or attachment disorders or those who have experienced trauma. Rather, the primary focus of treatment should begin with addressing the global anxiety. Once daytime anxiety has been addressed, nighttime fears can be treated with very gradual exposure.

In Practice

- Steps toward going to bed and sleeping independently are identified specific to the anxiety-provoking stimulus.
- For older children, steps may include going into the bedroom alone for 30 seconds, then 1 minute, then 3 minutes, and so on.
- For younger children, flashlight treasure hunts can help the child associate a fun activity with the feared dark room and provide the child increasingly longer opportunities to develop the ability to remain in the dark alone.
  - The parent places objects/toys in the child's room without the child knowing where they are.
  - The child is told to use a flashlight to go into the bedroom and locate the hidden objects.
  - Begin with objects hidden in simple locations that can be found quickly.
  - As the child's anxiety reduces, add more hidden objects or hide objects in more difficult locations to lengthen the time that the child is exposed to the dark room with the flashlight.

Handout 16 provides step-by-step instructions for parents on using flashlight treasure hunts.

- For both older and younger children, the time spent in the darkened room alone may also include positive self-talk and progressive muscle relaxation (see Exhibit 8.1), to assist with anxiety reduction during the exposure.
- Combining positive reinforcement with exposure and response prevention may be the most effective way to carry out the intervention.

Handout 17A provides step-by-step instructions for parents on how to implement exposure with response prevention; the companion, Handout 17B, provides instructions for children on the use of positive self-statements and diaphragmatic breathing. Both handouts include a Fear Scale to allow children to rate their fear during the exposure exercises.

EXHIBIT 8.1

Incorporating Progressive Muscle Relaxation

As an adjunct (rather than a stand-alone treatment), progressive muscle relaxation (PMR) can be a nice addition to help children and adolescents learn a self-calming strategy. Several books are available that use storytelling to guide children through progressive relaxation (see the Resources section). The following provides guidance on how to use this with children and adolescents.

- The child is guided in the office visit in slow, diaphragmatic breathing while sitting in a comfortable position.
  - Many children will do well to learn diaphragmatic breathing through the use of blowing bubbles or blowing on a pinwheel. The clinician can make a game of seeing how long the child can blow the pinwheel by using slow, steady exhalation.
- The child is then engaged in progressive muscle relaxation while continuing to practice diaphragmatic breathing.
- At home, the parents should guide the child in practicing both diaphragmatic breathing and PMR separate from bedtime. Once the child has mastered the combined skills, she should begin using them once in bed and prior to sleep.
- As with any new learned skill, relaxation takes practice to be effectively used, and children and their parents should be encouraged to practice it frequently (just like riding a bike) to fully acquire the skill.

Managing Potential Pitfalls

Find reinforcers that are more motivating than anxiety. Anxiety is a powerful motivator to avoid an activity, and as a result, the child may be resistant to starting the exposure process. Parents may need to be creative in finding positive, powerful reinforcers. If necessary, parents should be encouraged to use large reinforcers initially to help the child develop confidence that he is able to manage his anxiety. This is described further in the Positive Reinforcement section below.

Provide the child with anxiety management tools. The child's anxiety may be too high initially to manage the full length of time necessary to remain in the room. Adding progressive muscle relaxation and positive self-statements should provide the child with alternative behaviors and cognitions during the exposure. Use of distracting activities can also be helpful, such as reading a book, playing a game, or singing a song, depending on the child's interests.

The Bottom Line

Exposure with response prevention is commonly the first line of treatment for anxiety. When anxiety and fears are present at bedtime, the exposure needs to include being present in the bedroom, alone, and in the dark. Most children with significant anxiety will also require additional elements of intervention, such as cognitive strategies, positive reinforcement, and progressive muscle relaxation to experience success.

Cognitive Strategies

Cognitive strategies focus on decreasing the cognitive component of anxiety that has been interfering with sleep onset at bedtime and may include Worry Time, cognitive restructuring, and therapeutic storytelling. Each of these interventions aims to assist the child in managing worry by using healthier thought patterns.

CONTRAINDICATIONS AND CONSIDERATIONS FOR SPECIAL POPULATIONS

As with any cognitive intervention, children should have the cognitive capacity to comprehend the instructions and have metacognitive skills to question and dispute irrational thoughts. Younger children will benefit from more concrete strategies, whereas older children will be better able to directly challenge negative thoughts.

WORRY TIME

How It Works

By providing a dedicated time to worry each day, Worry Time serves as a somewhat paradoxical intervention. At bedtime, it enables the child to set the worries aside, without having to ignore them altogether (which can be difficult to achieve). Paradoxically, during the day, the child may ultimately find that she has difficulty filling all of her Worry Time with worries.

In Practice

- The child is told that she can worry for a set amount of time each day, typically 15 to 30 minutes (some children may require two to three Worry Times per day).
- The child chooses a specific time each day to practice Worry Time. This time should be separated from bedtime; typically, before or after dinner may be most appropriate for families.
- The child may choose to worry alone or with a parent present.

- The child may express any and all worries for Worry Time, and time may be spent problem solving ways to address worries.
- At any other time of the day or night that the child begins to worry, she should remind herself that worries will need to wait for the next Worry Time.
- If the child approaches the parent with worries at other times of the day, the parent, rather than providing reassurance, should direct the child to wait until Worry Time.
- After several Worry Times have not been filled with worries, the length or number of Worry Times should gradually decrease as Worry Time is faded.

Handout 18 provides step-by-step instructions for parents on how to use Worry Time.

Managing Potential Pitfalls

Identify the optimal time for Worry Time. After-school activities may interfere with established Worry Times. If this occurs, you should help the parent and child identify in advance an alternative time for Worry Time. For example, time spent driving in the car to and from activities could be used as Worry Time.

Consider suggesting additional Worry Times in some situations. A child with severe anxiety may experience increased worry as a result of waiting for just one Worry Time per day. Worry Time may need to occur multiple times per day but should always be separate from bedtime (e.g., before breakfast, when returning home from school, after dinner).

Use Worry Time for other positive activities, if possible. Some children find that they cannot fill all of Worry Time with worries. The parent may choose instead to engage in a preferred activity with the child, such as playing a game together. This may also indicate it is time to begin fading Worry Time.

Keep worries and reassurance seeking to Worry Time only. Some children with significant anxiety may repeatedly seek reassurance from parents and/or frequently express worries outside of Worry Time. Again, additional Worry Times may be needed and/or the child may require positive reinforcement for use of Worry Time.

The Bottom Line

Worry Time can be an effective and somewhat paradoxical intervention if used effectively. For greatest success, parents need to support the child in expressing worries and fears only during their established Worry Time. Most children are then able to ignore their worries while making efforts to leave them for Worry Time instead of ruminating on them all day and/or night. This can be a valuable skill not only at bedtime but throughout the day as well.

COGNITIVE RESTRUCTURING

How It Works

Through principles of cognitive therapy, children are taught strategies to change their thoughts from more negative irrational thoughts to more positive/rational thoughts. Initially, children are taught to identify negative thinking patterns that may contribute to their anxiety/fears and are then instructed in strategies to question the validity of the thoughts while replacing them with more positive helpful thoughts. Additional information on comprehensive cognitive restructuring interventions can be found in the Resources section.

In Practice, in Session

- Help the child identify his frequent worries and write them down.
- Ask the child to "think like a detective." The child should look for all evidence for and against the likelihood of the worry being true. For example, a child may state that he is worried that he will be kidnapped. Through a series of questions, help the child identify whether he has ever known anyone who was kidnapped or if his parents have known anyone who was ever kidnapped. In most cases, the child will say no. Then assist the child in identifying what a low-risk event kidnapping is and the safety measures his family uses (e.g., having the child play only where his parents can see him, staying together in public locations, having the carpool lane at school in which only an identified caregiver can pick him up). Handout 19 provides parents instructions on how to help their child think like a detective.
- A competing, more positive thought should be developed for those worries that have the most evidence against them. For a child with a fear of being kidnapped, for example, the competing thoughts may be "I know that my mom always knows where I am" or "I know that my school will not let me leave with anyone but a parent or grandparent."
- Worries that have the most evidence in their favor should be discussed with parents to determine the best way to protect and assure the child that adults are helping to keep him safe.

EXHIBIT 8.2

Monster Spray

Monster Spray can be a means of capitalizing on a child's fantasy play while also giving the child feelings of mastery over the monster or other feared object. To use Monster Spray, parents give the child a spray bottle of water that is labeled as "Monster Spray" (or "Ghost Spray," "Witch Spray," etc.). The child is told that monsters are allergic to this spray and will sneeze if they come too close to it. Alternatively, the child could be told that Monster Spray protects them from monsters the same way that bug spray protects them from bugs. At bedtime, the child is then encouraged to spray the Monster Spray anywhere that she believes the monster may hide. Handout 20 provides parents instructions on how to use Monster Spray.

- Younger children can be taught to replace their fearful statements with simple, positive self-statements, for example:
  - "I am brave."
  - "I am a big boy/girl."
  - "I can take care of myself."
  - "My room is a safe place."
- Younger children may also benefit from a number of more playful approaches. One example of such an approach, Monster Spray, is described in Exhibit 8.2, with parent instructions provided in Handout 20.

In Practice, at Home

- Parents can model the cognitive restructuring process for the child and encourage him to think like a detective and determine the evidence for or against the worry.
- The child should again identify positive self-statements that can be used as replacement thoughts when having the worry (e.g., "I know there is no evidence for this thought," "I don't have to listen to these worries," "I know my parents are keeping me safe").
  - Replacement thoughts can be more powerful with more detail (e.g., "I know my parents keep me safe by knowing where I am and who I am with").
- Children rehearse these statements during the day, when the bedtime anxiety is not present.
- Children then make the statements out loud as they are getting ready to go to bed.
- Children should continue to make the statements out loud in their room at bedtime once the parent has left.

Handout 21 provides guidelines for parents on using and practicing cognitive restructuring.

Managing Potential Pitfalls

Problem solve with parents when the child's worries are realistic. Ways to reduce the child's exposure to the anxiety-provoking stimulus should be identified, and parents should provide protection and reassurance as they are able. For example, the nightly news should not be left on the television while the family has dinner.

Provide additional instructions if the child is resistant to disputing a belief in irrational worries. These additional steps should provide more evidence against the fear, and/or encourage the child to participate in cognitive restructuring.

- Children can be given the homework of asking their friends, teachers, neighbors, family members, and so on, to rate the likelihood of worries occurring. Alternatively, for children who are cognitively capable, Internet searches can be performed along with the parents or clinician to determine the actual rates of events (e.g., house fires, burglaries in their zip code). Although not immediate, many children with anxiety will respond to contradictory evidence over time.
- Children who are resistant to challenging the reality of their worries may benefit from reinforcement of their cognitive restructuring. For each worry that they dispute, they may receive a token. Tokens can then be exchanged for tangible rewards.

The Bottom Line

Cognitive restructuring can be used to teach children to think differently about their fears and anxiety. The addition of concrete strategies such as Monster Spray takes advantage of imagination in younger children and may facilitate their sense of mastery over their fears. Older children and adolescents can be taught to think like a detective to independently dispute unhelpful thoughts that interfere with sleep and replace them with more realistic and helpful thoughts. With healthier thinking patterns, children should experience decreased presleep worry and reduced sleep onset time.

Case Example: Michael

Michael is a 10-year-old boy who has always been a worrier. As a young child, he was hesitant to go to a new classroom in day care and fearful of new activities. As Michael has gotten older, he has expressed increasingly more worries to his parents. Michael's worries typically relate to fears of breaking a rule at school, worries that his friends do not like him if they have chosen to play with another child, and fears of accidents or illnesses befalling his family members. His worries have recently begun to interfere with bedtime, as he is focused on worries that his house will be burglarized or catch on fire while the family is sleeping. Before bed, Michael will frequently check that all of the doors in the house are locked and that all of the smoke detectors have green lights. He then will repeatedly ask his parents to check the locks and smoke detectors. Once in bed, he will often leave his room to either ask his parents again if they have checked the locks and smoke detectors or to talk with his parents about other worries he is experiencing. His parents try to repeatedly reassure him, yet he continues to stay awake later than his target bedtime of 9:00 p.m. because of his worries. Michael must awaken for school by 6:45 a.m., and his parents are finding it increasingly difficult to awaken him because of his delayed sleep onset. When he does awaken, he is highly irritable and more prone to daytime anxiety.

Michael's parents chose a multifaceted approach to helping him manage his bedtime anxiety. Because some of the anxiety at bedtime related to specific worries about what might happen during the night (e.g., fires, the house being burglarized) and to more broad potential worries (e.g., family illnesses, school difficulties), Michael was provided with Worry Time twice during the day—once for 15 minutes before he left for school and once for 15 minutes just before dinner (to separate it clearly from bedtime). Because Michael was an avid baseball player, his evening Worry Time frequently had to be moved to accommodate his practice and game schedule. To do so, Michael chose to use the drive to the baseball fields as his Worry Time with his parents. He was resistant to the idea of Worry Time being helpful to him and tried many times throughout the day to talk with his parents about his worries and to seek reassurance that they had checked the smoke detector batteries and the burglar alarm. His parents identified specific reinforcers for Michael to wait to express his worries until Worry Time. Michael chose to have a packet of baseball cards for each day that he talked about his worries only during Worry Time. Initially, Michael easily filled every minute of his Worry Time, with his parents helping him think like a detective about the likelihood of each of his feared events. They then helped him identify which of his worries were most likely to happen, as well as the most likely outcome of each event. Michael's parents would help him problem solve how he would approach each feared event that he identified as most likely to occur. After only 4 days, Michael could no longer fill his full 15 minutes with worries. Sometimes he would use the remainder of the Worry Time to play a game with his parents, and other times he would simply go play with friends or watch TV. Michael was also taught progressive muscle relaxation, which he initially practiced when he returned home from school and then began using just before going to bed. He found that after a week of using progressive muscle relaxation at bedtime, he was very relaxed once it was time to go to sleep and would fall asleep in less than 15 minutes. After approximately 3 weeks, Michael told his parents that he did not think he needed to use Worry Time any longer. His parents noted that they would only have to remind him to think like a detective and he could use cognitive restructuring independently. At the end of treatment, Michael's parents described him as someone who still had a tendency to worry more than other children; however, he was more open to cognitive restructuring and was able to go to sleep more quickly at night without having night-time worries interfere with his sleep onset.

THERAPEUTIC STORYTELLING

How It Works

Based in a more playful approach to working with children, therapeutic storytelling works within the child's framework of learning from models.

In Practice

- The parent should help the child choose a character from television, movies, books, family stories, and so on, with whom the child identifies and/or enjoys.
- The child is then told either that he can pretend to be this character bravely battling the feared object or that the character is watching over the child to protect him. Children often may benefit from having a transitional object that is a stuffed replica of the character.
- Alternatively, children may have a stuffed replica of a character that they are required to protect and care for during the night (see Exhibit 8.3).

Managing Potential Pitfalls

Try multiple stories until the child finds one with which he or she most identifies. Some children will not easily identify with the story character that is initially presented. Clinicians may need to try different stories to find the one with which the child identifies best. A story can be successfully used when the child clearly seems engaged and is able to actively participate in telling the story together with the clinician.

Use therapeutic storytelling as an adjunct to additional cognitive–behavioral strategies recommended in this chapter. Many children may enjoy the story but do not seem to have anxiety reduction. In this case, the story may serve as an adjunct to other treatment components described in this chapter. Many times, therapeutic storytelling is not sufficient as a sole intervention to significantly reduce anxiety.

Huggy Puppy

Developed initially for children under extreme stress, the Huggy Puppy intervention has been shown to reduce nighttime fears in young children (Kushnir & Sadeh, 2012). The idea behind the Huggy Puppy is that providing the child with a transitional or security object to care for can reduce bedtime fears and help facilitate sleep onset.

To use the Huggy Puppy intervention, the child is given a stuffed puppy and told one of two stories:

1. The puppy is very sad and afraid and needs someone to take care of him at night. If the child provided the puppy with lots of hugs and reassurance, the puppy would feel less sad and scared.
2. The puppy is the child's friend and companion, and at night the child could confide his fears to the puppy and hug him when the child is scared; thus, the puppy will help the child overcome his fears at bedtime.

The use of both stories has been shown to reduce nighttime fears with the presence of the puppy (Kushnir & Sadeh, 2012).

The Bottom Line

Whereas children's imagination and fantasy orientation can sometimes induce significant anxiety and fear, therapeutic storytelling harnesses this fantasy orientation in a way that can be beneficial to the child. However, it often is not effective as a sole intervention and should be used as an adjunct to other cognitive–behavioral interventions for anxiety, such as exposure with response prevention and cognitive restructuring.

POSITIVE REINFORCEMENT

Positive reinforcement can often provide the child with a reason to face her fears rather than continue to avoid them. For most anxious children, the anxiety is so aversive that it can be difficult to convince the child to follow an exposure protocol or use brave behaviors. Positive reinforcement can help reduce bedtime struggles as the child has something positive to look forward to (the reinforcement) as opposed to focusing on a negative stimulus at bedtime. Thus, the added component of positive reinforcement may provide the push necessary to motivate the child to engage in the treatment plan.

How It Works

Based on operant conditioning, positive reinforcement is provided to the child for brave behaviors and statements, and fearful behaviors and statements are ignored.

In Practice

Many of the components described in Chapter 7 that use positive reinforcement, including Bedtime Charts/picture schedules and the Second Goodnight, can be used as part of the treatment package for a child with anxiety. Children who are fearful can also be provided with Bedtime Passes (as described in Chapter 7) to help them feel more comfortable, knowing that they can leave the room if their anxiety becomes overwhelming.

In addition, parents can provide the child with positive reinforcement for successfully completing steps outlined in some of the previously described anxiety management interventions.

- Reinforcement can be both verbal and tangible.
  - Verbal reinforcement can include praise for brave behaviors. Examples of this include
    - "Great job staying in your room with the light off" and
    - "I'm proud of you for being so brave to lie in your bed quietly."
  - Tangible reinforcement can include bravery tokens.
    - The child is given a token for each night that she remains in the bedroom making brave statements.
- For older children, tokens may also be used as a way to reinforce practice of anxiety-incompatible behaviors and statements, as well as for following steps of the bedtime routine.
- A set number of tokens may be traded in for identified prizes based on the child's interests (e.g., video game credits, nail polish, gift cards).
- For optimum effect, the clinician should build for success. Goals should be set that are relatively easy to achieve, such as providing one token for spending 30 seconds in the room alone, one token for 1 minute, one token for making a positive self-statement, one token for following one step of the bedtime routine, and so on. Once four tokens have been earned, the child earns a prize.
- After the child has earned the first prize, the goals should be increased for future prizes (e.g., after a prize is earned for four tokens, the goal becomes five tokens).
- To keep the child motivated, rewards should be changed regularly to make sure that the child does not satiate or become bored with the reinforcer.

Managing Potential Pitfalls

Consider using large reinforcers initially. For children with significant anxiety, the escape from the anxiety-provoking stimuli may seem more salient than the tangible reinforcer. If the child is not motivated by the reinforcer to face the anxiety-provoking stimulus, the parent may need to begin with a larger reinforcer. Most parents and children can identify together what most interests the child. Once the most powerful reinforcers are identified, they can be used initially to develop a sense of mastery over the anxiety.

Educate parents about the role of positive reinforcement in behavior change. Some parents will have concerns that they are bribing their children or giving them reinforcers for behaviors that they should already be doing independently. Parents can be encouraged with education and reassured that the reinforcers will eventually be faded and discontinued once the child has mastered the behavior. Reinforcers can also be conceptualized as helping the child get over the hump of the anxiety, providing something that is more motivating to attempt independent sleep than the level of motivation to avoid the anxiety of independent sleep. The clinician can work with the parents at the beginning of treatment to plan for fading and discontinuation of the reinforcers.

Strongly encourage parents to reduce the reassurance they are providing to the child. As with any anxiety intervention, excessive reassurance by parents can often become the primary pitfall. Parents very often fall into the trap of repeatedly reassuring their child that the feared stimulus is not real and that the child is safe. As this occurs, the child is frequently reinforced for exhibiting or expressing fear. The child is also often reinforced for leaving the bedroom to seek this reassurance, as the parent tells the child that she is safe and tucks her back into her bed. To avoid this pitfall, parents should be encouraged to provide reassurance only once and refocus the child's efforts toward positive self-statements, bravery tokens, and reinforcement for following the bedtime routine and remaining in bed. Parents often need to be reminded of the powerful role their attention plays in maintaining their child's behavior. Parents can be encouraged that by redirecting the child to use bravery statements and focus on earning tokens, they actually help the child acquire a skill that can be used in many areas to conquer the child's fears. The key to success is truly reinforcing the child's ability to practice bravery and avoid escaping the feared bedroom.

The Bottom Line

Positive reinforcement may be used to help a child engage in any treatment plan, but it can be particularly helpful for children with anxiety. However, positive reinforcement of brave behaviors must be paired with teaching the child how to use these behaviors, as described in the Cognitive Restructuring section. This additional element must be tweaked on the basis of the child's specific preferences and how well the child is responding to the intervention. If she is not earning any reinforcers, the reinforcers should be changed to be more motivating or the goals should be shortened. As the child begins to earn reinforcers quickly, the goals should be increased, always building for success.

Case Example: Isabel

Isabel is a 5-year-old girl who has always been a fairly "good sleeper," according to her parents. Since infancy, she has gone to sleep independently, without requiring her parents' presence. In the past few months, however, she has been stalling at bedtime by crying and repeatedly asking her parents to sleep with her. Although they have not done so, Isabel has repeatedly gotten out of her bed, crying and asking her parents to come back into her room. She has told her parents that she thinks she hears zombies in her room. Her parents have told her that there is no such thing as zombies, have opened the closet door to show her there are no zombies present, and have allowed her to look under her bed every night (sometimes repeatedly) to show her that there are no zombies. Regardless of their reassurances, Isabel continues to cry and repeatedly call for her parents. Isabel's behavior has resulted in her falling asleep well past her 8:00 p.m. bedtime, often at 10:00 p.m. She then must awaken by 6:30 a.m. for school. Isabel's parents note that she has been difficult to awaken in the morning and has been very irritable throughout the day. Now that she is in kindergarten, she is no longer napping, and her parents are concerned that she is not sleeping enough at night.

For Isabel's parents, the approach combined many elements to address her fears. First, Isabel's parents provided her with a bottle of "zombie spray." She went around her room spraying everywhere that zombies might have ever been and might ever hide. Isabel was told that zombies were terribly allergic to zombie spray and would sneeze so much that they would have to leave the house. She giggled as she was able to spray this all around her room, soaking the carpet in places. Her parents taught her to tell herself, "I am a brave girl. I know that the zombies can't be here because of how allergic they are to that spray. I can be a big girl and sleep in my bed." Each night that Isabel practiced her statements, she was given a bravery token. She then traded in three tokens for a new bottle of nail polish. Isabel was also provided with Bedtime Passes. At first, she was given three Bedtime Passes each night. On the first night, Isabel used all three passes. Her parents reassured her only on the first visit out of the room. After that, they gave her a kiss and a hug and told her they loved her while taking her back to her room and tucking her in. She did not get out of bed again and was asleep by 9:00 p.m. In the morning, she was reminded that she could trade in a pass for a reward if she chose to not use all three passes. On the second night, Isabel again sprayed her zombie spray throughout her room and practiced her brave statements. She then used only two Bedtime Passes, trading the third in for a piece of candy. By the third night, Isabel used only one Bedtime Pass. After 2 weeks, Isabel was falling asleep independently soon after her 8:00 p.m. bedtime without leaving her room and was able to go to sleep even without using her brave statements.

IMAGERY REHEARSAL THERAPY FOR TREATMENT OF RECURRENT NIGHTMARES

Nightmares are very common in young children and typically do not require treatment. For children who frequently have nightmares that disrupt their sleep or who become so fearful of having a nightmare that it interferes with sleep onset, IRT can be a highly effective intervention. The primary focus of IRT is to replace the child's frightening dream content with more benign content. The purpose is to help the child gain mastery over the negative dream content by encouraging her to have more self-efficacy in her ability to control her dream content. Before beginning IRT, it is critical to evaluate for trauma or significant stress.

Assessment Considerations

It is important for clinicians to remember that nightmares are more common in children who have had exposure to trauma. In particular, recurrent nightmares are one of the diagnostic criteria for posttraumatic stress disorder (PTSD). Children who present with an acute onset of recurrent nightmares should be fully evaluated to ensure that no history of trauma is present before beginning treatment of the nightmares. Even children who have had trauma exposure, including those with a diagnosis of PTSD, can benefit from interventions to reduce recurrent nightmares; however, more global treatment for PTSD is also indicated. In these cases, the child should be referred to a clinician with expertise in trauma-focused interventions in children.

How It Works

IRT is an intervention that addresses a child's nightmares through rescripting the dream (often with drawings) and then rehearsing the new dream both during the day and immediately following a nightmare. Through this process, the child learns to focus on more benign thoughts and reduce exposure to fearful thoughts. It also has the added benefit of assisting the child in developing self-efficacy and a sense of control over his own dreams.

The Evidence

IRT has been demonstrated to be an effective means of reducing the frequency and intensity of nightmares in both adults and children. In adults, IRT has been used effectively with individuals with a history of trauma (Davis & Wright, 2007), and in children, it has empirical support for use with adolescents with concurrent psychiatric illness and histories of trauma (Krakow et al., 2001). IRT can typically be completed in four sessions, with attention paid to the critical elements of the importance of imagery, selecting a dream, changing the dream in any way the patient chooses, and then rehearsing the new dream (Krakow & Zadra, 2006). Specific to children, adding an element of drawing the nightmare has been demonstrated to decrease distress related to their nightmares (Simard & Nielsen, 2009).

Contraindications and Considerations for Special Populations

Even children who have been exposed to trauma and have a diagnosis of PTSD have been shown to benefit from IRT. Therefore, this intervention is not contraindicated in a traumatized population, although they will also require interventions, such as trauma-focused cognitive–behavioral therapy. Also, even very young children may benefit from the concrete nature of IRT when drawing the rescripted dreams. Children with fine motor difficulties or who have vision impairments may have difficulty with the drawing component of IRT. If this is the case, the clinician may choose instead to use just verbal intervention and to discuss dream rescripting without having the child draw the dream content.

In Practice

- While awake, the child chooses to focus on a recent nightmare. The child describes the content of the nightmare in as much detail as possible. Similar to the use of guided imagery, for IRT the child should make efforts to involve all senses in the recounting of the nightmare. What does the child see, hear, feel, smell, taste, and so on?
- The child is instructed, "You can be the boss of your own dreams. You get to decide what your brain makes up."
- The child then changes the nightmare to have more positive content in any way he chooses. This may be by changing the ending of the dream to be more positive, by having the child take on the role of the powerful person in the dream or by replacing it with an entirely unrelated dream. For most young children, using

the same dream and placing the child in the powerful position assists with their understanding of the intervention, as well as with increasing self-efficacy.

- Many children, particularly younger children, benefit from drawing the content of the nightmare and the content of the new, more positive dream. This assists with improving visualization, as well as with making the task more concrete for the child. Some children enjoy tearing up the drawing of their nightmare while hanging the drawing of their positive dream next to their bed; this can help the parents while coaching children through rehearsal of their positive dream content.
- After drawing the newly scripted dream, the child should then rehearse the story by describing it repeatedly with the clinician, as well as with the parents. Start by having the child describe the dream during the day, and once he becomes comfortable, he should describe it just before going to sleep. Many children may benefit from having the drawing of the positive dream present to serve as a concrete prompt while describing it.
- When the child awakens following a nightmare, he should then practice in vivo with new, positive dream content. The parents should be coached in helping the child to do so upon awakening.

Handout 22 provides parents step-by-step instructions on how to work with their child on rescripting dreams.

Managing Potential Pitfalls

Continually allow the child to rehearse alternative dream content. Some children will experience a change in nightmare content while using the IRT. Because the parents should have already been coached in working with the child to rehearse the positive dream content, the parents can work with the child to construct a new, more positive dream that fits the content of the new nightmare. The child should then rehearse this positive dream throughout the day and at bedtime, as well as in vivo when awakening. Greater success may accompany this new dream if the child again draws the new nightmare and then draws the positive replacement dream.

The Bottom Line

IRT can be a fun intervention for children, particularly as they can incorporate creativity through drawing and using their imagination to create a new dream. It also provides the child with mastery over a feared object (the nightmare content) and can improve children's self-efficacy while eliminating the recurrent nightmares.

Case Example: Jada

Jada is a 5-year-old girl who has begun having nightmares on a nearly nightly basis over the past 3 months. Before that time, she had been having occasional nightmares that her family did not find to be disruptive. Since she began having nightmares nearly nightly, however, she has been waking her parents at night and having significant difficulty returning to sleep. She has also begun to talk frequently at night before going to bed about her nightmares and expresses worry about going to sleep for fear of having nightmares. Jada reports that her nightmares typically are about monsters eating her. With each nightmare, the monster frequently changes, but in the end of the dream she always awakens just as the monster begins to eat her. Both Jada and her parents have denied any recent history of trauma and report the only significant current stressor is the recent move of her best friend to another town.

Jada was able to offer a very detailed description of her most recent and disturbing nightmare. She described a large, hairy, purple monster with "1,000 eyes" coming toward her. She noted that the ground was shaking, and she could hear people screaming "everywhere." Even when she tried to run, her feet were stuck on the ground. Just as the monster opened his mouth over her head to bite her, she woke up. Jada spent considerable time drawing a picture of her nightmare and became very engaged, giggling as she drew the eyes all over the monster. When asked how she would like to change the dream, Jada decided that she wanted to have a "shrink ray" that would shrink the monster to the size of an ant. Once he was as big as an ant, she would then step on him. She then drew a series of pictures in which she shrank the monster and then stepped on him. She was very proud to show the drawings to her parents and looked forward to being able to practice this at home. Jada happily recounted getting to be the boss of her own dreams. Over the course of the next month, Jada had a significant reduction in the frequency of her nightmares, going from nightly to three times per week, to no nightmares at all.

Summary and Take-Home Points

Anxiety and worries can significantly interfere with sleep onset and perpetuate recurrent nightmares that can cause both sleep onset and sleep maintenance difficulties. Both cognitive and behavioral interventions can be used to decrease children's presleep anxiety. Several of the interventions can actually be fun for children, which helps the clinician have more buy-in from the patient. An added bonus for many of these children is acquiring an anxiety management skill that can be carried over into the daytime to help manage general anxiety around the clock. Specific points to remember are outlined below.

- Exposure with response prevention is the backbone of anxiety management. This can be used in a way that is more fun for the child by making a game of the exposure.
- Even preschool-age children can be taught cognitive strategies for managing anxiety if presented in a developmentally appropriate way, such as through storytelling or simple, positive statements.
- Positive reinforcement can go a long way in motivating children to participate in an intervention that may not sound very appealing (e.g., being exposed to a feared dark bedroom that he would rather avoid).
- Eliminating excessive reinforcement can be challenging for many families, particularly as they have developed this pattern in an effort to calm and comfort their child. Providing positive praise and tokens helps support both the parent and child in making changes to decrease presleep anxiety while encouraging a more positive bedtime experience for the family as a whole.

Insomnia 9

nsomnia, defined as difficulties initiating and/or maintaining sleep, is common in adolescents, with rates ranging from 3% to 36%, depending on the diagnostic criteria used. For most adolescents, obtaining sufficient sleep is challenging. Adolescents have an increasing number of academic demands, extracurricular activities and jobs, and social obligations, as well as technology in the bedroom. These factors often clash with early school start times, as well as the natural biological circadian rhythm changes that occur with puberty. School-age children also may have difficulty obtaining sufficient sleep, as they begin to have later bedtimes during the school week and sleep in on weekends even before the onset of puberty. Thus, a clear history that includes all of these factors is essential to provide an accurate differential diagnosis.

For example, Mark and Rob both presented with 11:00 p.m. bedtimes and the complaint of difficulty falling asleep before 1:00 a.m. If Rob goes to bed at 1:00 a.m., it still takes him 2 hours to fall asleep. But if Mark goes to bed at 1:00 a.m.,

http://dx.doi.org/10.1037/14645-010
Pediatric Sleep Problems: A Clinician's Guide to Behavioral Interventions, by L. J. Meltzer and V. M. Crabtree

he falls asleep quickly. In these cases, we would identify Rob as having insomnia, whereas Mark has a delayed circadian rhythm.

As most patients with insomnia will be adolescents, we refer to "adolescents" when describing interventions. However, it should be understood that these approaches also work with school-age children.

Assessment Considerations

For children, deciding whether the presenting problem is insomnia versus bedtime problems or night wakings can also be a challenge. Thus, it is important to carefully screen for potential sleep-onset associations, as well as possible reinforcements that the child receives for not falling asleep or staying asleep (e.g., being allowed to move to the parents' bed).

It is also important to assess for all children and adolescents what happens while they are trying to fall asleep, including behaviors (e.g., watching television) and thoughts (e.g., rehashing the day's events, planning for the next day, worries about not sleeping). The Dysfunctional Beliefs and Attitudes about Sleep Scale (DBAS; Morin, Vallières, & Ivers, 2007) may also be useful to identify possible cognitive distortions about sleep, helping to inform the need for cognitive restructuring.

Behavioral (and Cognitive–Behavioral) Interventions for Insomnia

Cognitive–behavioral therapy for insomnia (CBT-I) is a well-established treatment for insomnia that has been shown to be as effective as hypnotic medication in the short term, and more effective than hypnotic medication in the long-term management of insomnia in adults (Morgenthaler, Kramer, et al., 2006; Morin, Culbert, & Schwartz, 1994; Morin et al., 2006; National Institutes of Health, 2005). Brief behavioral therapy for insomnia (BBTI) is similar to CBT-I but with a reduced number of treatment visits (two visits over 4 weeks vs. six to eight visits over 8 weeks for CBT-I; Buysse et al., 2011; Edinger & Sampson, 2003; Troxel, Germain, & Buysse, 2012). Notably, both treatments include stimulus control therapy (SCT) and sleep restriction therapy, the key components of insomnia treatment. The additional visits in CBT-I are used to further refine these two interventions, as well as to address dysfunctional beliefs and attitudes about sleep (cognitive restructuring).

For many adolescents, BBTI is sufficient to resolve their sleep difficulties. However, adolescents who hold negative beliefs about their insomnia and the consequences of poor sleep will likely need CBT-I. Although this chapter focuses on the core components (SCT, sleep restriction therapy, and cognitive restructuring), a number of adjunct interventions have been shown to enhance treatment for insomnia, including education about healthy sleep habits and progressive muscle relaxation. However, compared with the core components of CBT-I, the independent use of education and relaxation has been shown to be less effective in the treatment of insomnia, whereas the use of education and relaxation in combination with the core components has been shown to increase the effectiveness of CBT-I (Morin et al., 2006). More information on complete volumes dedicated to CBT-I and adjunct interventions can be found in Appendix A.

THE EVIDENCE

As previously stated, CBT-I is a well-established intervention for the treatment of chronic insomnia (Morgenthaler, Kramer, et al., 2006; Morin et al., 2006; National Institutes of Health, 2005). A number of studies have demonstrated the effectiveness of this approach, especially when compared with pharmacological interventions (e.g., Jacobs, Pace-Schott, Stickgold, & Otto, 2004; Morin et al., 2009; Sivertsen et al., 2006). However, only a limited number of studies have examined the effectiveness of CBT-I in children and adolescents. Paine and Gradisar (2011) examined an intervention for children ages 7 to 13 years that included education, bedtime fading (similar to sleep restriction), and cognitive components to address anxiety. Although total sleep time was not greater in the CBT group versus the wait-list controls, significant improvements were found for sleep-onset latency (SOL), wake after sleep onset, and sleep efficiency. Bootzin and Stevens (2005) found that adolescents who completed four or more sessions of CBT-I, as part of a multicomponent intervention for substance abuse, had significantly longer total sleep, shorter SOL, fewer nighttime awakenings, higher sleep efficiency, and a greater subjective report of sleep quality. Finally, a recent study of both group and Internet-based CBT-I by de Bruin, Oort, Bögels, and Meijer (2014) found significant improvements in SOL, wake after sleep onset, and sleep efficiency, by both sleep diary and actigraphy. Total sleep time was also improved by sleep diary but not actigraphy. Although clearly more evidence is needed to support the use of CBT-I with children and adolescents, we have found great success with this approach in our clinical practices.

INTERVENTION FOR INSOMNIA BEGINS WITH EDUCATION

Before initiating any component of insomnia treatment, the first step is to provide adolescents (and their parents) education about sleep regulation and insomnia. Two models are particularly important.

The first model is the two-process model of sleep. It is essential for adolescents and their parents to understand the mechanisms of sleep regulation, as this provides rationale for treatment recommendations. Please see Chapter 2, this volume, for a review of the two-process model of sleep regulation (i.e., circadian rhythm and homeostatic sleep pressure).

The second model is Spielman's 3P model of insomnia. There are three different factors associated with the development and maintenance of insomnia that help guide the treatment process (Spielman & Glovinsky, 1991). These factors are outlined below.

1. Predisposing factors: Some people have factors that increase the likelihood of developing sleep difficulties (e.g., family history, hyperarousal, anxiety).
2. Precipitating factors: Life events and medical, environmental, and/or psychological factors can trigger sleep difficulties that result in insomnia (e.g., divorce, death of a family member, surgery, social or academic stressors).
3. Perpetuating factors: These are the behaviors (e.g., napping, extending time in bed to attempt to increase sleep duration) and/or beliefs, attitudes, or cognitions that develop to cope with sleep difficulties (e.g., anxiety about not falling asleep, worry about daytime consequences of not sleeping)

The treatment components described in this chapter aim to identify and remove the factors that perpetuate insomnia.

STIMULUS CONTROL THERAPY

For adolescents with insomnia, the bed and bedroom have become conditioned to create physiological arousal (e.g., racing thoughts, anxiety around sleeping) that is not compatible with sleep. Many adolescents will complain that they are completely exhausted and ready to fall asleep while watching television or doing homework, but the moment they enter the bedroom and/or the bed, they immediately wake up and begin to worry. Thus, the goal of SCT is to recondition the adolescent's association with the bed and bedtime such that decreased SOL is associated with the rapid onset of sleep.

How It Works

Based on classical conditioning, difficulty initiating sleep is conceptualized as a learned behavior that has been conditioned by repeated unsuccessful attempts to sleep. This results in a negative association with the sleep environment, in particular, the bed. SCT creates a positive association by pairing bedtime with a rapid sleep onset.

Contraindications and Considerations for Special Populations

Although there are no significant contraindications for SCT, the adolescent must have the cognitive capacity to understand and follow the rules of SCT. That said, if there is a parent or caregiver who understands these rules, SCT can still be used. However, the adolescent (or his parent/caregiver) needs to be highly motivated, as getting out of bed repeatedly (especially if it is cold and dark) can be the most challenging part of treatment for insomnia. For youth with severe anxiety who do not like to be alone at night, SCT can be even more challenging when other members of the family are sleeping.

In Practice

- Provide education about the conditioning aspect of stimulus control, in particular, the fact that despite an overwhelming feeling of sleepiness, the adolescent becomes instantly awake as soon as he closes his eyes. When the adolescent understands this association, introduce the following rules of SCT.
  1. Use the bed only for sleep. The adolescent should be instructed to avoid any activities in bed, including reading, watching TV, texting, using social media, doing homework, and so on, because this prevents the brain from making the association between the bed and sleep.
  2. Sleep should occur only in bed. Instruct the adolescent to sleep only in his bed and not on the couch or other location. Again, it is important to emphasize creating the connection between sleep and the adolescent's bed.
  3. Have a consistent bedtime and wake time. This should be in place with the implementation of sleep restriction (but often the two are introduced simultaneously). Adolescent bedtimes and wake times should not differ on the weekends. In addition, adolescents should not nap during the day. Regardless of SOL or night waking duration, morning wake time should not change (i.e., no sleeping in to try and make up for lost sleep).

4. Go to bed only when sleepy. The adolescent should be discouraged from going to bed earlier than the agreed-upon time in an attempt to increase sleep duration. Rather, the adolescent should get into bed only when he feels sleepy, even if this is after the set bedtime.

5. If unable to fall asleep in 15 to 20 minutes, the adolescent should get out of bed and engage in a quiet, boring activity in dim light until he feels sleepy again. Rather than watch the clock (which should be removed from the bedroom or turned away from the adolescent), he should simply guess when this time has passed. Most adolescents can identify that point when they know sleep is not going to happen. This step should be repeated as many times as needed until the adolescent falls asleep. This is the hardest, but most important, step.

6. If the adolescent wakes during the night and is unable to return to sleep in 15 to 20 minutes (again, at that point when he knows sleep is not going to happen or when he starts counting how many hours are left until the alarm goes off), he should again get out of bed and engage in a quiet, boring activity until he feels sleepy again. The activity should not involve electronics or light-emitting devices, as this can delay the onset of feeling sleepy.

▪ Handout 23 provides step-by-step instructions that can be provided to adolescents for the implementation of SCT.

Managing Potential Pitfalls

Identify activities to engage in when out of bed. It is important to work with the adolescent to identify what he can do when he gets out of bed. The activities should be engaging enough to keep the adolescent distracted but boring enough that he will become relaxed and sleepy. Examples include reading a book (in dim light) that he has read many times before (so could easily put down when he feels sleepy); reading magazines; rearranging the bookshelf (by size, by author, by color); folding a basket of laundry, dumping it out, and folding it again; writing in a journal or drawing; or playing solitaire (with cards, not on an electronic device).

Address concerns related to getting out of bed at bedtime and during the night. "It's cold and dark!" is the most common complaint from adolescents who do not follow the rules of SCT. It is important to recognize that getting out of bed is the most challenging part of stimulus control, especially when it is cold and dark and the rest of the family is sleeping. As many adolescents also complain about being alone and the unfairness of getting out of bed, it is important to validate their concerns (and/or inability) so they can get out of bed as recommended. Further, cognitive restructuring (see the next section), can be used to address these concerns. Additional education about retraining the body that the bed is only for sleep may be necessary.

Assist the adolescent in finding a place to sit when he is not in bed. Adolescents will often tell you that "there is nothing in my room other than the bed." Sitting on the bed is not sufficient for the stimulus control. If there is another room in the house the adolescent can go that will not disturb other family members, this is the best solution. If not, it is important to problem solve other possibilities (e.g., sit on the floor leaning against the bed, put pillows or a beanbag chair in the corner of the room).

The Bottom Line

Although SCT can be used alone or in combination with other components of cognitive–behavioral therapy for insomnia (e.g., sleep restriction therapy, cognitive restructuring), it typically serves as the frontline treatment for insomnia in older children and adolescents. The actual implementation of SCT can be challenging, however, especially for youth who are anxious or unmotivated. Thus, it is essential to provide detailed education to adolescents and their parents about sleep, insomnia, and how SCT works. In addition, proactive problem solving will increase the likelihood of treatment adherence and success.

SLEEP RESTRICTION THERAPY

One factor that perpetuates insomnia is spending a significant amount of time in bed not sleeping. When adolescents go to bed too early, they often do not have enough homeostatic sleep pressure to facilitate sleep. In other words, their sleep drive is not sufficient to help them fall asleep. The goal of sleep restriction therapy is to create mild sleep deprivation to increase homeostatic drive and sleep consolidation. The end goal is a sleep efficiency greater than or equal to 85%. *Sleep efficiency* is defined as the time spent asleep divided by the time in bed times 100, expressed as a percentage. For example, if a patient is sleeping only 6.5 hours per night, but spending 9.5 hours in bed (10:30 p.m. to 8:00 a.m.), she would have a sleep efficiency of 68.4% (6.5 hour sleeping / 9.5 hour time in bed × 100 = 68.4%).

How It Works

By creating minor sleep deprivation, the therapy increases homeostatic sleep pressure, reduces SOL, and consolidates overnight sleep.

Contraindications and Considerations for Special Populations

The increased sleep drive at the start of sleep restriction therapy will result in increased daytime sleepiness. Thus, it is not recommended to use sleep restriction therapy at a time of high stress or when academic functioning is a concern (e.g., midsemester or during finals). When daytime sleepiness may compromise safety (e.g., teen driving to school, summer job painting houses), adolescents should not engage in sleep restriction therapy. In addition, adolescents who have comorbid conditions that are sensitive to sleep deprivation (e.g., epilepsy) and adolescents with comorbid sleep disorders (e.g., obstructive sleep apnea [OSA], parasomnias, narcolepsy) should not use sleep restriction therapy. Finally, clinical judgment should be used in cases in which anxiety may interfere with treatment success.

In Practice

- Using a sleep diary for 7 to 14 days, determine the adolescent's average sleep duration (number of hours asleep between bedtime and wake time) and add 30 minutes to account for SOL (e.g., average of 6.5 hours; then prescribed time in bed would be 7 hours).
- Work with the adolescent to set a wake time based on required rise time for school. This wake time must remain consistent on weekends. Adolescents should get out of bed within 15 minutes of waking to prevent falling back to sleep.
- Starting with the set wake time, count backward around the clock the number of hours the adolescent typically sleeps to find the set bedtime (e.g., prescribed time in bed is 7 hours, wake time is set at 6:30 a.m., bedtime should be 11:30 p.m.).
- Have the adolescent maintain a daily sleep diary (see Handout 3), from which the clinician can calculate sleep efficiency at each appointment. Exhibit 9.1 provides one way to present the sleep diary data to the adolescent.

Note: Although the recommendation for adults being treated for insomnia is a minimum of 5 hours in bed, we recommend that time in bed for adolescents should never be less than 6.5 hours. For school-age children, a minimum time in bed should never be less than 7.5 hours.

At Follow-Up (Approximately 1–3 Weeks After Initial Visit)

- If the average sleep efficiency is more than or equal to 85%, time in bed is increased by 15 minutes (or 30 minutes if sleep need is high).
- If the average sleep efficiency is 80% to 85%, time in bed does not change.
- If the average sleep efficiency is less than 80%, then time in bed is reduced by 15 minutes.
- Handout 24 provides adolescents step-by-step instructions for using sleep restriction therapy.

EXHIBIT 9.1

Graphing Sleep Diary Data in Treatment

Reviewing and calculating sleep diary data can be timely and unwieldy, so it may be beneficial to create a program within a spreadsheet that allows for a quick calculation and review of the data. In addition, although not required, it is often helpful for the adolescent and clinician to graph the sleep diary data. This allows for a visual examination of changes to sleep patterns. For example, these graphs represent an adolescent's initial nonadherence to the recommended bedtimes and wake times, resulting in continued difficulties with sleep initiation and maintenance, as well as inconsistencies in sleep duration and sleep efficiency.

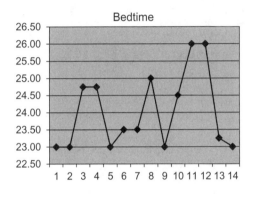

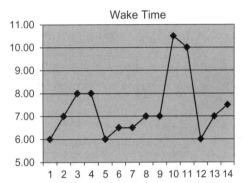

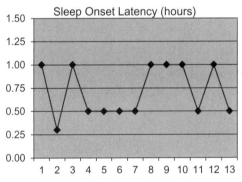

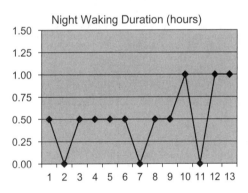

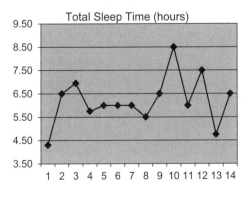

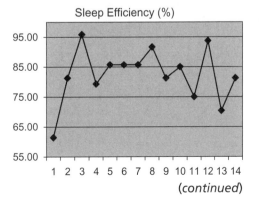

(continued)

EXHIBIT 9.1 *(Continued)*

Using many of the recommendations described in the Managing Potential Pitfalls sections for both sleep restriction therapy and stimulus control therapy, the adolescent returned after 2 additional weeks with sleep diary data demonstrating increased adherence to treatment recommendations and significant improvements to sleep-onset latency, night waking duration, and overall sleep efficiency.

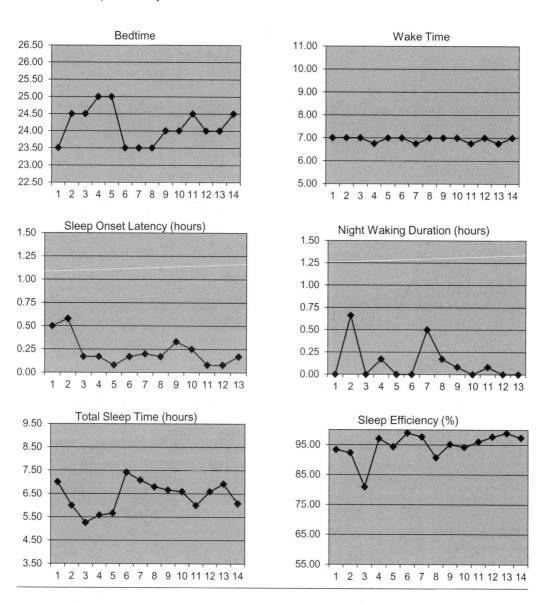

Managing Potential Pitfalls

Ensure that the adolescent is in agreement with the target wake time on weekends. A desire to sleep in on the weekends is the most common factor that will prevent an adolescent from following through on sleep restriction. Most adolescents (and their parents) believe that the weekend is a time to catch up on their sleep. In addition, some parents may balk at having to get up early to ensure the adolescent wakes up. A detailed review of the two-process model of sleep is essential to help families understand the reasons it is important to maintain this consistent wake time. In addition, adolescents should be reminded that this is a short-term sacrifice for the long-term gain of improved sleep quantity and quality. Finally, it is helpful to query adolescents about whether sleeping in on weekends has been helpful to either their sleep or their daytime functioning.

Emphasize the importance of maintaining a consistent weekend bedtime. Although bedtime is less of an issue than wake time, some adolescents may want to stay up later than the prescribed bedtime on weekends (e.g., sleepover with friends, video gaming, party at school). Again, adolescents should be reminded that the prescribed sleep schedule is part of the treatment and will not always be this way. In addition, it is often helpful to gently remind adolescents that they have come to you to improve their sleep and without a consistent sleep pattern, things will not improve.

Address concerns that the adolescent (or parent) has that she will be able to stay awake until the set bedtime. When this concern arises, it should be explained that the adolescent is currently not falling asleep until around the prescribed time anyway, so you are working with their current biological rhythm. Other recommendations may include avoiding reclining positions for the last 1 to 3 hours before bedtime or engaging in physical activity in the evening to help the adolescent stay awake.

Recognize concerns that the adolescent is not getting enough sleep. Adolescents and parents may have concerns about the negative impact of a limited amount of time in bed. It is true that for the first week or two, sleep duration may decrease. However, using the baseline sleep diary data, clinicians should emphasize that the adolescent is currently sleeping less than the prescribed time in bed and that the use of sleep restriction will increase her sleep efficiency and, ultimately, her sleep duration.

Encourage the adolescent to return the sleep diary. It is critical to have the sleep diary to track progress with treatment recommendations. When introducing the sleep diary, it is important to spend time explaining the value of the diary as a tool to assess treatment progress and determine whether to titrate time in bed. In addition, daily diaries prevent adolescents from the subjective biases of recalling only the last night and the worst night. To ensure adherence, complete a sample diary with the adolescent so that she understands the instructions. In addition, work with the adolescent to find a way to ensure daily completion (e.g., put a diary on the table to be completed while eating breakfast, set daily alarm on phone as a reminder to complete diary). If there is a reminder call about the follow-up appointment, it may also be helpful to remind adolescents to bring the sleep diary to the appointment (a completed diary left on the adolescent's bed is not going to help in the treatment session!). Finally, there are a number of sleep diary apps that may be used if the adolescent will simply not complete a paper diary. However, it is important to ensure that the selected diary includes the necessary information (bedtime, wake time, SOL, and wake after sleep onset) to calculate sleep efficiency. It is also important to determine ahead of time how to get the information from the app.

The Bottom Line

Although sleep restriction therapy feels counterintuitive to many adolescents and their families (e.g., "What do you mean you want her to stay up later?!"), this well-validated treatment is known to make a rapid change to an adolescent's experience of insomnia, with regular consolidated sleep replacing irregular and disrupted sleep. Further, the increase of sleep pressure results in deeper sleep rather than the intermittent light sleep commonly experienced by adolescents with insomnia. However, the success of this treatment is heavily dependent on both adolescent and parent buy-in because adherence to the schedule (both staying up late and then waking consistently in the morning, even on weekends) requires a highly motivated adolescent.

COGNITIVE RESTRUCTURING

For many adolescents, simply making behavioral changes with SCT and sleep restriction therapy is sufficient for addressing their insomnia. However, for a group of youth, dysfunctional attitudes and beliefs about sleep can interfere with sleep onset or sleep maintenance. For these adolescents, cognitive restructuring is needed to change and reduce these negative and counterproductive thoughts that are not compatible with falling asleep or staying asleep.

How It Works

Negative beliefs, attitudes, expectations and attributions contribute to a negative cycle of heightened arousal, inability to fall asleep, and negative thoughts about sleep. By identifying and reframing negative cognitions, this cycle is disrupted. For children and adolescents who have difficulties falling asleep because of worries unrelated to sleep, the use of Worry Time (see Chapter 8, this volume) can be used in place of cognitive restructuring.

Contraindications and Considerations for Special Populations

As the primary goal of cognitive restructuring is addressing negative cognitions, adolescents need to not only have dysfunctional attitudes and beliefs about sleep but must also have the cognitive capacity to identify and challenge these thoughts. Thus, cognitive restructuring should not be used with adolescents who have severe developmental disorders and/or reduced cognitive capacity.

In Practice

- Using a thought record (see Table 9.1 for an example and Handout 25 for adolescents to use at home), work with the adolescent to identify a situation in which he experienced a strong negative feeling or distressing thought related to his insomnia. Write this in the Situation column.
- Then query about associated mood or feelings that he experienced in this situation. Write this in the Mood column and rate the intensity (0%–100%).
- Identify thoughts associated with the situation. This could include thoughts about daytime consequences of not falling asleep (e.g., "I'll fail my test") or predicting he will never fall asleep. The adolescent should be encouraged to write all thoughts down, even if they seem silly.

TABLE 9.1

Example of Thought Record

Situation (date/time)	Automatic Thoughts (what were you thinking?)	Emotions (rate intensity of each one from 0%–100%)	Alternate Thoughts/ Adaptive Coping Statements	Emotions (rate intensity of each one from 0%–100%)
3/29, 1:30 p.m. sitting in class feeling tired	I'm never going to get through today I'm going to fail this class	Frustrated (100%) Worried (80%) Exhausted (100%)	I may not feel good, but somehow I always make it through the day I've had insomnia for 2 years and have not gotten below a B	Frustrated (60%) Worried (20%) Exhausted (70%)

- Identify adaptive alternative thoughts. This can include citing evidence for and against the thought/belief (e.g., "I've never not fallen asleep"), identifying the impact the thought has on his emotions (e.g., "Even though I'm really frustrated that I have trouble sleeping, I'm still doing well in school"), or estimating how likely it is that the negative outcome will actually happen (e.g., "I've had trouble sleeping for a long time and my girlfriend still likes me").
- Finally, reassess the adolescent's emotions in light of the adaptive thoughts.

Managing Potential Pitfalls

Emphasize the importance of practicing these skills on a daily basis. Self-monitoring is a challenging activity that requires a lot of practice. More important, this exercise should be done during the day and not when the adolescent is trying to sleep. It is helpful to find examples to emphasize the need for practice (e.g., you can't expect to get an *A* on a test without studying; if you haven't done the drills over and over during practice, you will not score goals during the soccer game).

Identify situations in which the adolescent misattributes his or her mood or fatigue to insomnia, and provide education about what is "normal." Many adolescents have unrealistic expectations about sleep that will interfere with their treatment progress. Thus, it is important to provide education about SOL (the time to fall asleep), which is considered typical if less than 30 minutes; *sleep inertia*, the feeling of grogginess most people experience in the first 30 to 60 minutes after awakening in the morning, regardless of sleep duration or sleep quality; as well as the increase in sleepiness in the early afternoon that corresponds to the natural circadian dip in alertness in the early afternoon (typically after lunch). Provide strategies to deal with these situations, including coping statements such as "this feeling will pass soon," going for a short walk, or getting fresh air.

Help adolescents identify other cognitive distortions. Similar to traditional cognitive therapy, adolescents with insomnia experience catastrophizing (e.g., "I'm going to go crazy if I don't sleep"), self-fulfilling prophecy (e.g., "I'm going to have a terrible day because I didn't sleep well last night"), all-or-none thinking (e.g., "I never sleep"), discounting the positive/focusing on the negative (e.g., one time the adolescent fell asleep at school after a bad night of sleep but has stayed awake every other day of the school year), and other cognitive distortions. It is important to identify these thoughts using the thought record and work with the adolescent to restructure these distortions.

The Bottom Line

Although not all adolescents require cognitive restructuring as part of their treatment for insomnia, for the subset of adolescents who have dysfunctional attitudes and beliefs about sleep, cognitive restructuring is a well-supported intervention that addresses these negative thoughts. However, as with traditional cognitive therapy, cognitive restructuring requires the adolescent to regularly practice and complete homework (thought record), especially at times other than when the adolescent is trying to sleep.

Case Example: Sydney

Sydney is a 17-year-old girl who has had difficulty falling asleep for the past 2 years following knee surgery. When she presented in clinic, her evening routine included sports practice, dinner, and homework (done in bed, often on her laptop). At 10:30 p.m., she would turn off the computer and lights and attempt to fall asleep. SOL was typically 1 to 2 hours. On weekends or during the summer, she would go to bed around midnight but still had difficulties falling asleep, reporting that she was rarely asleep before 1:30 a.m. Once asleep, Sydney reported frequent nighttime awakenings and said she was "annoyed" if she could not return to sleep quickly. She would set her alarm for 7:00 a.m. on school days. However, even with multiple reminders from her parents, she often slept until 8:00 a.m., making her late for school. Sydney's average sleep duration was around 6.5 hours, with her prolonged SOL and nighttime awakenings. On Saturdays, she would wake around 7:45 a.m. if she had a sporting event; otherwise, she'd sleep until 11:00 a.m. On Sundays, she would wake at 8:00 a.m. for church.

Sydney had no symptoms of an underlying sleep disorder (i.e., OSA, periodic limb movements in sleep, restless legs syndrome). She had tried a prescription hypnotic, melatonin, and playing soothing music, with no benefits. However, turning the clock around and removing the television from her room had helped a little with falling asleep. She was a high-achieving student with multiple honors courses and was captain of her sports teams. Other than finding it difficult to wake in the morning, Sydney denied sleepiness and fatigue during the day. However, she reported concerns that her sleep difficulties might interfere with her academic or athletic performance, although until this point that had not been the case.

With a typical sleep duration of 6.5 hours, Sydney was prescribed 7 hours of time in bed. Because she had to wake at 7:00 a.m. for school, she was instructed to go to bed at midnight and wake at 7:00 a.m. every day (including weekends). In addition, the rules of stimulus control were discussed, and Sydney stated that she would read magazines, draw, or rearrange the books on her shelf if she needed to get out of bed. Although no formal cognitive intervention was provided, ways to challenge her "frustrated thinking" during the night were provided. This included writing statements such as "I always fall asleep eventually" and

"Tomorrow will be okay even though I'm not sleeping now" on note cards and placing these next to her bed to read as needed at bedtime or during the night. Finally, the rules of sleep hygiene were reviewed.

Sydney returned for follow-up 2 weeks after her initial appointment and reported attempting to follow the recommended schedule during the first week. By the end of the first week, she was no longer having to get out of bed at bedtime or during the night. However, the second week was fall break from school, so she had a progressively later bedtime and would sleep in most mornings until noon. With that routine, she also had a return of her multiple nighttime awakenings requiring her to get out of bed. The importance of maintaining a consistent bedtime and wake time for the plan to be effective was again reviewed. Sydney's feelings that it was challenging to maintain a sleep schedule with only a 7-hour time-in-bed window were validated, yet it was also reinforced that the ultimate benefit would be reduced SOL and more consolidated sleep.

Sydney's second follow-up was 2 weeks later, and her sleep diary revealed improved adherence to treatment recommendations, with a consistent bedtime between 11:45 p.m. and 12:00 a.m., with the exception of one night when there was an end-of-season party for her sports team. However, she woke the next morning by 8:30 a.m. She reported being able to wake to her alarm clock now, with less reliance on her mother to wake her, and she would get out of bed by 7:15 a.m. Notably, she no longer felt tired upon waking or the need to go back to sleep. Her SOL was reduced to 15 minutes, and she reported no night wakings in the past week. During the day, she reported feeling less "cranky" and "happier" because of the changes in her sleep.

As her sleep efficiency was now 90%, her time in bed was titrated by 15 minutes, with a bedtime of 11:45 p.m. It was discussed how each week if she continued to fall asleep quickly and not wake during the night, she could add 15 minutes on to her time in bed each week. However, she should not add on more than 15 minutes per week, and if she was finding it difficult to fall asleep or stay asleep, she should return to the time in bed used for the previous week for an additional 1 to 2 weeks.

Summary and Take-Home Points

For many children and adolescents, difficulties falling asleep and staying asleep are a result of increased cognitive and physiological arousal at bedtime. However, cognitive–behavioral therapy for insomnia, a well-validated and effective treatment, can be used to help adolescents fall asleep faster and obtain more consolidated sleep. Specific points to remember are outlined below.

- Although effective, CBT-I can be challenging and requires a highly motivated adolescent and supportive parent. Consistency and follow-through are essential for treatment success.
- Use of SCT and sleep restriction therapy may be sufficient for many adolescents, but a subset of adolescents will also need cognitive restructuring to address all aspects of their insomnia.

Delayed Sleep–Wake Phase 10

C ircadian rhythm sleep–wake disorders are diagnosed when the timing of an individual's sleep–wake cycle is not consistent with the needs of his daytime functioning. The most common circadian rhythm sleep–wake disorder, by far, in adolescents is delayed sleep–wake phase disorder (DSP), occurring in up to 16% of adolescents and young adults (American Academy of Sleep Medicine [AASM], 2014). The hallmark of DSP is the inability to fall asleep at a "normal" time (in other words, rarely falling asleep before 1:00 to 3:00 a.m.), but once asleep, the adolescent has no problems sleeping. However, with early school start times in middle and high school, the clinical presentation of DSP is typically a youth who takes 2 or more hours to fall asleep at bedtime and then is "impossible" to awaken for school. Many parents will even say, "He has his days and nights backward, up all night and sleeping all day."

Along with difficulty falling asleep and waking up on weekdays, the adolescent also experiences poor functioning

http://dx.doi.org/10.1037/14645-011
Pediatric Sleep Problems: A Clinician's Guide to Behavioral Interventions, by L. J. Meltzer and V. M. Crabtree

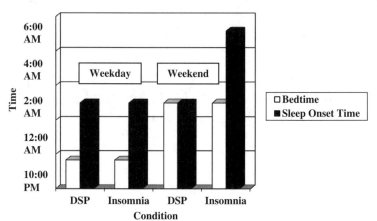

Distinguishing delayed sleep–wake phase (DSP) from insomnia.

at school, for morning classes in particular. By the time they present to a clinician, many youth with DSP are no longer in school because of their inability to obtain sleep at night and/or rise in the morning. DSP has also been associated with mood problems (in particular, depression), suicidal ideation, academic achievement difficulties, truancy, social isolation and difficulties, family conflict, substance abuse, and job loss (AASM, 2014; Crowley et al., 2007; Liu, 2004).

Although DSP and insomnia can certainly co-occur, DSP can be distinguished from insomnia in that if the adolescent goes to bed at his body's desired bedtime (rather than the required bedtime needed to obtain sufficient sleep), he will typically fall asleep rather quickly. In an adolescent with insomnia without a circadian rhythm component, oftentimes, if he goes to bed very late, he will continue to have a delayed sleep onset. Figure 10.1 provides a visual comparison of the scheduled bedtime versus the actual sleep-onset time of patients with DSP versus insomnia on weekdays when two teens are attempting an earlier bedtime versus on a weekend when they are going to bed much later.

Assessment Considerations

Because adolescents with DSP often have co-occurring conditions, such as depression and truancy, a thorough assessment is essential. Adolescents should be assessed for substance use and abuse, depression, and suicidal ideation. Further, psychoeducational assessment should be considered for those adolescents who may avoid school secondary to academic struggles.

Behavioral Interventions for Delayed Sleep–Wake Phase

NEGOTIATING SLEEP SCHEDULES

In every treatment approach to DSP, a preferred bedtime and wake time must be established for the intervention to work effectively. For adolescents, the target bedtime should be set on the basis of required wake time for school. As stated in Chapter 1, many high schools start their day very early, and adolescents must awaken by 5:30 a.m. to catch the school bus. Because most adolescents require 8 to 9 hours of sleep per night, this would then make the bedtime between 8:30 and 9:30 p.m., which is significantly earlier than most adolescent circadian rhythms will allow but is particularly difficult for adolescents with DSP. In these cases, careful negotiation with the adolescent and parent should occur to determine the most feasible bedtime that will allow for sufficient sleep for the adolescent to adequately function.

BRIGHT LIGHT THERAPY

With the use of bright light therapy (BLT), delayed circadian rhythms can be advanced to make sleep timing much more appropriate to the adolescent's academic needs. There are a number of commercially available BLT models that can be purchased online, including light boxes or visors that the adolescent wears. Some models contain dawn simulators, although this can increase the cost and may not be necessary to advance circadian rhythm.

The Evidence

Circadian timing in humans is strongly influenced by external cues—most important, the light–dark cycle. In particular, BLT has been demonstrated to effectively entrain the circadian rhythm in mammals, and the timing of bright light exposure is crucial for appropriate circadian rhythmicity with light administered in the morning causing the circadian rhythm to be advanced (Dodson & Zee, 2010). By exposing the adolescent to bright light at the appropriate time, the circadian rhythm can be shifted earlier, allowing for earlier sleep onset. BLT has been demonstrated to be a very effective treatment for advancing circadian rhythm in adolescents with delayed sleep–wake phase and has been shown to improve adolescents' abilities to attend school on time following treatment (Chesson et al., 1999; Okawa, Uchiyama, Ozaki, Shibui, & Ichikawa, 1998).

Contraindications and Considerations for Special Populations

BLT should not be used in any adolescent with photophobia or light sensitivity, as this can increase ocular symptoms. Adolescents with migraine headaches triggered by light should also avoid BLT. Furthermore, because BLT can elevate mood, caution should be exercised in its use with adolescents with a history of mania or bipolar disorder. Although most BLT units do not contain ultraviolet rays, this should be verified with the manufacturer before the use of BLT in adolescents who are taking photosensitizing medications. Adolescents with retinopathy or other eye disorders may not be appropriate candidates for BLT, and they should thus have approval from their treating ophthalmologists. Furthermore, because light boxes are not regulated by the Food and Drug Administration (FDA), families should research each company's claims and ensure that the company provides data to support claims of efficacy of their product.

In Practice

- The patient should sit approximately 12 to 18 inches from the light box (or wear the light visor) for approximately 30 minutes upon awakening each day (7 days per week).
- Adolescents should not sit and stare at the light but rather engage in other activities in front of the light, only occasionally glancing toward the light box but without looking directly at the light, as this can cause significant eye strain and/or headaches.
  - Patients can
    - do homework;
    - eat breakfast; or
    - watch TV, play handheld video games, and so on.
- The timing of BLT is highly important.
  - BLT must be used just after the lowest core body temperature, which most often occurs 2 hours before the circadian wake time.
  - Collaboratively establish with the adolescent a preferred wake-up time to use the light box each day.
- Most adolescents will do well with starting the BLT at the time they are currently typically awakening.
- Then, the wake-up time (and BLT application time) can be gradually moved earlier by 15 to 30 minutes every other day.

- As the wake-up time is moved earlier, the bedtime should also be moved earlier at a corresponding rate.
- Light should be presented from just above eye level to have its greatest impact on the retina. If not using a visor, the adolescent may choose to place the light box on an elevated counter while sitting in front of it. See Handout 26 for a sample BLT schedule for an adolescent with DSP.
- To motivate adolescents to wake early and spend 30 minutes in front of a light (when they would prefer not to wake up at all), it is often helpful to discuss that many patients report feeling more alert and attentive during the day when using BLT, even before moving bedtimes earlier (and increasing sleep duration).

Managing Potential Pitfalls

Ensure that bright light therapy is applied at the appropriate time. If the adolescent waits until too long after awakening to use the light box, this can further delay circadian rhythms. Patients should be cautioned to not use the light therapy box if they oversleep in the morning. If the adolescent awakens 30 minutes too late or forgets to use the light box within 30 minutes of awakening, he should be told to not use the light therapy box on that day.

Pay careful attention to the side effects, particularly eye strain. Adolescents should be cautioned to not look directly at the light box, as the light is very bright and can be bothersome to the eyes. They should be reminded to only occasionally briefly glance toward the light (not looking directly at it) while engaging in another activity. If eye strain occurs or is very bothersome, use of the light box should be discontinued.

Monitor mood. Although not common, some patients may experience hypomania or mania in conjunction with the use of the light box. If this occurs, they should immediately discontinue using BLT.

The Bottom Line

BLT is a highly effective means of resetting the circadian rhythm. With proper timing and positioning of the BLT box, adolescents can see rapid improvement in alertness, mood, and sleep schedule.

MELATONIN

Melatonin is a hormone that is naturally secreted by the pineal gland in response to dim light. This hormone is essential in regulating the circadian rhythm and promoting a feeling of drowsiness. Dim light melatonin onset (DLMO) generally occurs 2 hours before sleep onset and begins to ready the body for sleep. For adolescents with DSP, the

DLMO is significantly delayed, resulting in a lack of drowsiness at the appropriate time. Small doses of exogenous melatonin given at the correct time can shift circadian rhythm to promote drowsiness earlier in the evening.

Melatonin is sold as an over-the-counter herbal supplement and therefore is not regulated by the FDA. As a result, no oversight is provided to the accuracy of the dosing listed on the packaging. If one brand of melatonin does not seem effective for an adolescent, she may need to try an alternative brand in the event that the proper dosage is not present in the bottle. A melatonin agonist is available by prescription, if the patient's physician chooses to prescribe this medication.

The Evidence

By administering exogenous melatonin in the early evening, the DLMO is earlier than would otherwise naturally occur, resulting in an earlier experience of drowsiness and sleep onset. In this instance, melatonin is used as a chronobiotic (meaning it affects circadian timing) rather than a hypnotic (meaning it induces sleepiness—see Exhibit 10.1). Exogenous melatonin given in the early evening has been demonstrated to both lower the core body temperature and advance the circadian rhythm,

---

EXHIBIT 10.1

Melatonin as a Hypnotic

Research suggests that melatonin may be a more powerful chronobiotic (i.e., working to change circadian rhythm) than hypnotic (i.e., working to induce sleepiness). However, for children and adolescents who have difficulty with sleep-onset initiation that does not have a circadian component (i.e., sleep-onset insomnia in children with autism or attention-deficit/hyperactivity disorder), melatonin can be tried as a hypnotic. However, behavioral interventions should be implemented before, or concurrently with, the use of melatonin.

- Larger doses may be needed (e.g., 1–6 mg) for melatonin to be an effective hypnotic.
- When used as a hypnotic, the timing of the melatonin administration is much closer to bedtime (30 minutes to 1 hour before the desired bedtime).
- Again, care should be taken to use the lowest dose possible. If not effective in 1 week, the dose may be increased by 1 mg.
- For children who are falling asleep much later than the desired bedtime, melatonin may be used in conjunction with bedtime fading such that the melatonin is administered 30 minutes before the current bedtime, gradually moving both melatonin administration and bedtime earlier.
- Melatonin should not be given too early or too late to avoid shifting the circadian rhythm.
- Melatonin has a short half-life, and as a result typically does not provide improvement for sleep maintenance. While some extended release preparations are available on the market, the research support tends to be less robust than for sleep-onset difficulties.

resulting in earlier sleep onset (Arendt & Skene, 2005). It is important to note that higher doses of melatonin do not appear to advance the circadian rhythm any more than do low doses; therefore, using a lower dose (0.3–0.5 mg) approximately five hours before bedtime has been shown to effectively advance the circadian rhythm (Revell et al., 2006).

Contraindications and Considerations for Special Populations

Although not routinely found, a lowered seizure threshold in children taking melatonin has been found by some studies. Therefore, any child or adolescent with a history of seizure disorder or propensity toward seizures should not use melatonin without approval by her physician. Although unlikely, some people may also experience fatigue or depressed mood with melatonin, and it should be discontinued should significant depression occur.

In Practice

- Studies have shown variability in individual response to the dosage and timing of melatonin.
- Care should be taken to start at the lowest dose of melatonin (e.g., 0.3 mg) with gradual increases (e.g., no more than once/ week) if a response is not shown.
- Because exogenous melatonin has its greatest impact on advancing the circadian rhythm if given several hours before DLMO, the key to effective melatonin dosing in DSP is to use the lowest dose possible (0.3 mg–0.5 mg) at the earliest time that the adolescent can tolerate it (without becoming too sleepy too early in the evening), typically 3 to 6 hours before the desired bedtime.
- For most adolescents, starting at 0.3 mg of melatonin 3 hours before bedtime may be sufficient. Doses and administration time can then be adjusted from there as necessary.
- Because most providers will not be able to determine DLMO in a clinical setting (saliva samples must be collected every 30–60 minutes in the late afternoon and into the night for several hours, in a constantly dim environment, and sent to a lab for analysis to determine the rise in endogenous melatonin), the timing of the dosage must be tailored to the individual patient on the basis of her initial response.
- If the patient feels too sleepy before the desired bedtime, the timing of the melatonin can be moved to later in the evening (approximately one hour later).
  - If the patient does not experience benefit, the dosage can be increased (i.e., from 0.3 to 0.5 mg or from 1 mg to 2 mg) or the timing can be moved earlier by approximately 1 hour.

▪ Melatonin can be combined with BLT such that the adolescent takes the prescribed melatonin several hours before the target bedtime while simultaneously using bright light for 30 minutes upon awakening.

Managing Potential Pitfalls

Ensure that the adolescent is fully alert to complete tasks in the evening. If an adolescent complains that he feels too sleepy too early in the evening (particularly during homework time), this may be an indication that he is taking the melatonin too early. In this case, the adolescent should take the melatonin 1 hour later.

Make dosage adjustments as necessary. Some adolescents may complain that they do not feel any sleepier at the desired bedtime. In this case, the patient may require a higher dose of melatonin. Dosage can be increased in 0.5-mg or 1.0-mg increments. In addition, the adolescent may require a different brand of melatonin. As previously mentioned, because melatonin is considered an herbal supplement and not monitored by the FDA, label claims may not match the actual dosage of melatonin in the bottle. Alternatively, if the adolescent complains that he feels groggy the following day, the dosage should be reduced. For those already on the lowest dosage, either move the timing of the melatonin earlier in the evening or discontinue use of the melatonin.

The Bottom Line

Although melatonin can be used as a hypnotic, it has the greatest support for its use as a chronobiotic. The chronobiotic effect of melatonin is dependent on an adolescent's DLMO, which is impractical to establish in clinical practice. Because of this, much finesse and trial-and-error are necessary to determine the optimal dosage and timing of melatonin. Patients and parents should be counseled that determining the optimal dosage and timing can be a multiweek and somewhat labor-intensive process that requires close collaboration between the patient, family, and treating clinician. Melatonin may also be used effectively in combination with BLT for a combined treatment approach.

CHRONOTHERAPY

Because the human circadian rhythm is naturally slightly longer than a 24-hour day (Wever, 1984), it is far easier for people to go to bed and fall asleep later each day than it is to go to bed and fall asleep earlier. Harnessing this biological propensity, chronotherapy moves the circadian rhythm forward each day rather than fighting against the delayed circadian rhythm in an attempt to move it earlier. This allows for larger shifts in the sleep timing than are possible when advancing the sleep onset. Because the shifts in bedtime are so large in chronotherapy, the circadian rhythm can be reset very quickly, often in 1 to 2 weeks. For adolescents, this can allow for a quick treatment during school breaks.

The Evidence

Chronotherapy has been demonstrated to effectively substantially delay the circadian rhythm until such time that the desired bedtime and wake time have been achieved. This approach has been demonstrated as effective in treatment of DSP, particularly when used in conjunction with BLT (Lack & Wright, 2007; Weitzman et al., 1981). Lack and Wright (2007) recommended choosing chronotherapy as an intervention for patients who have typical wake times later than noon or in those who find BLT to be highly aversive (e.g., those with eye strain or headaches). With the use of chronotherapy, phase shifting should be able to occur to achieve the target bedtime and wake time within 1 to 2 weeks (Lack & Wright, 2007; Weitzman et al., 1981).

How It Works

By moving bedtime and wake-up time later by several hours each day, the adolescent then locks in a bedtime and wake time that is more consistent with what is required for school schedules.

Contraindications and Considerations for Special Populations

Many patients with DSP are already not attending school, but for patients who are still managing to make it to school each day, chronotherapy should only be used during school vacations, unless an individual school is willing to permit an adolescent to miss school while she is sleeping during daytime hours. This is occasionally permitted by schools, particularly for those students who have been excessively truant. Chronotherapy can also affect the timing of prescription medications. For adolescents with diabetes, it should be avoided, as this can negatively impact administration of insulin. For other adolescents taking prescription medications, the treating clinician should consult with the patient's prescribing physician to have chronotherapy approved, as well as to determine optimal timing of prescription medications. In patients with a history of bipolar disorder, care should be taken to avoid a manic episode. Chronotherapy should be discontinued if the patient shows a decreased need for sleep, indicating early signs of mania.

In Practice

- The patient should maintain her bedtime, sleep-onset time, and wake time consistently for 1 week to ensure ability to adhere to a treatment protocol and provide a solid baseline from which to work.
- Once this has been established, the patient should move her bedtime and wake time 2 to 3 hours later, allowing for approximately 8 to 9 hours of sleep.
- Each night, continue to move the bedtime and wake time 2 to 3 hours later until the desired bedtime is reached (see Exhibit 10.2).
- Once the desired bedtime is reached, the patient should lock in both the bedtime and the wake time to ensure that her sleep-onset time does not continue to move later. This means that the sleep schedule needs to be maintained every single night, including weekends!
- It can also be helpful to ensure that the adolescent is having light exposure (either outdoor light or bright light) upon awakening to help maintain this wake time.
- Melatonin should be avoided when using chronotherapy, as it can be exceedingly difficult or impossible to time the melatonin in relation to DLMO, given the rapidly changing sleep cycle.

Handout 27 provides detailed step-by-step instructions for patients on how to use chronotherapy.

Managing Potential Pitfalls

Be sure to lock in the bedtime and wake time once the desired schedule has been reached. Chronotherapy runs the risk of continuing if adolescents are not diligent about maintaining the preestablished bedtime after it has been reached, particularly on weekends (see Exhibit 10.3). If the new schedule is not maintained, the patient may develop a free-running circadian rhythm in which the sleep-onset time continues to advance

---

EXHIBIT 10.2

Sample Chronotherapy Schedule

Night 1: Bedtime 7:00 a.m., Wake time 3:00 p.m.
Night 2: Bedtime 10:00 a.m., Wake time 6:00 p.m.
Night 3: Bedtime 1:00 p.m., Wake time 9:00 p.m.
Night 4: Bedtime 4:00 p.m., Wake time 12:00 a.m.
Night 5: Bedtime 7:00 p.m., Wake time 3:00 a.m.
Night 6: Bedtime 10:00 p.m., Wake time 6:00 a.m.
Night 7: Bedtime 10:00 p.m., Wake time 6:00 a.m.

EXHIBIT 10.3

A Word About Weekends

All treatments for delayed sleep–wake phase (DSP) rely heavily on establishing and maintaining a desired bedtime and wake time every single night. That said, adolescents frequently prefer to sleep in on weekends as a result of insufficient sleep during the school week (particularly for those attending schools with early start times). This can create problems for all adolescents, but especially for those with DSP. Because of the likelihood of treatment failure if the sleep schedule is not consistent, adolescents with DSP and their parents should be strongly cautioned about the tendency for the circadian rhythm to be further delayed by later weekend wake times. Specifically, wake times for all adolescents, but especially those with DSP, should not vary by more than 30 minutes to 1 hour from the weekday wake times.

around the clock. Because a free-running cycle can be very problematic, the adolescent and parent should be strongly cautioned against this. Use of melatonin in the early evening and BLT upon awakening can help adolescents maintain this wake time without continuing to advance their rhythm around the clock.

Find activities for the presleep period. The inability to remain awake until the preestablished bedtime does not occur very often, particularly in adolescents who have a delayed circadian rhythm. In the event it does occur, however, adolescents should be encouraged to engage in stimulating activities (e.g., spending time with friends, exercising) until the desired bedtime.

Provide motivation to awaken at the desired time. Because of individual variability in sleep requirements, some adolescents require more sleep and may have difficulty awakening at the target rise time. For these patients, the target bedtime should remain the same, but the wake time should be moved even 1 hour later (e.g., bedtime of 4:00 a.m., wake time of 1:00 p.m.). It is also important to have an adult monitoring the rise time. Either a parent needs to be present to awaken the adolescent or the adolescent should be required to call a parent to verify that he has awakened at the target rise time.

Monitor for the development of insomnia. Some adolescents will have difficulty falling asleep once the established bedtime during the chronotherapy cycle is at an unnatural time (e.g., 3:00 p.m.). In this case, chronotherapy may need to be discontinued and a focus placed on BLT and/or melatonin administration.

The Bottom Line

Chronotherapy can be a quick and effective approach to treating DSP. It typically needs to be carried out during school breaks, unless an adolescent's school is willing to work closely with the treating clinician and provide excused absences during the days in which the patient is sleeping during daytime hours. A significant risk exists that delayed sleep onset will continue and develop into a free-running cycle if the treatment is not closely followed. As a result, adolescents and their parents must be cautioned to maintain a very strict bedtime and wake time, particularly on weekends, to lock in the circadian rhythm.

Case Example: Dallas

Dallas is a 15-year-old boy who reports ongoing and very severe insomnia. He and his mother complain that he has not been able to fall asleep for hours after going to bed. Because Dallas needs to awaken by 6:00 a.m. for school, his mother has tried to have him go to bed by 10:00 p.m. each night. Approximately 2 years ago, he began having increasing difficulty falling asleep at bedtime. Now, even if he goes to bed at 10:00 or 11:00 p.m., he very often does not fall asleep until 4:00 a.m. When his mother tries to wake him up for school at 6:00 a.m., he either refuses to get out of bed or simply will not wake up. Dallas typically then will sleep until 10:00 or 11:00 a.m., long after his mother has left for work and he has missed the school bus. This has then led to reports of truancy, failing grades, and his school threatening to expel him. On weekends, Dallas usually does not even try to go to sleep until between 3:00 and 4:00 a.m., and he will fall asleep without difficulty on those nights. He then sleeps until 12:00 p.m. As his difficulties with falling asleep have gotten worse, so has Dallas's mood. His mother now describes him as moody, irritable, and withdrawn, which is substantially different than his mood before his sleep problems. Dallas has tried meditating, progressive muscle relaxation, and journaling in an effort to improve his sleep onset, but with little benefit.

Dallas arrived for treatment 3 weeks before his school's spring break. Through discussion of the different treatment options with Dallas and his mother, the family chose to begin with use of melatonin and BLT. Dallas began by taking 0.5 mg of melatonin at 7:00 p.m. and attempting a bedtime of 2:00 a.m. He was then instructed to awaken at 9:00 a.m. and use his light box for 30 minutes while eating breakfast and completing homework. He had a goal of moving his bedtime and wake time earlier by 30 minutes after he was able to go to sleep within 30 minutes of his 2:00 a.m. bedtime. The clinician provided a note to Dallas's school providing information about DSP, as well as requesting excused tardies while his wake time was gradually moved earlier. The school agreed to allow for this, as they were concerned about the number of unexcused absences Dallas had acquired. He initially reported that he felt more alert during the day and was not falling asleep in his first classes. He reported, however, that he continued to have difficulty falling asleep at 2:00 a.m. His melatonin dosage was increased to 1.0 mg, and he was encouraged to continue to make efforts to go to bed at 2:00 a.m. After 2 weeks of having ongoing difficulty falling asleep at the desired time (though continuing to report less daytime sleepiness), Dallas and his mother elected to attempt chronotherapy during his spring break. He discontinued use of the melatonin but continued to use the BLT box upon awakening each day. Dallas was able to fall asleep relatively quickly each day within minutes of his desired time. By the end of spring break, he was falling asleep within 30 minutes of his 10:00 p.m. bedtime and waking up at 6:00 each morning to use his light therapy box before school. Dallas and his mother reported improved mood, school attendance, and grades for the remainder of the school year. Over the summer, however, Dallas quickly reverted back to his previous sleep pattern. Two weeks before the start of the next school year, Dallas again used chronotherapy in combination with BLT to reestablish an appropriate circadian rhythm.

Summary and Take-Home Points

Delayed sleep–wake phase can be a very difficult experience for adolescents and their parents. The difficulty falling asleep and waking in relation to required school start times can lead to academic struggles, truancy, mood problems, and family conflict. Understanding the role of the circadian rhythm in promoting sleep and wake is essential for an effective treatment of patients with DSP. Points to remember are outlined below.

- Light is the strongest cue for the circadian rhythm. Use of BLT upon awakening can help patients move their circadian rhythms earlier, promoting earlier sleep onset.
- Melatonin works better as a chronobiotic than a hypnotic. For this reason, if given in small doses early in the evening, it can help promote earlier sleep onset in those with DSP.
- Chronotherapy can be a quick and effective intervention in adolescents who are able to miss school for approximately one week while their bedtimes and wake times are moved forward in large increments, taking advantage of our natural circadian rhythm that is longer than a 24-hour day.

Confusional Arousals, Sleep Terrors, and Sleepwalking

11

Confusional arousals, sleep terrors, and sleepwalking are all disorders of arousal, also known as *partial arousal parasomnias* or *nonrapid eye movement (NREM) parasomnias*. These events occur during the transition out of slow-wave sleep to lighter sleep, rapid eye movement (REM) sleep, or a brief arousal. Because most slow-wave sleep occurs in the first part of the night, NREM parasomnias typically occur during the first few hours after sleep onset. In addition, because slow-wave sleep decreases with age, events become less common in older school-age children and adolescents. Although less common, NREM parasomnias can also occur during daytime naps for younger children (thus the term *sleep terrors* rather than *night terrors*).

There are also REM parasomnias that can occur, including REM-sleep behavior disorder, hypnagogic/hypnopompic hallucinations, and nightmares. The treatment of nightmares is covered in Chapter 8, and the other two disorders are rare in children and adolescents, and thus are not covered in this chapter.

http://dx.doi.org/10.1037/14645-012
Pediatric Sleep Problems: A Clinician's Guide to Behavioral Interventions, by L. J. Meltzer and V. M. Crabtree

Each type of NREM parasomnia has a different presentation. Confusional arousals can be seen in infants as young as 6 months and are characterized by confusion, disorientation, grogginess, and possible agitation. Sleep terrors are most common in preschool and early school age children and present with a child waking suddenly and appearing frightened and/or significantly distressed (i.e., screaming, crying). Many children (up to 40%) will have at least one episode of sleepwalking in their life. These children will appear dazed and confused, with their eyes open, and may mumble or talk nonsensically. In addition, some sleepwalkers will engage in unusual behaviors (e.g., walking down the hall and urinating in a closet, making a sandwich and then not eating it or cleaning up, wandering out of the house).

Despite the different presentations, there are a number of common features for these events. Most are brief in duration (i.e., 5–10 minutes) and end spontaneously, although some children may experience more severe NREM parasomnias that last up to an hour. Children will often not respond to, not interact with, or not be comforted by parents during an event, and if they do, the child will often appear confused or noncoherent. Attempting to wake a child who is having an NREM parasomnia event will likely make the event last longer. Finally, children will have retrograde amnesia and thus will not recall the event in the morning.

Assessment Considerations

There are two primary ways to differentiate NREM parasomnias from nightmares. First, as mentioned, NREM parasomnias occur in the first part of the night (usually the first third), whereas nightmares occur in the last part of the night (as REM sleep mostly occurs in the last part of the night). Second, it is helpful to ask who is more upset by the episode. If it is the parent who is distressed by responding to a child who is upset, unresponsive, and/or does not recognize the parent, then it is a sleep terror. However, if the child is distressed and can clearly describe why she is afraid after waking, then she is likely experiencing nightmares.

NREM parasomnias are generally considered benign and self-limiting disorders. However, it is important to assess family history for these events, as NREM parasomnias commonly run in families, with up to 65% of patients having a first-degree relative with a history of at least one type of NREM parasomnia event. In other words, a child who has sleep terrors may have a parent who has a history of sleepwalking but never had a sleep terror. Finally, the primary trigger for NREM parasomnias is deficient or poor-quality sleep. Lack of sleep or disrupted sleep increases the pressure for slow-wave sleep and thus increases the likelihood of an NREM parasomnia event. Thus, a detailed history to identify whether and why the child is not getting adequate or quality sleep is essential.

Behavioral Interventions for Nonrapid Eye Movement Parasomnias

THE EVIDENCE

Although no studies have demonstrated the benefits of providing education, safety, and reassurance about NREM parasomnias, this is generally suggested as the frontline treatment (Mason & Pack, 2007; Mindell & Owens, 2010). Several studies have clearly shown the benefits of scheduled awakenings for children with predictable NREM parasomnia events (N. C. Frank, Spirito, Stark, & Owens-Stively, 1997; Lask, 1988, 1993).

EDUCATION, SAFETY, AND REASSURANCE

When a child has a sleep terror, she appears quite distressed, which is concerning for parents, who commonly worry that the sleep terror is a sign of underlying trauma or an early sign of psychopathology. For sleepwalkers, parents are often concerned about the child ending up injured or even lost if she wanders out of the house. Further, parents of patients with NREM parasomnias frequently report concerns about the child's sleep quantity and quality. The goal of education, safety, and reassurance is to provide families information about NREM parasomnias, as well as ways to decrease events and ensure the child's safety during the night.

How It Works

NREM parasomnias are typically benign, self-limited, and resolve on their own. Thus, education about the disorder and safety recommendations are the frontline behavioral treatments for infrequent and/or uncomplicated NREM parasomnias.

In Practice

- Basic information about NREM parasomnias should be provided to parents both verbally and in written format (Handout 28). This should include the following information.
  - NREM parasomnias are common in children. Up to 40% of children will have at least one NREM parasomnia event in their life.
  - For children predisposed to NREM parasomnias, these events are triggered by poor-quality or insufficient sleep. When a child does not get enough sleep or has poor-quality sleep, this will increase the likelihood of events, so it is important to educate parents about triggers (e.g., underlying sleep disorder, illnesses, sleeping in an unfamiliar environment on vacation).

- NREM parasomnias are a benign condition. This means these events do not indicate any underlying psychopathology or traumatic event has occurred. That said, children who have experienced trauma or have comorbid psychiatric issues, as well as a family history of NREM parasomnias, may be at increased risk for events if their sleep is disrupted because of the trauma or comorbid conditions.
- NREM parasomnias are not triggered by fears or exposure to scary stimuli such as frightening television shows or movies. That said, a child who is afraid to go to sleep after watching a scary movie may become sleep deprived, which in turn may trigger a NREM parasomnia event.
- Attempting to wake a child from an NREM parasomnia will likely only prolong the event.
- Parents and other family members should not discuss the events in the morning with the child, as this may cause the child to become anxious about having an event. This can lead to a cycle where the child has difficulty falling asleep because of fears of having an event, and this prolonged sleep onset results in decreased sleep duration and increased event frequency.
- Work with parents to identify ways to improve the child's sleep quantity and/or quality. It is helpful to have parents track sleep patterns and NREM parasomnia events to identify any patterns that may be addressed through behavioral interventions. In addition, the child should be carefully screened for underlying physiological sleep disorders (e.g., obstructive sleep apnea [OSA]), as well as behaviorally related sleep difficulties (e.g., bedtime stalling) and poor sleep hygiene (e.g., inconsistent late bedtimes) that will respond to behavioral interventions.
- To increase sleep duration move the child's bedtime up by 15 minutes. For many children, this increased sleep opportunity (i.e., an extra 1.75 hours over the course of 1 week) may be sufficient to decrease the frequency of events.
- Safety is essential, in particular, for children who sleepwalk. Safety recommendations include the following:
  - Installing some type of alarm or bell on the child's door to alert parents that she is up during the night. This could include hanging a jingle bell on the doorknob or using a wireless door alarm installed in her room.
  - Installing security systems to alert parents if the child attempts to open a window or leave the house. This can include a full home security system or a simple wireless door or window alarm that can be purchased at any hardware or home improvement store.

- Lock all exterior doors and windows.
- Encourage the child to not sleep on the top bunk and/or move the mattress to the floor if falling out of bed is a concern.
- Remove any objects in the sleeping environment and hallways that may cause the child injury.

Managing Potential Pitfalls

Inform alternative caregivers about the child's history of parasomnia events. If the child is sleeping at a friend's house or going to overnight camp, caregivers should be alerted that she might have an event.

Identify situations in which an event will be more likely to occur. When a child stays up late for a special event (e.g., a sleepover) he may be at increased risk for an NREM parasomnia event 1 or 2 nights later. Helping families identify situations such as this can provide additional reassurance about the normalcy of the events.

The Bottom Line

For most patients with NREM parasomnias, simply providing education, safety, and reassurance is enough of an intervention to decrease the frequency of the events. But a careful screening of sleep patterns, sleep habits, and underlying sleep disorders is also needed to help identify alternative points of intervention (e.g., earlier bedtime, treatment of OSA).

SCHEDULED AWAKENINGS

Although most pediatric patients with NREM parasomnias will respond to education, safety, and reassurance, some patients have more severe NREM parasomnia events that occur almost every night, with or without a prolonged duration. For these patients, a more intensive intervention, scheduled awakenings, is used to decrease the frequency of or eliminate NREM parasomnia events.

How It Works

Scheduled awakenings occur before the child has an NREM parasomnia event by gently awakening him from sleep. Although the specific mechanism remains unclear, the two primary hypotheses are (a) scheduled awakenings may alter the child's sleep physiology by preventing or interrupting the partial arousal and (b) conditioning occurs with the child learning to spontaneously arouse just before an event due to the repetition of scheduled awakenings.

Contraindications and Considerations for Special Populations

As described below, scheduled awakenings require a significant commitment from the parents, which results in parental sleep disruption. Therefore, scheduled awakenings should not be used (a) for patients with an untreated underlying sleep disorder, such as OSA; (b) if the events do not occur around the same time every night; (c) if the events occur fewer than one to two times per week; or (d) when the scheduled awakenings may result in deficient sleep (e.g., once the child is awakened, she is unable to return to sleep for 1 to 2 hours).

In Practice

- Instruct the parents to monitor the child's sleep patterns for at least 2 weeks, including bedtime, wake time, and the timing of the NREM parasomnia events.
- Using the parents' report of the child's sleep patterns, determine whether there is a consistent pattern to the events. If one is identified, use the data from the diary to (a) determine the average clock time for NREM parasomnia events and (b) calculate the average time from sleep onset until the NREM parasomnia event.
- With the understanding that scheduled awakenings should occur 15 to 30 minutes before the event, determine the optimal time for the scheduled awakenings based on the two data points from the sleep diary.
- Instruct parents to gently awaken the child with a light touch or verbal prompt at the designated time each night. After the child arouses (i.e., opens eyes, changes positions, and/or verbalizes that he is awake), he should be allowed to return to sleep.
- Parents should continue scheduled awakenings every night for 2 to 4 weeks.

Handout 29 provides parents detailed instructions on using scheduled awakenings for NREM parasomnias.

Managing Potential Pitfalls

Select the use of scheduled awakenings only if a consistent pattern of NREM parasomnia events is identified. Following the 2 weeks of monitoring by sleep diary, if a clear pattern is not discernible, then scheduled awakenings should not be used.

Explain to parents that NREM parasomnia events can start again after treatment completion. If the NREM parasomnia events return following the termination of treatment, parents should be encouraged to again use the strategies outlined above.

Discuss the challenges of having a scheduled awakening time that occurs after the parent's bedtime. When a parent has to wake up to wake the child, poor treatment adherence often results. Parents should be encouraged to set their alarm clock to remind them to wake the child. As parental sleep will be significantly disrupted during treatment, it also may be useful to remind parents that this is a short-term treatment with a long-term benefit (their own sleep will be less disrupted once the NREM parasomnias resolve). In addition, for children with nightly events, parents should also be reminded that they will be awakened regardless and at least this way it is a predictable time and to an alarm clock rather than a distressed child.

Inform parents that scheduled awakenings may trigger an NREM parasomnia event or fully wake the child. This is the most common side effects of scheduled awakenings, and if it occurs on more than one occasion, then the scheduled awakening time should be moved earlier by 15 minutes. Advancing the scheduled awakening time may also be necessary if the NREM parasomnia event occurs before the scheduled time.

The Bottom Line

Scheduled awakenings is an effective behavioral intervention for children with moderate to severe NREM parasomnias that occur regularly and around the same time each night. However, because of the difficulty in implementing the intervention (as the parent may have to wake to an alarm clock in the middle of the night), the decision to use scheduled awakenings should be made cautiously and only for cases that do not respond to education, safety, and reassurance, or where other potential causes for the events (e.g., OSA) are not identified.

Case Example: Logan

Logan was a 6-year-old boy who presented with sleep terrors that have been occurring intermittently for approximately 1 year. He had a consistent evening routine, with a bedtime between 8:00 and 8:30 p.m. If his mother put him to bed (which was most nights), he would stall and make curtain calls for about 30 minutes until she stayed with him to fall asleep. If his mom went out and dad put him to bed, he would go to sleep independently in approximately 15 to 20 minutes without any trouble. Once asleep, Logan would have sleep terrors 3 to 4 nights per week, somewhere between 10:30 p.m. and 1:00 a.m. He was described as difficult to wake in the morning between 7:00 and 7:30 a.m. Logan would take unplanned naps approximately twice a week in the car after school. During the summer his bedtime was the same, but he would wake spontaneously at 8:00 a.m.

Logan was an otherwise healthy child with no developmental concerns. Family history was significant for sleepwalking in Logan's mother when she was an adolescent, and his mother also reported that when she is stressed at work she continues to talk in her sleep.

To address his sleep terrors, Logan's mother was provided verbal and written education about these events. This included the fact that his sleep terrors were not likely caused by any trauma but rather were because of a family history of sleepwalking. In addition, he was not obtaining sufficient sleep, as evidenced by the difficulty waking him in the morning for school and the shorter sleep duration obtained during the school year compared with the summer.

A number of factors were identified for treatment. Because his sleep terrors did not occur on a nightly basis at the same time, scheduled awakenings were not considered. However, his bedtime stalling was addressed using strategies from Chapter 6. In addition, using bedtime fading, his bedtime was moved earlier to consistently be 8:00 p.m., increasing his nightly sleep duration.

Summary and Take-Home Points

Confusional arousals, sleep terrors, and sleepwalking are all disorders of arousal. Although different in presentation, these issues have similar features, including onset in the first third of the night, the child being unresponsive to parents or caregivers, the events typically ending spontaneously in a short period of time, and the child having no memory of the event the next day. For most patients with NREM parasomnias, ensuring an adequate sleep opportunity and sufficient sleep duration, as well as providing education, safety, and reassurance, is enough to treat their events. However, for children with more severe (both frequency and duration) events, scheduled awakenings may be used. Other specific points to remember are outlined below.

- NREM parasomnias are benign and self-limiting, which means they are not signs of underlying trauma or psychopathology.
- The most common triggers for NREM parasomnias are deficient or poor-quality sleep; therefore, it is important to review sleep patterns and sleep habits, as well as to screen for underlying sleep disorders in patients.
- Events will increase in frequency when a child's sleep schedule is thrown off, when she is sick, or when the family travels or has another disruption to their normal routines.

Nocturnal Enuresis | 12

N octurnal enuresis (as defined by the *Diagnostic and Statistical Manual of Mental Disorders;* 5th ed.; American Psychiatric Association, 2013) or *sleep enuresis* (as defined by the *International Classification of Sleep Disorders;* 3rd ed.; American Academy of Sleep Medicine, 2014) is diagnosed when a child repeatedly urinates into his bed or clothing while asleep at least twice per week for the past 3 months. If a child does not have this frequency of nighttime urination during sleep but the enuresis causes significant distress, then the diagnosis is still given, and the symptoms should be treated. Nocturnal enuresis is more common than daytime enuresis, is twice as prevalent in boys as in girls, and has a strong hereditary component. Nocturnal enuresis is a relatively common condition, with approximately 10% of all 6-year-olds and 3% to 5% of 10-year-olds meeting diagnostic criteria for nocturnal enuresis.

Before the age of 5 years, nocturnal enuresis is developmentally appropriate, and no treatment is required. However, for typically developing children, after the age of 5 years behavioral interventions for nocturnal enuresis can be very

http://dx.doi.org/10.1037/14645-013
Pediatric Sleep Problems: A Clinician's Guide to Behavioral Interventions, by L. J. Meltzer and V. M. Crabtree

effective not only in resolving the issues but also for improving self-efficacy in those who may be very embarrassed by the enuresis. Behavioral treatments for enuresis require a significant amount of work during the night and often take several weeks to be effective. Thus, before starting treatment, it is important to ensure that both the child and the parent are motivated to follow through on treatment recommendations. Social interactions often serve as the strongest motivator for both children and parents (e.g., wanting to spend the night at a friend's house or attend overnight camp). For families that are not yet motivated to implement an intervention, motivational interviewing (MI) strategies may be employed before prescribing the behavioral interventions.

Assessment Considerations

For both diagnosis and treatment, it is essential to identify whether a child's enuresis is primary or secondary. *Primary enuresis* occurs when a child has no history of established nighttime dryness. *Secondary enuresis*, on the other hand, is a new onset of bed-wetting after an established period (typically 6 months or more) of remaining dry at night. For children with secondary enuresis, additional evaluation is warranted to identify other potential etiologies, including physiological (e.g., illness, obstructive sleep apnea) and psychological (e.g., trauma, life stressors). Treatment is then dependent on whether the enuresis is primary or secondary. For primary enuresis, behavioral interventions are highly effective and are the frontline treatment. For secondary enuresis, further workup is essential in helping to identify the underlying etiology, which will become the primary area for treatment. If the child's enuresis persists after the underlying etiology has been treated, behavioral interventions may be used. Whether enuresis is primary or secondary, medical factors may contribute to the enuresis and should be formally evaluated by the child's physician (see Exhibit 12.1). In addition, enuresis is sometimes associated with encopresis (fecal soiling). Children who also present with encopresis should have the encopresis treated before the nocturnal enuresis (Hjalmas et al., 2004).

Pharmacologic Interventions for Nocturnal Enuresis

Although beyond the scope of this book, pharmacologic approaches are available for treatment of nocturnal enuresis. A number of medications have been used to treat this condition in children older than 7 years,

EXHIBIT 12.1

Medical Factors That Contribute to Enuresis

Because there are a number of underlying medical factors that contribute to the development/maintenance of enuresis, children with nocturnal enuresis symptoms should be referred to their primary care physician to rule out medical etiologies before beginning any behavioral intervention. These may include but are not limited to

- urinary tract infections,
- constipation,
- genitourinary abnormalities,
- structural defects,
- diabetes, and
- spina bifida.

including imipramine, desmopressin, oxybutynin, and tolterodine. However, pharmacological interventions for nocturnal enuresis are not effective for many children. For example, desmopressin does not work for 30% to 40% of children who use it (Glazener et al., 2005), and for those who do respond, only 30% will be "cured" annually (Hjalmas et al., 2004), leaving many children with ongoing enuresis symptoms. When choosing an intervention, it is important to keep in mind that all medications have potential side effects, and for most children, the medication is a temporary treatment but not a cure. In other words, medications work when you use them, but symptoms commonly return after medication is discontinued. It has been well established that behavioral interventions are more effective in the long-term resolution of nocturnal enuresis (Glazener et al., 2005; Hjalmas et al., 2004). That said, the behavioral treatments outlined in this chapter all take time to succeed. Thus, in cases of short-term treatment needs (e.g., 1-night sleepover, 2 weeks of summer camp), pharmacological options may be preferred.

Behavioral Interventions for Nocturnal Enuresis

URINE ALARM INTERVENTION

Urine alarms are one of the oldest behavioral interventions that continue to be used for nocturnal enuresis, and they represent the most effective current treatment, with lower cost and fewer side effects than medications. Originally presented in 1937 and then published in 1938 by Mowrer, the urine alarm improves arousal from sleep to the sensation of a full bladder. Unlike the original bell and pad alarm, many types of alarms are commercially available, typically ranging in cost from $50 to $150. These alarms include an auditory tone, vibration, or both. Some models provide wireless technology that enables a parent to have a monitor in a separate room. This can be beneficial when children have difficulty awakening to the alarm.

The Evidence

A large Cochrane Review of 56 trials revealed that the urine alarm is an effective behavioral intervention for nocturnal enuresis (Glazener et al., 2005). Approximately two thirds of children became dry at night while using the alarm. However, although the urine alarm intervention is very effective, it can take several weeks for treatment to succeed, and the relapse rate is relatively high, up to 45%. Relapse can be corrected with additional courses of the alarm intervention or additional interventions. Of note, punishment for bed-wetting has been found to not be beneficial in resolving the complaint and may in fact cause additional wetting (Glazener et al., 2005).

How It Works

Moisture coming into contact with the sensor completes a circuit that turns on the alarm. Through classical conditioning, the sound or vibration of the alarm is aversive. It then produces a conditioned response of either contracting the sphincter to retain urine or awakening the patient to empty the bladder in response to the stimulus of a full bladder.

Contraindications and Considerations for Special Populations

Urine alarm interventions should generally not be used before children are fully toilet trained during the day. A child who continues to have daytime wetting accidents should typically have the daytime enuresis addressed first before starting treatment for nocturnal enuresis. Additionally, we typically do not recommend treatment of nocturnal enuresis in a child who has a developmental age younger than 6 years. That said, children with developmental disabilities and/or autism spectrum disorders may still benefit from urine alarm training if provided with enough guidance and supervision from their parents.

In Practice

- Explain to the parent that most children with enuresis simply are not awakening to the feeling of a full bladder. The purpose of the urine alarm is to teach the child to wake up when her bladder

EXHIBIT 12.2

Cleanliness Training

Cleanliness training can help children make a clear connection between having a nighttime wetting accident and the aversive consequence of waking up fully during the night (Azrin, Sneed, & Foxx, 1974) and is a helpful adjunct for all enuresis interventions. Specifically:

▪ The child is taught to change his sheets and pajamas as independently as possible.
  ▪ For children who cannot change sheets and pajamas completely independently because of age or motor development, parents should assist as minimally as they can, while having the child participate in the process as fully as possible.
▪ The child should be required to place dirty clothes and sheets in the washer before going to bed.

Because cleanliness training is meant truly to teach rather than to punish, parents should not be punitive throughout the cleaning. Rather, they should remain neutral and praise the child for completing the cleanliness steps.

is full. Parents should understand that the alarm will begin to sound and/or vibrate as soon as urine comes in contact with the sensor. This should then help the child immediately understand: Full bladder = wake up!

▪ The child places the alarm sensor on her underwear before bedtime.
▪ The alarm monitor must be turned on to ensure that it will sound/vibrate when moisture comes into contact with the sensor.
▪ If the alarm sounds/vibrates, the child gets out of bed to finish urinating in the bathroom.
▪ A tracking sheet should be maintained to record dry versus wet nights (see Handout 30).
▪ Once the child has remained dry throughout the night for 14 nights, the alarm can be discontinued.
▪ An important additional element to include is cleanliness training, as described in Exhibit 12.2.

Handout 31 provides step-by-step instructions for parents on the use of the urine alarm intervention.

Managing Potential Pitfalls

Provide a cost analysis of urine alarm versus ongoing bed-wetting. Because urine alarms are not covered by insurance, many parents may express concern that the intervention is too expensive. If the parent chooses to not use the urine alarm because of cost, the clinician may spend time helping parents do a cost analysis of pull-up diapers and laundry versus the cost of the least expensive alarm system available. For providers with the financial means to do so, purchasing alarms to provide to families may help overcome this barrier.

Consider use of a vibrating alarm or a wireless monitor. Many parents of children with nocturnal enuresis will describe their child as a "deep sleeper." In reality, many children with nocturnal enuresis have higher arousal thresholds than their peers, which may be a cause, effect, or perpetuating factor in the enuresis. Because of their difficulty awakening to stimuli, many children will have difficulty awakening to the sound/sensation of the alarm. For children who do not awaken to auditory alarms, a trial of a vibrating alarm may be sufficient. For those who still do not awaken, parents may purchase a wireless monitor to place in their own bedroom. Alternative options are for one parent to sleep in a separate bed in the child's bedroom to quickly awaken the child following an alarm to complete urination in the bathroom.

Ensure that the child awakens fully to the alarm. Many parents may say that their child walks "half asleep" to the restroom after the alarm sounds. It is important for the child to be fully awake to ensure that she is learning from the alarm. If the child does not appear fully awake, the parent may use a wet washcloth on the child's face to awaken her fully.

Work with families to make sure that the child will cooperate with setting the alarm at the beginning of the night. Some children will forget or choose to not set the alarm at the beginning of the night. If it is a matter of the child forgetting, parents will need to ensure that the alarm has been placed on the underwear and turned on before the child goes to bed. For children who purposely choose to not set the alarm, a discussion with the child and her parents may be needed to identify reasons the child does not want to use it. In this instance, the child may also benefit from the additional element of positive reinforcement.

Parents should monitor their children to make sure they replace the alarm after a nighttime awakening. Many children with nocturnal enuresis have multiple wetting episodes throughout the night. Once the child has awakened, finished urinating, and changed pajamas and sheets during the middle of her sleep, she may be reluctant to reset the alarm or may genuinely forget to do so. Although the child should be completing these tasks as independently as possible, parents should supervise the tasks and ensure that the alarm is reset before the child returns to bed. Positive reinforcement for the use of the alarm can help children maintain adherence to the intervention. Once the child is using the alarm appropriately, providing positive reinforcement for dry nights can also encourage the child to awaken to the alarm and urinate in the bathroom.

Address relapses immediately. It is common for children to relapse after the alarm has been discontinued. Relapses can be corrected with additional use of the alarm intervention. It may be helpful to include additional elements of full spectrum training, as described in the next section.

Encourage patience. It usually takes at least 6 weeks (and sometimes several months) for treatment to succeed. Because the urine alarm is not a quick fix, it is critical to ensure that both the child and the parent are motivated to consistently follow through with this treatment every night. MI techniques may be used to increase motivation and improve treatment adherence.

The Bottom Line

Urine alarm training is one of the oldest and most widely accepted behavioral interventions available for nocturnal enuresis. It can be a time- and labor-intensive intervention that requires close parental supervision, and often the clinician must provide additional guidance, including adding positive reinforcement and ensuring that the tracking of dry versus wet nights is occurring. Urine alarm interventions can also be challenging in children who are difficult to awaken, so additional elements of the intervention may need to be considered, including changing the type of alarm and having the parent sleep near the child. Some families who are not able or willing to use a urine alarm can attempt nighttime awakenings to address the enuresis (see Exhibit 12.3).

FULL SPECTRUM TREATMENT

Full spectrum treatment incorporates the use of alarm intervention with positive reinforcement and cleanliness training, while also including additional elements of retention control training and overlearning (Houts, Peterson, & Whelan, 1986). These additional elements can help the child stop bed-wetting more quickly and have been shown to reduce the likelihood of relapse by up to half (Azrin, Sneed, & Foxx, 1974).

The Evidence

Retention control training as an additional element has not been shown to improve response rates during treatment, but it has been found to reduce relapse rates (Glazener et al., 2005). In particular, in the original studies using full spectrum home treatment, the addition of overlearning resulted in more initial treatment failures, likely related to the child's increased liquid consumption leading to more episodes of bedwetting. Those children who had the additional component of overlearning, however, had lower relapse rates than those who did not have overlearning (10% vs. 45%; Houts, 1996). Typically, children should achieve dryness within 12 weeks of treatment (Houts, 1996). Although these original studies had small samples, they point to the importance of the additional elements of treatment to improve learning, and the Cochrane Review concluded that these additional elements appear to reduce relapse rates (Glazener et al., 2005).

EXHIBIT 12.3

Nighttime Awakenings

For families who cannot afford urine alarms, choose not to use them, or have children who cannot awaken to the alarm, use of nighttime awakenings is an alternative intervention. However, to increase the effectiveness of nighttime awakenings, the treatment package should also include additional elements described in this chapter, such as positive reinforcement, cleanliness training, retention control training, and overlearning. The following are specific instructions for nighttime awakenings:

▪ The initial night of the intervention is very intense, with the parent waking the child every hour until 1:00 a.m. and having the child go to the bathroom to urinate each time (Azrin & Thienes, 1978).
  ▪ Because this first night is so intense, this intervention should not be used with any child who is at risk of experiencing serious daytime consequences of disrupted sleep. This includes children with disorders of arousal, seizure disorders, obstructive sleep apnea, and severe mood disturbance.
▪ If the child is wet at the time the parent awakens the child, she should then complete the cleanliness training component of changing pajamas and sheets as independently as possible.
▪ After the first night, the parent awakens the child just before the parent goes to bed and again 5 hours prior to the child's typical rise time (e.g., 10:30 p.m. and 2:00 a.m. for a child who awakens at 7:00 a.m.).
  ▪ If the child is dry, she should be praised and go to the bathroom to urinate.
  ▪ If the child is wet, she should begin cleanliness training procedures.
▪ After 6 consecutive dry nights, the child should be awakened for the second awakening one hour earlier (e.g., now at 10:30 p.m. and 1:00 a.m.). Similar procedures for dryness and wetness should occur each night.
▪ Continue in this fashion until the second awakening approaches the parent's bedtime.
▪ After 14 consecutive dry nights, nighttime awakenings can be stopped.

It is important to keep in mind that nighttime awakenings alone tend to be less effective than and do not have the degree of research support as urine alarms.

How It Works

Full spectrum treatment is based on a number of behavioral principles. As previously described, the urine alarm pairs the alarm with an arousal in response to a full bladder. Through the use of classical and operant conditioning, the child is taught during the day to pair the constriction of the sphincter muscles (a voluntary activity) with the sensation of a full bladder. With repeated pairings, the constriction of the sphincter muscles will become a conditioned response to a full bladder. Finally, a consistent reward schedule helps to maintain motivation and increase the desired behavior, in this case waking to a full bladder and/or having dry nights.

In Practice

▪ The child continues to use the urine alarm, including tracking dry vs. wet nights and cleaning up after himself, as previously described.

- Explain to the parent that many children will again begin wetting the bed once the alarm has been stopped:

  "To try to help prevent this, we are going to add some extra steps to really teach your child to stop himself from wetting the bed. Some of these things may be hard to do, but my hope is that by learning how to squeeze those muscles when his bladder is full, he will be better able to do the same thing when he is asleep."

- During the day, the child is taught to interrupt the stream of urine by constricting and releasing urinary muscles repeatedly while urinating (retention control training). This helps him to understand the voluntary muscle control required to postpone urination.

- Once the child has mastered the skill of stream interruption, he is then taught to postpone urination when he feels the sensation of a full bladder.

  - The child starts with waiting 1 minute to urinate when he feels that he has a full bladder.
  - The child then gradually increases the wait time to up to 45 minutes. This can be increased in 5-minute increments on a daily basis (i.e., wait 1 minute today, 5 minutes tomorrow, 10 minutes the next day, etc., until the child is able to wait 45 minutes).

- For overlearning, the child is taught to actually consume more liquids before bed to allow more opportunities to experience a full bladder during sleep.

- After the child has had 14 consecutive dry nights, the child should drink water 1 hour before bedtime.

  - The clinician calculates how much water the child should drink by using 2 ounces per year of age plus another 2 ounces (e.g., a 9-year-old child should drink 20 ounces of water 1 hour before bedtime).

- The child should urinate before going to bed and continue to use the urine alarm.

- The water consumption before bed should continue nightly until the child achieves 14 additional dry nights. At that time, both the increased water consumption and the urine alarm can be discontinued.

Handout 32 provides parents step-by-step instructions for implementing full spectrum treatment.

Managing Potential Pitfalls

Choose smaller increments of time for postponing urination, if necessary. For a child who is unable to postpone urination, smaller increments of time should be used. The child should be encouraged to engage in distracting activities rather than focus on the sensation of the full bladder while postponing urination. If the child still cannot postpone urination for 15 minutes after he was able to do so for 10 minutes, reduce the time frame to 12 minutes. Once he has been successful, the time frame can increase once again.

Explain the rationale behind overlearning. Sometimes, the parent and/or child are reluctant to drink extra water after dryness has finally been achieved. Of course, clinicians should always meet families where they are most comfortable in following through on an intervention. However, it is important to explain carefully to parents and children the importance of the additional element in helping learning occur and in reducing long-term relapse rates. If families understand that 45% of children are likely to relapse and that this additional element (which may cause a resumption of symptoms for a week) can reduce their likelihood of relapse to 20%, they may feel more motivated to attempt the intervention.

Expect a relapse once overlearning has been added. This element of the intervention should not be used until the child has achieved 2 weeks of dryness at night. It is anticipated that large volumes of water will cause the child to wet the bed again. The clinician should predict the relapse for the parent and child and explain this as a method whereby the child is being provided with additional opportunities to learn to control urination, even with a very full bladder.

The Bottom Line

Full spectrum treatment takes advantage of using the urine alarm as well as adding overlearning as a strategy to reduce the likelihood of relapse. Because relapse rates can be relatively high in children treated with urine alarms, this additional element may help a child more fully achieve nighttime dryness. For some families, however, the knowledge that the additional water consumption will likely trigger a relapse may be too unappealing to attempt.

Case Example: Gabriel

Gabriel is a 9-year-old boy who has wet the bed throughout his life. He has never had an extended period of dryness that his mother can recall, and he produces large volumes of urine multiple times throughout the night, every night. His mother has attempted restricting the volume of fluids that he drinks after dinner, waking him up in the middle of the night to prompt him to use the restroom, paying him to stay dry throughout the night, and insisting that he clean his own pajamas and sheets when he wets. No improvement in his nighttime wetting has occurred with any of these attempts. Gabriel now has been invited to spend the night at two different friends' homes and wants to stop wetting the bed so that he can feel comfortable going on sleepovers.

Although Gabriel's mother had attempted elements of different interventions, Gabriel had not yet tried a urine alarm, and they had not made efforts at a systematic approach to his bed-wetting. Gabriel began using a urine alarm that had both an auditory and vibrating function, but he would frequently sleep through the alarm while he wet the bed. By the time his mother arrived in his room, he typically had fully wet and would need to change his sheets and pajamas, which he could do independently, as she had already taught him to do so. Because he continued to not awaken consistently to the alarm, his mother began sleeping on the floor of his bedroom. When she heard the alarm begin to sound, she would awaken Gabriel at that time. Once his mother was present in the room to awaken him, Gabriel was able to then stop his stream of urination to go to the restroom to finish urinating. This typically then allowed him to need to change only his pajamas and not his sheets, as he had not fully wet the bed, resulting in less time awake during the night. Gabriel kept a chart in which he indicated when he wet the bed fully, when he was able to go to the bathroom to finish urinating, and when he had completely dry nights. His mother began by rewarding him with a new game app on his tablet for every 3 nights that he was able to stop his urination in bed and go to the bathroom to finish urinating. After 2 weeks of Gabriel no longer fully wetting the bed, his mother was able to return to her bedroom, and he awakened to the sound and vibration of the alarm without her help. He then began to earn apps for 3 nights of remaining fully dry. After 2 consecutive weeks of dryness, Gabriel began the overlearning process and would drink 20 ounces of water 1 hour before bedtime. Three nights of bed-wetting followed this, but then began to remain dry through the night again. After 2 weeks of dryness, even after drinking additional water, the alarm and the additional water consumption were stopped. Approximately 3 months later, Gabriel began to wet the bed again. Neither he nor his mother could identify any changes in his routine that contributed to this. Gabriel again began using the alarm, and his bed-wetting resolved after 2 weeks. He had no further relapses after that time.

Summary and Take-Home Points

Nocturnal enuresis can be a distressing experience for children and parents. It can prevent children from engaging in activities they would enjoy (e.g., spending the night at a friend's house), and it creates embarrassment, additional time cleaning up each morning, and the financial burden of purchasing additional pull-up diapers and frequent laundering.

Enuresis can also be quite distressing to families who have siblings sleeping in a bed together. Behavioral approaches are the intervention of choice and have been shown to be superior to pharmacologic interventions in long-term management of enuresis, with almost no side effects. It is important to keep in mind, however, that both the child and parent must be motivated, as alarm interventions are time- and labor-intensive and require close parental monitoring. Specific points to remember are outlined below.

- Urine alarms are by far the most effective behavioral intervention for nocturnal enuresis.
- Relapse rates are relatively high, occurring in up to 45% of children.
- Likelihood of relapse can be reduced by adding additional elements to the intervention, including cleanliness training, retention training, and overlearning.
- Maintaining a record of dry versus wet nights can help in managing a positive reinforcement schedule.
- In families who cannot afford or choose not to purchase a urine alarm, nighttime awakenings in combination with overlearning, retention control training, and cleanliness training can be used.

Nonadherence to Positive Airway Pressure Therapy   13

T he frontline treatment for pediatric obstructive sleep apnea (OSA) is adenotonsillectomy (AT). However, for a small percentage of children, positive airway pressure (PAP) therapy is required. PAP uses mild air pressure to keep the airway open during sleep. Although PAP does not "cure" OSA, when used, it is the most effective treatment for children who have OSA that is not treatable with AT. A PAP machine includes (a) a mask or nasal interface that provides the air pressure, (b) a headgear or strap that holds the interface in place during sleep, (c) a tube that connects the interface to the machine, and (d) the machine that blows the air into the tube. There are a number of different types of masks and nasal interfaces, as well as machines that have different features, including heated humidity; a ramp-up feature that increases air pressure over a set time (e.g., 20 minutes); and/or a monitoring feature that records when the machine is turned on and used at full pressure, enabling the clinician to download information about and track daily use.

http://dx.doi.org/10.1037/14645-014
Pediatric Sleep Problems: A Clinician's Guide to Behavioral Interventions, by L. J. Meltzer and V. M. Crabtree

When regularly used, PAP therapy is highly effective in managing OSA in children and adolescents. However, when it is not used, there is no benefit. This is problematic, as adherence to PAP therapy in pediatrics is poor for a variety of reasons. In this chapter, we present information about the importance of patient education, factors that contribute to nonadherence (in particular, discomfort), and a multicomponent validated treatment to improve adherence.

Behavioral Interventions for Nonadherence to PAP Therapy

THE EVIDENCE

Only a handful of studies have examined adherence to PAP therapy in pediatric populations. The first case series was published in 1995, reporting on the benefits of a multicomponent behavioral intervention (including parent training, modeling, and desensitization) in four children with craniofacial anomalies requiring the use of PAP therapy (Rains, 1995). All patients were adherent for 3 months, with three of the four children still adherent 9 months after treatment. Koontz, Slifer, Cataldo, and Marcus (2003) also examined multicomponent behavior therapy intervention in 20 children, ages 1 to 17, and reported that 75% of children who received the intervention tolerated PAP, with an increase in PAP usage. Using a similar intervention in four preschool children, Slifer et al. (2007) reported that all of the children tolerated PAP therapy during sleep following treatment. Finally, in 2013, Harford et al. reported on the development of a multicomponent behaviorally based PAP adherence program for pediatric patients. Although data were descriptive (collected in clinic), short-term improvements were found in terms of the consistency of PAP usage.

PATIENT EDUCATION ABOUT OBSTRUCTIVE SLEEP APNEA TO IMPROVE PAP ADHERENCE

For all patients, education about OSA (i.e., what it is, what happens during sleep, the consequences of untreated OSA) is the essential first step of any treatment. Parents are key for the treatment of OSA with PAP, regardless of the patient's age. Although this intuitively makes sense for younger children or children with developmental delays (e.g., Down syndrome), it is also essential for adolescents. Research has shown that adherence to treatments for chronic illness is better in adolescents who have parental involvement. However, many parents believe that adolescents should be able manage their treatment independently. Motivational interviewing (see Chapter 5, this volume) and patient education are critical to treatment success.

Because of a lack of knowledge about OSA, PAP, and the consequences when OSA is left untreated, parents and patients may undervalue the need for PAP therapy. For some families, learning that a child needs PAP to manage OSA (a chronic illness) is very challenging to accept. Thus, any education about the disease and its treatment may need to be repeated more than once. In addition, unlike other chronic illnesses (e.g., asthma, diabetes), if a patient does not use her PAP regularly, there are few immediate consequences, reducing the perceived urgency for treatment. Thus, it is important to provide education about the current and future consequences of untreated OSA (i.e., neurocognitive deficits, behavior problems, and daytime sleepiness, as well as increased risk for developing hypertension, cardiovascular disease, and stroke). In addition, families need education in how the machine treats OSA, as well as the physiologic health and neurocognitive benefits of using PAP every day.

CASE EXAMPLE: MAKAYLA

Makayla is a 14-year-old girl with obesity who was prescribed PAP therapy after an overnight polysomnography found residual OSA following AT. At her first follow-up appointment, Makayla's smart card download showed that the mask was on but was not reaching full pressure. Her mother reported that the durable medical equipment company had shown Makayla how to use the machine, so she expected Makayla to put the mask on herself each night before bed. Mom also could hear the machine each night, so she was unaware of the lack of use. Makayla stated that she was embarrassed that she had to wear the PAP, found it uncomfortable, and did not really see the point because she felt fine. Both Makayla and her mother were hoping that instead of using PAP, there was a pill she could take or an alternative treatment for her OSA.

Detailed information was provided to Makayla and her mother about OSA, including the causes of OSA (i.e., obesity, anatomical features that create a narrow airway), what happens during sleep when you have OSA (i.e., the airway collapses, multiple arousals cause fragmented sleep), the short-term consequences of untreated OSA (i.e., daytime sleepiness, difficulties concentrating, mood swings), and the long-term consequences of untreated OSA (i.e., hypertension, cardiovascular disease, stroke). The following example was provided to help Makayla and her mother understand that OSA is a chronic illness and that PAP therapy is important.

> An adolescent with Type 1 diabetes who does not take his insulin will become hyperglycemic and may need to go to the emergency room. Similarly, an adolescent who does not regularly take her daily asthma medications will likely have an exacerbation and require medical care. OSA is also a chronic illness like asthma and diabetes. However, if you don't use your PAP regularly, you may not notice any immediate problems. But every night while you are sleeping, your OSA is waking you up multiple times every hour. This is similar to if someone poked you over and over so that you never got a good night of sleep. Over time, this lack of sleep will have significant consequences for your health and well-being.

Empathy and active listening (motivational interviewing techniques) were used to reflect Makayla's frustrations about the fact that she already had surgery and now she had to do something every day that her friends did not have to do. It was also discussed that although a simple daily pill would be desirable, that is not an option. More than an hour was spent on education and discussions related to the need for and benefits of PAP use. At that point, Makayla and her mother were appreciative of the time spent discussing their concerns and stated they were willing to begin working together to improve her adherence.

It is not surprising that adolescents are commonly nonadherent to PAP therapy. This is seen across chronic illnesses. As previously stated, the literature has clearly shown that when parents are involved, adolescents are more adherent to medical treatments. Thus, education for older children and adolescents and their parents is key to improving adherence. Although any type of behavioral intervention requires parent buy-in, it is critical to work together with both the patient and the parent to increase their understanding of the disease (OSA), the treatment (PAP therapy), and the consequences of nonadherence. Initially, it may seem like a considerable amount of clinician time is required to provide education and get the patient and parent to agree to work on adherence. However, in most cases, PAP therapy is not a short-term intervention, so in the long run the payoff is significant, with patients becoming adherent to their PAP therapy at night (and hopefully lifelong users of PAP). Further, regular use of PAP therapy will result in improved daytime and long-term functioning, including cognitive and health outcomes.

ADDRESSING DISCOMFORT TO IMPROVE PAP ADHERENCE

Although not a behavioral intervention, it is critical to partner with a medical team member, such as a respiratory therapist, to ensure that the PAP is as comfortable as possible. As previously described, the PAP machine has multiple components and hence multiple points where comfort may be improved. The primary points to consider when a patient is nonadherent are described below.

Proper Mask Fitting

The three primary types of mask interfaces that a patient can use are *nasal air pillows*, for which small soft silicone pillows go into each nostril; *nasal mask*, the most common type used that covers only the nose; and *full face mask*, an interface that covers both the patient's nose and mouth. As there are a number of different manufacturers of these interfaces, it may take several tries before the most comfortable mask is identified. If the mask does not fit properly, the result is an air leak, which is not only uncomfortable for the patient but also results in the PAP machine being unable to provide full pressure or benefit to the patient. Because of skin irritation or breakdown, it may be necessary for a patient to alternate between two different types of masks. Appropriate adjustment of the straps should be discussed to provide comfort while also keeping the mask well sealed to prevent air leakage.

Nasal Discomfort

Patients may experience congestion, runny nose, and/or nosebleeds while using PAP. Some of these symptoms may be treated by the medical team with saline nasal washes or nasal steroid sprays. In addition, a heated humidifier can also help alleviate these issues.

Sleep Positioning

Patients may need help in finding comfortable sleep positions to allow for the mask to stay in place, particularly if they are accustomed to sleeping in a certain position or if they feel uncomfortable breathing if they are lying flat while the machine is on.

Feelings of Choking or Suffocating From Air Pressure

The air pressure from PAP is strong to keep the airway open. However, this pressure can be uncomfortable on lower settings and downright terrifying to some children when higher settings are used. It is never a good idea to initially introduce PAP therapy while a child is sleeping as the trauma of waking up with a mask and air pressure may result in the child never using the device again. Once the machine is introduced more gradually (as described in the next section), patients may benefit from a ramp-up feature on the machine that increases the air pressure over a period of time (e.g., 20 minutes). Thus, while falling asleep the pressure is not as intense and more tolerable.

MULTICOMPONENT BEHAVIOR THERAPY APPROACH TO IMPROVE PAP ADHERENCE

The most common reason for not using PAP therapy is anxiety, which can result in negative behaviors (e.g., tantrums, hitting). Although this is seen across all ages, a significant number of pediatric patients who need PAP therapy have developmental delays, which further contributes to the challenge of introducing and reinforcing the use of PAP therapy.

Young children and children with anxiety, behavior problems, or developmental delays often struggle to use PAP. The patient will resist any attempt to put the mask on the face (this includes pushing it away or covering her face, crying, or turning away). This can result in learned escape and avoidance behaviors, as well as conditioned anxiety from the combination of discomfort (mask and/or air pressure) and the physiological arousal that results from behavioral resistance. Thus, it is important to teach children how to relax when using PAP therapy to increase adherence.

How It Works

Using multiple components from behavior analysis and behavior therapy, a task analysis is used to break down the steps required to begin using PAP. Distraction and differential reinforcement (positive reinforcement while ignoring negative behaviors) techniques are also used to encourage success for each step (thus resulting in counterconditioning of the child's anxiety or emotional distress), as well as extinguishing escape and avoidance behaviors.

Contraindications and Considerations for Special Populations

A multicomponent behavior therapy approach can be used with patients of any age or any developmental disorder. The steps described below focus on primarily younger children or children with developmental delays, as these are the groups that benefit the most from this type of intervention. That said, older children and adolescents with anxiety, claustrophobia, or a negative experience with PAP therapy would also benefit from a multicomponent approach. For these populations, the steps below should be modified with more age-appropriate rewards and distraction techniques.

In Practice

Differential reinforcement provides positive reinforcement for appropriate behaviors (i.e., wearing the mask) while ignoring or not responding to unwanted behaviors (crying, hitting, screaming "no"). Before introducing the first steps of the intervention, one should identify favorite activities (e.g., music, videos, games on computer or tablet) and preferred rewards (e.g., stickers, bubbles, snacks). These will be used for distraction (see below) and rewards. Children should earn a sticker or token for each successful step of the graduated exposure, exchanging these immediate rewards for the preferred reward at the end of the session. Any attempt to wear the mask is praised and reinforced (i.e., "Good job putting the mask to your face!"), and any refusal behaviors are ignored, showing the child that wearing the mask results in positive parental attention. Parents are also guided to ignore refusal behaviors and to not use negative forms of attention such as, "Stop hitting" or "Why can't you just put the mask on?"

- Use graduated exposure. To introduce the mask, headgear, and air pressure, the process should be broken down into very small steps (see Exhibit 13.1 for a sample task analysis and Handout 33 for a chart that can be completed for parents/patients). Older children

---

EXHIBIT 13.1

Sample Task Analysis for Graduated Exposure

This analysis can be modified based on the child's age and cognitive functioning. For example, the following steps could be outlined in the task analysis.

- Child holds mask.
- Child places mask on face of stuffed animal.
- Child places mask on parent's face.
- Child holds mask up to his face and counts to 3 (5, 10, etc.).
- Child holds mask up to his face and sings "ABCs."
- Mask is attached to headgear and placed on child for 3 seconds (increasing length of time with each success until reach 1 minute).
- Mask (but not headgear) is placed on child and air is turned on for 3 seconds (increasing length of time until reach 1 minute).
- Mask with headgear placed on child and air is turned on for 3 seconds (increasing length of time until reach 15 minutes).

During a session, parents should be actively involved with each step of the exposure. Depending on how quickly a child progresses, homework between sessions should be prescribed to help continued progression. Once this task analysis is completed, a new one should be created to assist parents in the introduction of positive airway pressure at bedtime (e.g., wearing the mask while lying down and reading stories, introducing the air plus the mask while reading stories, having the child fall asleep with the mask and air).

will likely progress quickly through this process, and younger children and those with developmental delays will likely take much longer. Each time a new task is introduced, it should be done for 5 seconds initially. The length of time is then increased at a rate the child can tolerate (10 seconds, 30 seconds, 1 minute). As the time gets longer for each task, younger children can be encouraged to sing a favorite song (e.g., "ABCs" or "Twinkle, Twinkle, Little Star") rather than counting. Using a timer is often helpful for young children or special populations, as it provides a neutral and concrete cue of when the mask can come off. This also removes the parent from being viewed as the decision maker. Children with anxiety also benefit from holding the timer to keep them distracted with a timekeeping job, rather than focusing on worries. In addition, holding the timer keeps hands occupied to avoid removal attempts.

▪ Use distraction. The graduated exposure should be completed alongside enjoyable or favored activities (e.g., music, videos, games on computer or tablet). Not only does this distract the child from potentially uncomfortable new sensations, it also pairs these new sensations with positive activities, reducing anxiety and distress.

▪ Extinguish escape/avoidance behaviors. It is essential to teach the child that attempts to remove or avoid the PAP equipment will not be tolerated. Gentle reminders and encouragement should be used (e.g., "The timer hasn't said we are ready to take the mask off" or "It's okay, you can do it!"). If the child removes the mask, it should be immediately put back in place and held there until the goal time is reached. If the child becomes combative, the mask should be held in place as long as possible—long enough not to reinforce its being removed simply because of the hitting/combative behavior but short enough to build toward success without a lengthy struggle. For example, place the mask, block the child's hands, replace the mask and go a few seconds while providing distraction, then remove the mask and provide the reward for completion.

Managing Potential Pitfalls

Spend the necessary time to get parents to buy in. Because the graduated exposure needs to be practiced at home, without parent buy-in success will be challenging. As previously described, as much time as needed should be spent with parents providing education, empathy, and support. In addition, it is helpful to assist parents with problem-solving obstacles that may interfere with practice (e.g., parent's work schedule, illness, child shares room with sibling, inconsistent bedtime routines or sleep schedule).

Work at a pace at which the child and family will be successful (in other words, don't go too quickly!). Although some children will progress through the graduated exposure quickly and easily, for many children this is not a fast process. If the clinician goes too quickly, the child and parent may become discouraged and frustrated. This may lead to the patient not attending follow-up visits and, ultimately, not using PAP therapy as prescribed.

Continue to use reinforcement as long as necessary to ensure adherence. To maintain the behavior of wearing PAP, reinforcement should be gradually faded rather than just stopped once the child is successful. For example, a child becomes successful with PAP by receiving a sticker every night to earn a special outing with a parent on the weekend. Next, increase the special outing to every 2 weeks for a month. Then move to once a month, and so on.

Address physical discomfort and side effects. It is critical that clinicians who are using this type of behavioral intervention work closely with the medical team who prescribed the PAP therapy. Issues that commonly lead to nonadherence are mask leaks, ill-fitting masks, nasal congestion, and an incorrect pressure (i.e., child may feel like he is suffocating if the air pressure is too low).

Maintain frequent contact and follow up. This is an essential step for success, in particular, in the first few weeks of PAP therapy. Patients should be called approximately 48 hours and then 1 week after PAP initiation. Follow-up with the clinician should occur approximately 4 weeks (i.e., 2–6 weeks) after initiation. Once the patient is adherent, follow-up should occur quarterly to reinforce success or problem solve barriers to adherence.

Recognize the demands graduated exposure makes on the family. This is not a quick process and requires regular practice at home. Thus, it is important to take into consideration family resources (i.e., work schedules, other children, parent physical and emotional health) and family dynamics (i.e., does one parent believe PAP therapy is not necessary so sabotages home practice? Does a sibling tease the patient about wearing the mask?). These factors should be queried and should be a part of the regular problem solving that occurs at the initial and follow-up visits.

The Bottom Line

Although a multicomponent behavioral intervention is not a quick fix to improve adherence to PAP therapy, it is important to remember that there is a short-term cost (i.e., not wearing PAP immediately after diagnosis of OSA) for the long-term gain (i.e., a patient who learns to tolerate PAP and remains adherent to treatment over time). Multiple studies have demonstrated the effectiveness of this type of approach, especially with younger children and those with developmental delay. But clinician time, patience, and empathy are critical factors for treatment success.

Case Example: Carlos

Carlos is a 6-year-old boy with Down syndrome who was referred because of nonadherence to his PAP therapy. Mom reports that Carlos screams every time she tries to put the mask on him. At first, she would try to hold it on, but he became so combative that now she removes it. Most days when she brings the mask out, he simply runs away and cries. She has tried putting the mask on after he falls asleep, but he either wakes up immediately, removes the mask, and becomes very upset; if he does sleep for a short period with the mask on, without fail he will remove it a couple of hours later. Mom is exhausted and frustrated. After trying for a couple of weeks, she states that she has given up.

A lengthy conversation with Carlos's mother identified the primary stressors related to PAP therapy and his nonadherence. First, she stated that Carlos already had so much to deal with because of his Down syndrome that she felt guilty trying to make him wear "that terrible machine." Second, Carlos's father (who had not come to any medical appointments) did not believe that Carlos really needed PAP therapy. This left mom with little support with PAP therapy practice at home.

The next session was scheduled at a time when Carlos, his mother, and his father were able to attend. Additional education about OSA and PAP therapy was provided, and the parents were encouraged to work together on the recommended gradual exposure. Once both parents agreed, Carlos and his parents identified a favorite activity (train game on the tablet) and reward (toy dinosaurs). A graduated exposure protocol was implemented, with Carlos playing on the tablet and earning tokens for each successful step. For every five tokens he earned, Carlos could get a small dinosaur. If Carlos became combative or removed the mask, the tablet was taken away until he calmed down and was ready to repeat that step. At a follow-up visit 2 weeks later, the machine download showed Carlos was wearing his mask for about 3 hours a night. His mother reported that he fell asleep with the mask and machine on but took it off sometime during the night. As Carlos's father usually worked late, it was agreed that he would check on Carlos when he came home around midnight and replace the mask if needed. On nights dad did not work, the parents agreed to set their alarm for midnight to wake them to replace the mask. Carlos's adherence continued to increase over time. At each follow-up visit, new issues were identified and addressed as needed.

USE OF DATA FROM PAP MACHINE TO IMPROVE ADHERENCE

Most machines include a way to monitor adherence. Not only should patients bring their mask and machine to every appointment to ensure that the mask is fitting properly and the machine is working properly, but the data from the machine should also be downloaded and analyzed at follow-up appointments. Observing the patterns of PAP use can provide a clinician with useful information that can be incorporated into a plan for improving PAP adherence. The following are descriptions of commonly seen patterns of PAP usage data, along with explanations for what the pattern means and suggestions for how to address the issue.

Machine on But Not Achieving Full Pressure

Machine monitors can identify when the PAP machine is on and whether it is achieving full pressure. There are several reasons for not reaching full pressure.

- Mask leak. If the patient and parent provide a credible report that the child is wearing the PAP, it is possible the mask is leaking and thus not allowing full pressure to be achieved.
- Machine is on but mask is not. As with the first case example, patients will sometimes turn the machine on but not wear the mask. Some patients may even be as creative as putting the mask on a stuffed animal.
- Mask is removed during the night. It is common for the mask to be removed (intentionally or unintentionally) during the night. Typically, the machine's alarm will sound, alerting the child and/or parent that the mask is off and needs to be replaced. However, some patients/parents sleep through the alarm and may not be aware that the mask has come off. A baby monitor can be used to amplify the alarm. Alternatively, using the monitoring data, a pattern may be detected. For example, the mask is worn until at least midnight but never after 2:00 a.m. Parents can be instructed to set their own alarm clock to wake at 2:00 a.m. to check on the child and replace the mask as needed. This sleep disruption is temporary, as the child will quickly adapt to sleeping through the night with the mask on. This also shows the child how important it is to wear the mask and that the parent is invested in their efforts.

PAP Holiday

Patterns of use can help create a dialogue about why the PAP is not regularly used. For example, some patients may not wear the PAP on weekends, believing they have earned a "PAP holiday." It may be acceptable for some patients to have such a holiday; however, this is a decision that needs to be made by the medical team. In addition, the primary concern with a PAP holiday is that it may be difficult to restart use. For patients taking a PAP holiday, it is important to help identify incorrect beliefs or frustrations related to PAP therapy, especially in older children and adolescents. This may be helpful for teens who are embarrassed by their PAP and do not want to take it when they spend the night out. If a PAP holiday is not recommended, providing a script for teens as to how to explain why they have the regimen may help remove the anxiety of explaining PAP to their peers or relatives.

"Oh No, I'm Going to See the Doctor!"

Another pattern that may be seen is that a child's adherence increases immediately before and after an appointment but then tapers off in between appointments. For this type of patient, more frequent contact and monitor downloads can be used to increase adherence.

Summary and Take-Home Points

For most children with OSA, surgery is the primary treatment. However, when surgery is not successful in curing the OSA, or when surgery is not an option, PAP is required. Nonadherence to PAP therapy is common, with multiple factors contributing. These include a lack of understanding about OSA and the consequences if left untreated, the patient or parent not accepting that OSA is a chronic illness, discomfort from the PAP equipment, and anxiety about using the machine. Specific points to remember for intervention are outlined below.

- It takes significant time, patience, and empathy to connect with families and get their buy-in for treatment. Unlike treatments for other chronic illnesses, many patients and families do not see the immediate benefits or understand the long-term consequences of nonadherence to PAP therapy.
- Working together with the medical team will ensure that discomfort due to the equipment and/or side effects are addressed, allowing for the focus to be on behavioral interventions.
- Together with the patient and family, it is important to choose rewards and distractions that are motivating enough to ensure success with the multicomponent behavioral approach.
- Objective data provide clinicians with a wealth of information about PAP adherence, allowing for an easy discussion entry point with patients on ways to improve PAP usage.

Appendix A

Resources for Clinicians and Families

Sleep Resources

American Academy of Sleep Medicine
(http://www.aasmnet.org)

The American Academy of Sleep Medicine (AASM) is the primary membership organization for professionals practicing sleep medicine. The AASM aims to promote health by providing access to tools and resources for disordered sleep.

AASM-Accredited Sleep Centers
(http://www.sleepeducation.com/find-a-center)

This consumer resource, provided by the AASM, enables patients to find a sleep center in their area (within the United States) that has been accredited by the AASM.

Society of Behavioral Sleep Medicine
(http://www.behavioralsleep.org/FindSpecialist.aspx)

The Society of Behavioral Sleep Medicine is a professional membership organization dedicated to setting standards and promoting excellence in behavioral sleep medicine. The website provides information for clinicians, as well as a list of behavioral sleep medicine specialists in the United States.

National Sleep Foundation (http://www.sleepfoundation.org)

The National Sleep Foundation is a nonprofit organization that is dedicated to improving health through sleep education and advocacy. Their website provides a range of general information related to healthy sleep habits, sleep disorders, and tools and tips to improve sleep.

Narcolepsy Network (http://www.narcolepsynetwork.org)

The Narcolepsy Network serves as a membership opportunity for individuals experiencing narcolepsy and provides information about the disorder and treatment options.

American Sleep Apnea Association (http://www.sleepapnea.org)

This consumer-oriented organization provides resources for individuals living with sleep apnea. Additional resources include gently used continuous positive airway pressure machines for those who are unable to afford to purchase new machines.

Willis–Ekbom Disease Foundation (http://www.rls.org)

The Willis–Ekbom Disease Foundation provides resources for consumers, clinicians, and researchers related to restless legs syndrome/Willis–Ekbom disease.

Start School Later (http://www.startschoollater.net)

This nonprofit organization is composed of scientists, parents, and educators whose goal is to promote health, safety, learning, and equity in all public schools by means of appropriate hours of attendance. The primary aim is to promote later school start times for middle and high schools in the United States.

Enuresis Alarms (http://www.bedwettingstore.com)

The Bed Wetting Store offers a variety of products to assist in the process of treating enuresis. This includes different types of alarms, dry night tracking sheets, and other products. A team of trained consultants are available to assist if there are any questions about products or the process.

Other Resources

American Psychological Association (http://www.apa.org)

The American Psychological Association is the largest membership organization representing the field of psychology in the United States. It is composed of students, clinicians, researchers, and educators.

American Academy of Pediatrics (http://www.aap.org)

The American Academy of Pediatrics is the primary membership organization for pediatricians and offers a wide variety of resources for pediatric providers as well as for parents.

Motivational Interviewing (http://www.motivationalinterviewing.org)

This site offers manuals, training tools, and an overview of motivational interviewing techniques in an effort to disseminate motivational interviewing as a tool in treatment.

Books for Clinicians

PEDIATRIC SLEEP

Mindell, J. A., & Owens, J. A. (2010). *A clinical guide to pediatric sleep: diagnosis and management of sleep problems* (2nd ed.) Philadelphia, PA: Lippincott, Williams, & Wilkins.

This clinical guide to pediatric sleep disorders and their treatment is aimed at primary care providers. Symptom checklists are included, and a companion website offers handouts for providers and families.

Sheldon, S. H., Ferber, R., Kryger, M. H., & Gozal, D. (Eds.). (2014). *Principles and practice of pediatric sleep medicine* (2nd ed.). Philadelphia, PA: Elsevier Saunders.

This text is a comprehensive resource for diagnosing and managing sleep disorders and their co-occurring conditions in children and adolescents. Both print and online access are available.

Wolfson, A., & Montgomery-Downs, H. E. (Eds.). (2013). *The Oxford handbook of infant, child, and adolescent sleep and behavior.* New York, NY: Oxford University Press.

This edited volume provides information on typical sleep, as well as both research and clinical intervention for sleep disorders in infants, children, and adolescents.

GENERAL SLEEP

American Academy of Sleep Medicine. (2014). *International classification of sleep disorders: Diagnostic and coding manual* (3rd ed.). Darien, IL: Author.

The *International Classification of Sleep Disorders (3rd ed.)* is the most up-to-date diagnostic manual for both behavioral and medical sleep disorders. It is available in an electronic format and provides epidemiologic and diagnostic information on sleep disorders.

Kryger, M. H., Roth, T., & Dement, W. C. (Eds.). (2010). *Principles and practice of sleep medicine* (5th ed.). Philadelphia, PA: Elsevier Saunders.

This text provides updated information on the diagnosis and management of all clinical sleep disorders, with an emphasis on empirically based treatments. The book provides both print and electronic resources.

COGNITIVE–BEHAVIORAL THERAPY FOR INSOMNIA

Edinger, J. D., & Carney, C. E. (2014). *Overcoming insomnia: A cognitive-behavioral therapy approach therapist guide* (2nd ed.). Oxford, England: Oxford University Press.

As part of the "Treatments that Work" series, this updated version of *Overcoming Insomnia* has been revised to be consistent with the *Diagnostic and Statistical Manual of Mental Disorders* (5th ed.). Specificinstruction in cognitive–behavioral therapy for insomnia is provided.

Morin, C. M., & Espie, C. A. (2003). *Insomnia: A clinical guide to assessment and treatment.* New York, NY: Kluwer Academic/Plenum.

This clinical handbook provides information for clinicians in the diagnosis and management of insomnia in adults. This can be a useful guide for treatment of older adolescents.

Perlis, M. L., Aloia, M., & Kuhn, B. R. (Eds.). (2010). *Behavioral treatments for sleep disorders: A comprehensive primer of behavioral sleep medicine interventions.* Burlington, MA: Academic Press.

This comprehensive resource provides step-by-step instruction in the behavioral management of sleep problems from childhood through adulthood.

Perlis, M. L., Jungquist, C., Smith, M. T., & Posner, D. (2008). *Cognitive behavioral treatment of insomnia: A session-by-session guide.* New York, NY: Springer.

This clinician's guide provides session-by-session instruction in the implementation of cognitive–behavioral therapy for insomnia.

TEXTS ON BEHAVIOR THEORY

Malott, R. W., & Shane, J. T. (2013). *Principles of behavior.* (7th ed.) New York, NY: Pearson Education.

This textbook presents a broad range of information on behavioral principles, ranging from behavioral theories to applied behavior analysis.

Martin, G. L., & Pear, J. (2014). *Behavior modification: What it is and how to do it* (10th ed.). Prentice Hall.

This basic introduction to behavior modification addresses both behavior theory and its application.

Thorpe, G. L., & Olson, S. L. (1997). *Behavior therapy: Concepts, procedures, and applications.* (2nd ed.) New York, NY: Pearson.

Included in this book are behavior theories, principles of behavior change, and specific behavior therapy techniques.

MANAGEMENT OF ANXIETY IN CHILDREN

Frank, T., & Frank, K. (2003). *The handbook for helping kids with anxiety and stress.* Chapin, SC: YouthLight.

This book includes a section for professionals on using cognitive strategies to manage anxiety in children, as well as a section targeted directly to children with activities to reduce anxiety.

Friedberg, M. D., McClure, J. M., & Garcia, J. H. (2009). *Cognitive therapy techniques for children and adolescents: Tools for enhancing practice.* New York, NY: Guilford Press.

This book provides modules for anxiety management with children and adolescents in clinical practice. Child-friendly activities to engage patients in cognitive therapy are included.

Kendall, P. C., & Hedtke, K. A. (2006). *Coping CAT workbook* (2nd ed.). Philadelphia, PA: Temple University.

This modular format workbook provides session-by-session instruction in empirically supported cognitive–behavioral therapy for anxiety in children.

Kendall, P. C., & Hedtke, K. A. (2006). *Cognitive–behavioral therapy for anxious children: Therapist manual* (3rd ed.). Philadelphia, PA: Temple University.

This therapist guide that accompanies the Coping CAT Workbook provides instructions to clinicians in the implementation of the Coping CAT program.

Vernon, A. (2006). *Thinking, feeling, behaving: An emotional educational curriculum for children Grades 1–6* (Rev. ed.). Champaign, IL: Research Press.

This workbook provides a curriculum-based format, targeted toward specific grade levels and includes specific strategies for cognitive restructuring to manage anxiety.

Books and Resources for Parents

SLEEP

Autism Treatment Network Sleep Tool Kit (http://www.autismspeaks.org/science/resources-programs/autism-treatment-network/tools-you-can-use/sleep-tool-kit)

This website provides resources and tools for parents of youth with autism spectrum disorder to assist with sleep problems in their children.

Ferber, R. (2006). *Solve your child's sleep problems.* New York, NY: Fireside.

This book is oriented toward parents and provides a guide to understanding sleep problems and incorporating strategies to improve children's sleep difficulties.

Katz, T., & Malow, B. A. (2014). *Solving sleep problems in children with autism spectrum disorders: A guide for frazzled families.* Bethesda, MD: Woodbine House.

For parents of children on the autism spectrum, this book provides education about sleep in children with autism, as well as practical strategies for improving sleep in this population.

Mindell, J. A. (2005). *Sleeping through the night: How infants, toddlers, and their parents can get a good night's sleep* (Rev. ed.) New York, NY: HarperCollins.

Sleeping Through the Night serves as a guide to solving infants' and toddlers' sleep problems, with a focus on bedtime rather than the middle of the night. The book also includes frequently asked questions, tips, and techniques.

Owens, J. A., & Mindell, J. A. (2005). *Take charge of your child's sleep: The all-in-one resource for solving sleep problems in kids and teens.* New York, NY: Marlow.

This book provides information concerning the importance of sleep, sleep issues, and the tools and treatments of sleep problems targeted to parents of older children and teens.

Weissbluth, M. (2003). *Healthy sleep habits, happy child* (3rd ed.). New York, NY: Ballantine Books.

This book focuses on both prevention of, and intervention for, a broad range of sleep problems in childhood.

PARENTING, ATTENTION-DEFICIT/ HYPERACTIVITY DISORDER, AND CHILD ANXIETY

Barkley, R. A. (2013). *Taking charge of ADHD: The complete authoritative guide for parents.* New York, NY: Guilford Press.

Taking Charge of ADHD is a comprehensive guide to empirically based information about attention-deficit/hyperactivity disorder, treatment, and behavior planning for children ages 6 to 18.

Chansky, T. E. (2014). *Freeing your child from anxiety: Powerful, practical solutions to overcome your child's fears, worries, and phobias.* New York, NY: Harmony Books.

This book enables parents to help their children with anxiety. It includes activities and tools to enable children to be in control of their thoughts and emotions.

Clark L. (2005). *SOS help for parents: A practical guide for handling common everyday behavior problems* (3rd ed.). Bowling Green, KY: SOS Programs & Parents Press. See also http://www.sosprograms.com

SOS is a parent-friendly resource for self-help materials ranging from books, videos, and worksheets for parents with a focus on improving children's behavior.

Phelan, T. W. (2010). *1-2-3 magic: Effective discipline for children 2–12* (4th ed.). Glen Ellyn, IL: Parent Magic.

This parent-oriented book offers guidance on behavior management for children ages 2 to 12.

Books for Children

Crist, J. J. (2004). *What to do when you're scared and worried: A guide for kids*. Minneapolis, MN: Free Spirit.

This children's book is focused on helping children understand the root of their worries and fears while providing ways to manage these emotions.

Culbert, T., & Kajander, R. (2007). *Be the boss of your sleep*. Minneapolis, MN: Free Spirit.

This book encourages children to take control of their daily routines and make behavioral and environmental changes to promote better sleep.

Huebner, D. (2006). *What to do when you worry too much*. Washington, DC: Magination Press.

As part of the "What to Do" series, *What to Do When You Worry Too Much* is targeted to children ages 6 to 12. This workbook includes cognitive–behavioral strategies to assist children (and their parents) in managing anxiety.

Huebner, D. (2008). *What to do when you dread your bed*. Washington, DC: Magination Press.

Also part of a series of "What to Do" books published by Magination Press, *What to Do When You Dread Your Bed* is a self-help workbook that guides parents and children through cognitive–behavioral techniques to facilitate a more peaceful bedtime experience and decrease bedtime struggles.

Lite, L. (1996). *A boy and a bear: The children's relaxation book*. Marietta, GA: Stress Free Kids.

As part of a series of relaxation books, children ages 3 to 10 are instructed on relaxation strategies for self-calming.

Lite, L. (2007). *A boy and a turtle: A children's relaxation story*. Marietta, GA: Stress Free Kids.

Another book in Lori Lite's relaxation series, this book uses imagination and visualization techniques in an effort to teach children to manage stress.

Lite, L. (2007). *The goodnight caterpillar: A children's relaxation story*. Marietta, GA: Stress Free Kids.

The Goodnight Caterpillar uses a story-based format to teach the technique of progressive muscle relaxation to children.

Lite, L. (2008). *Angry octopus: A relaxation story.* Marietta, GA: Stress Free Kids.

This book offers another story to assist children in learning to implement progressive muscle relaxation and deep breathing to manage anger.

Peterson, J., & Peterson, M. (2004). *The sleep fairy.* Omaha, NE: Behave'n Kids Press.

The Sleep Fairy uses a playful approach to encourage children to stay in bed with the promise of a surprise treat.

Shapiro, L. E., & Sprague, R. K. (2009). *The relaxation and stress reduction workbook for kids: Help for children to cope with stress, anxiety, and transitions.* Oakland, CA: New Harbinger.

This interactive workbook provides more than 50 activities for families to complete together in an effort to teach and demonstrate to children how to feel more relaxed and calm.

Williams, M. L. (2007). *Cool cats, calm kids: Relaxation and stress management for young people.* Atascadero, CA: Impact.

Cool Cats, Calm Kids is targeted to children ages 7 to 12 as a tool for stress management.

Appendix B

Handouts

The following handouts were designed to support the information provided to patients/parents during a clinical visit, including step-by-step instructions or guidance on how to implement many of the treatments described in Part III, a brief rationale for the intervention, and reminders to help families be successful. All of the handouts are also available for free online at http://pubs.apa.org/books/supp/meltzer/.

HANDOUT 1

Healthy Sleep Habits

The following recommendations are given to provide the best quality sleep every night.

1. **Have a consistent sleep schedule.** Wake up and go to bed at about the same time on weeknights and weekend nights. Bedtime and wake time should not differ from day to day by more than an hour.
2. **Establish a regular, relaxing bedtime routine.** Make the 30 minutes before bed wind-down time. Do not watch TV, use electronic devices (smartphones, tablets, etc.), the Internet, or exercise during this time; rather, do something relaxing, such as playing with quiet toys, reading a book, or listening to soothing music.
3. **Create an environment that is only for sleeping.** This means the bedroom should be comfortable, quiet, and dark. Also, make sure the room is not too warm (75 degrees or higher), as warm temperatures interfere with sleep. It is also very important to get all technology (TV, cell phones, computers, tablets, etc.) out of the bedroom.
4. **Have a light snack before bed.** Eat regular meals throughout the day and have a light snack before bed. There is truth to cookies and milk helping facilitate sleep! Healthier snack choices include yogurt, milk, or cheese. Do not eat large amounts of sugar or chocolate.
5. **Exercise regularly (but not too close to bedtime).** The best time to exercise is first thing in the morning or in the late afternoon. Avoid strenuous physical exertion right before bed.
6. **Enjoy the sunshine in the morning.** Spend time outside every day, especially in the morning, as exposure to sunlight or bright light helps to keep the body's internal clock on track. However, it is important to limit light exposure in the evening, especially after dinner. This means turning down overhead lights and reducing the brightness of screens (e.g., computers, tablets).
7. **Avoid naps if you are having trouble falling asleep at bedtime.** Naps are developmentally appropriate in young children, and some adolescents benefit from a short afternoon nap (45 minutes right after school). However, for those who have difficulties falling asleep at bedtime, naps can make this even worse.
8. **Do not consume caffeine after 4 p.m. or within 6 hours of bedtime.** Caffeine has a half-life of 4 to 6 hours, which means it should still be helping you stay awake 4 to 6 hours after you take it but then can also make it hard to fall asleep! Be aware of all the things that have caffeine. You may know that many sodas, coffee, iced tea, and dark chocolate have caffeine. But you can also find caffeine in less obvious products like certain waters, juice drinks, gum, and candy bars. Some medications also contain caffeine. In general, children should not be consuming caffeine.

Just like the dentist asks you to brush and floss twice a day or your doctor asks you to eat five fruits and vegetables and exercise 30 minutes every day, healthy sleep habits will help you fall asleep faster, stay asleep, and wake more refreshed in the morning. However, consistency in following these rules is essential to achieve quality sleep.

HANDOUT 2

Sleep Log Instructions

▪ Please keep a daily log of your child's sleep for 2 weeks.
▪ To show the time your child gets in bed, please mark that time with a down arrow (↓).
▪ Please shade in the time that your child is asleep.
▪ To show the time your child wakes up and/or gets out of bed (either during the night or in the morning), please mark that time with an up arrow (↑).

On the bottom of your sleep log is an example line. The markings show this child went to bed at 9:30 p.m. (↓), was asleep from 10:00 p.m. to 2:00 a.m., was awake and/or out of bed from 2:00–3:00 a.m. (↑), and was asleep again from 3:00 a.m. to 7:00 a.m., and got out of bed at 7:30 a.m. This child also took a nap from 1:00 p.m. to 3:00 p.m.

Please note, each day of the sleep diary starts at 6 p.m., so if you are recording for Tuesday, you will start with Tuesday at 6 p.m. and record through Wednesday 6 p.m. on the first line. The second line will be Wednesday 6 p.m. through Thursday 6 p.m., and so on.

(continued)

HANDOUT 2 (Continued)

Sleep Log

Name: _____ Dob: __ / __ / __

Date Started: __ / __ / __ Date Ended: __ / __ / __

List Medications: _____

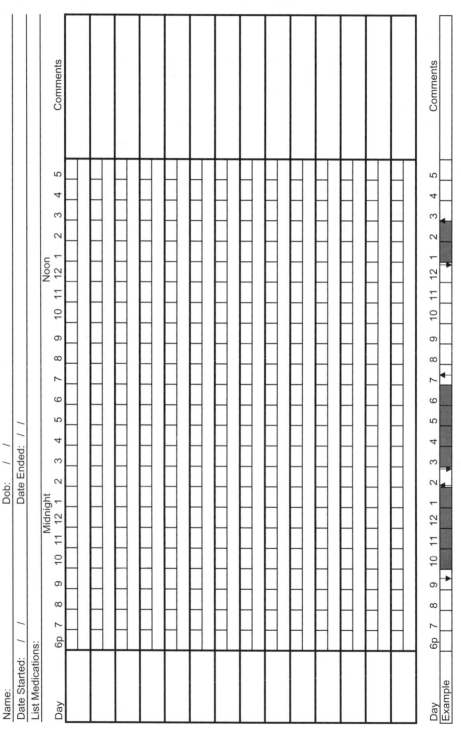

Key: down arrow = in bed   up arrow = out of bed   shaded = asleep (can have unshaded space between arrows, in bed not asleep)

HANDOUT 3

Sleep Diary Instructions

- Please fill out this sleep diary every day. If possible, please fill it out within 1 hour of waking up in the morning. One way to remember is to put it on the table and fill it out while you are eating breakfast.
- **Do not worry about giving exact times and do not watch the clock**. Just give your best guess when answering the questions.

The following tell you what is being asked for each item.
Date: Write the date of the *morning* that you are filling out the diary (so today's date if you are filling it out about last night)

1. <u>What time did you get into bed?</u> Write the time that you got into bed last night. This may or may not be the same time that you tried to fall asleep. For example, if you got into bed at 10:15 p.m. and then read for 15 minutes before you closed your eyes and tried to sleep, then you got into bed at 10:15 p.m.
2. <u>What time did you try to go to sleep?</u> Write what time you tried to fall asleep. This may or may not be the same time that you got into bed. For our example, after reading for 15 minutes you closed your eyes and tried to fall asleep at 10:30 p.m.
3. <u>How long did it take you to fall asleep?</u> Starting with the time in question 2, estimate how long it took you to fall asleep.
4. <u>How many times did you wake up, not counting your final awakening?</u> Write how many times you woke up during the night between the time that you first fell asleep and your final awakening.
5. <u>In total, how long did these awakenings last?</u> Write how long you were awake between the time you first fell asleep and your final awakening. For example, if you woke up 3 times for 45 minutes, 30 minutes, and 15 minutes, add them up (45 + 30 + 15 = 90 minutes or 1 hour and 30 minutes).
6. <u>What time was your final awakening?</u> Write what time you woke up in the morning for the last time (this is usually the time your alarm goes off or someone wakes up you, but if you wake before your alarm and never go back to sleep, that is the time you would record here).
7. <u>What time did you get out of bed for the day?</u> Write what time you got out of bed to start your day. This may be different from your final awakening time. For example, your alarm may have woken you up at 6:30 a.m. (what you would write for question 6), but you did not get up to get ready for school until 6:45 a.m. (what you would write for question 7).
8. <u>How would you rate the quality of your sleep?</u> Select which answer best describes whether you thought your sleep was good or poor.
9. <u>Comments (if applicable).</u> This space is for you to record anything about your day or night that you think may have affected your sleep.

From "The Consensus Sleep Diary: Standardizing Prospective Sleep Self-Monitoring," by C. E. Carney, D. J. Buysse, S. Ancoli-Israel, J. D. Edinger, A. D. Krystal, K. L. Lichstein, and C. M. Morin, 2012, *Sleep*, 35, pp. 287–302. Consensus Sleep Diary copyright 2011 by C. E. Carney, D. J. Buysse, S. Ancoli-Israel, J. D. Edinger, A. D. Krystal, K. L. Lichstein, and C. M. Morin. Adapted with permission.

(continued)

SLEEP DIARY

Name: _____

Today's date	4/5/11						
What time did you get into bed?	10:15 p.m.						
What time did you try to go to sleep?	10:30 p.m.						
How long did it take you to fall asleep?	1 hour						
How many times did you wake up, not counting your final awakening?	3 times						
In total, how long did these awakenings last?	1 hour 30 min						
What time was your final awakening?	6:30 a.m.						
What time did you get out of bed for the day?	6:45 a.m.						
How would you rate the quality of your sleep?	Very poor / (Poor) / Fair / Good / Very good	Very poor Poor Fair Good Very good	Very poor Poor Fair Good Very good	Very poor Poor Fair Good Very good	Very poor Poor Fair Good Very good	Very poor Poor Fair Good Very good	Very poor Poor Fair Good Very good
Comments (if applicable)	I have a cold						

HANDOUT 4

Nighttime Awakenings—Sleep Training

Nighttime arousals are normal. All children (and adults) wake approximately two to six times every night. Problematic nighttime awakenings occur when your child cannot return to sleep without your help after he has a normal nighttime arousal. To teach your child to return to sleep during the night, you must first teach him to fall asleep independently at bedtime. **This treatment can be very challenging, as it does involve a fair bit of crying, so it is strongly recommended that you have support from your spouse/partner, a friend, or a family member.** That said, in less than 1 week, you should see significant improvements in your child's ability to fall asleep independently at bedtime and to return to sleep following normal nighttime arousals. The following provides guidance on how to help teach your child to fall asleep at bedtime without your help.

1. Have a consistent bedtime routine and a consistent bedtime in place. For your child, this routine should include the following: _____
   _____ and should end
   at _____ p.m.
2. At the end of the routine, you should place your child in his crib awake and leave the room.
3. You should go in to check on your child only if you are concerned about safety (e.g., his leg is stuck in the crib) or health issues (e.g., he has thrown up).
4. When your child wakes during the night, you should ignore protests, again checking on your child only if you are concerned about safety or health.

Important Things to Remember
■ Your child is crying at bedtime because he is tired and knows how to fall asleep only with your help. He will still be very happy to see you in the morning, and there will be no short-term or long-term damage by doing this sleep training.
■ The second night will likely be worse than the first night! On average, most children cry 45 minutes the first night at bedtime. On the second night, most children cry 90 minutes. By the third night, most children cry about 20 minutes. So you have to be prepared to do at least 3 nights of this intervention. If you "rescue" your child after prolonged crying and then help him fall asleep (e.g., rocking, nursing), all he has learned is that prolonged crying will get him what he ultimately wants, which is you helping him to fall asleep.
■ Although unlikely, it is possible that your child will throw up. To prepare, have a second set of sheets on the crib/bed with a pad in between and a second set of pajamas ready to go. If your child vomits, take him out of the crib/bed and remove the dirty sheets, clean him up and change his pajamas. Then return him to the crib/bed. Although this sounds terrible, it is necessary because children as young as 6 months can learn to vomit on demand. So, if you help your child fall asleep after he vomits, then he may learn to vomit every night until he gets what he wants, which is you helping him fall asleep.

(continued)

HANDOUT 4 *(Continued)*

▪ Listening to a baby cry when he is learning to sleep independently is <u>very</u> challenging. Here are some strategies you could use to help yourself manage your frustration, worry, guilt, and irritation (all of which are normal feelings!):
  ▪ take a bath;
  ▪ listen to music;
  ▪ meditate;
  ▪ exercise;
  ▪ talk on the phone;
  ▪ play a game; or
  ▪ enlist the support of your partner, friends, and/or family to take turns monitoring your child so that you can take a break to have time for yourself.

  Although challenging, this treatment is very successful as long as you are consistent and follow through with all of the recommended steps. Keep in mind that you are doing this to help your child learn to sleep. The short-term benefit is that both you and your child will start sleeping better. The long-term benefits are numerous, including improved child and parent mood, improved parent–child interactions, and improved family functioning.

HANDOUT 5

Nighttime Awakenings—Checking Method

Nighttime arousals are normal. All children (and adults) wake approximately two to six times every night. Problematic nighttime awakenings occur when your child cannot return to sleep without your help after she has a normal nighttime arousal. To teach your child to return to sleep during the night, you must first teach her to fall asleep independently at bedtime. Once she has learned how to fall asleep without your help, in about 2 weeks, you will see that she starts to sleep longer and longer stretches at night without waking. **Keep in mind that this treatment focuses only on bedtime, so your child's nighttime awakenings will continue for at least the next few weeks.**

If you are currently nursing/feeding or rocking your child to sleep, you must first make changes to this behavior. For example, move the nursing/feeding to the first part of your bedtime routine and then rock her to sleep. After a few nights of rocking your child to sleep, rock her for only a few minutes before placing her in the crib awake. The following provides guidance on how to help teach your child to fall asleep at bedtime without your help once you are ready to place your child into the crib awake.

1. **Have a consistent bedtime routine and a consistent bedtime in place.** For your child, this routine should include the following: _____ _____ and should end at _____ p.m.
2. **At the end of the routine, you should place your child in her crib awake and leave the room.**
3. **You can then check on your child as often as you want, but the longer you can stay out of the room, the better!** If your child gets more upset by your visits, then don't go in as often. For the first few nights you should check on your child every _____. After that, the time between checks should increase by _____ every night.
4. **When you check on your child, the visit is brief and boring.** These checks are for you to say, "I love you, it's sleeping time!" and to make sure your child is safe and okay.
5. **It is best if you do not pick your child up to comfort her, as she could snuggle into your shoulder and go right to sleep.** Then all she has learned is that if she cries long enough you will "rescue" her. However, if you feel as if your child is past the point where she will be able to calm down without a brief interaction, you may pick her up for a couple of minutes to try and calm her down. However, she must be returned to her crib awake. If when you put her back in the crib she becomes even more distressed, it may be better in the future to not pick her up again.
6. **When your child wakes during the night, you should respond immediately and consistently.** For your family, this response should be _____ _____.

(continued)

HANDOUT 5 (*Continued*)

Important Things to Remember

- Your child is crying at bedtime because she is tired and knows how to fall asleep only with your help. She will still be very happy to see you in the morning and there will be no short-term or long-term damage by doing this sleep training.
- The second night will likely be worse than the first night! On average, most children cry 45 minutes the first night at bedtime. On the second night, most children cry 90 minutes. By the third night, most children cry about 20 minutes. So, you have to be prepared to do at least 3 nights of this intervention. If you "rescue" your child after prolonged crying and then help her fall asleep (e.g., rocking, nursing), all she has learned is that prolonged crying will get her what she ultimately wants, which is you helping her to fall asleep.
- Although unlikely, it is possible that your child will throw up. To prepare, have a second set of sheets on the bed with a pad in between and a second set of pajamas ready to go. If your child vomits, take her out of the crib and remove the dirty sheets, clean her up and change her pajamas. Then return her to the crib. Although this sounds terrible, it is necessary because children as young as 6 months can learn to vomit on demand. So if you help your child fall asleep after she vomits, she may learn to vomit every night until she gets what she wants, which is you helping her fall asleep.
- Listening to a baby cry when she is learning to sleep independently is <u>very</u> challenging. Here are some strategies you can use to help yourself manage your frustration, worry, guilt, and irritation (all of which are normal feelings!):
  - take a bath;
  - listen to music;
  - meditate;
  - exercise;
  - talk on the phone;
  - play a game;
  - enlist the support of your partner, friends, and/or family to take turns with you monitoring your child so that you can take a break to have time for yourself. This can also be very help-ful for children who need their sleep managed in the middle of the night. Taking turns with a partner can help each of you get much needed rest.

  Although challenging, this treatment is very successful as long as you are consistent and follow through with all of the recommended steps. Keep in mind that you are doing this to help your child learn to sleep. The short-term benefit is that both you and your child will start sleeping better. The long-term benefits are numerous, including improved child and parent mood, improved parent-child interactions, and improved family functioning.

HANDOUT 6

Nighttime Awakenings—Parental Presence

Nighttime arousals are normal. All children (and adults) wake approximately two to six times every night. Problematic nighttime awakenings occur when your child cannot return to sleep without your help after he has a normal nighttime arousal. To teach your child to return to sleep during the night, you must first teach him to fall asleep independently at bedtime. Once he has learned how to fall asleep without your help, in about 2 weeks, you will see that he starts to sleep longer and longer stretches at night without waking. **Keep in mind that this treatment focuses only on bedtime, so your child's nighttime awakenings will continue for at least the next few weeks.**

If you are currently nursing/feeding or rocking your child to sleep, you must first make changes to this behavior. For example, move the nursing/feeding to the first part of your bedtime routine and then rock your child to sleep. After a few nights of rocking your child to sleep, rock him for only a few minutes before placing him in the crib awake. The following provides guidance on how to help teach your child to fall asleep at bedtime without your help once you are ready to place your child into the crib awake.

1. **Have a consistent bedtime routine and a consistent bedtime in place.** For your child this routine should include the following: _____
   _____ and should end
   at _____ p.m.
2. **At the end of the routine, you should place your child in the crib awake and then stay with him until he is asleep.** For the first few nights, you can comfort or interact with your child by rubbing his head or providing verbal reassurances ("I love you, it's sleeping time").
3. **After a few nights of your child falling asleep in the crib with you present, you have two choices:**
   a. *Move half the distance from the crib to the door and stay on the floor until your child is asleep.* After 3 to 5 successful nights (e.g., limited crying), move to the doorway and remain until your child is asleep. After an additional 3 to 5 nights, move into the hallway and remain until your child is asleep.
   b. *Stay with your child for a few minutes and then take a short break (1–2 minutes), returning and staying with your child until he is asleep.* Each night, the break should get longer and longer, with the goal of your child falling asleep when you are not in the room. You should always return to ensure your child is asleep, and if not, stay with him until he does fall asleep.
4. **It is best if you do not pick your child up to comfort him, as he could snuggle into your shoulder and go right to sleep.** Then all he has learned is that if he cries long enough you will "rescue" him. However, if you feel as if your child is past the point where he will be able to calm down without a brief interaction, you may pick him up for a couple of minutes to try and calm him down. However, he must be returned to his crib awake. If when you put him back in the crib he becomes even more distressed, it may be better in the future to not pick him up again.
5. **When your child wakes during the night, you should respond immediately and consistently.** For your family, this response should be _____
   _____.

(*continued*)

HANDOUT 6 (*Continued*)

Important Things to Remember

- Your child is crying at bedtime because he is tired and knows how to fall asleep only with your help. He will still be very happy to see you in the morning, and there will be no short-term or long-term damage by doing this sleep training.
- The second night will likely be worse than the first night!
- Although unlikely, it is possible that your child will throw up. To prepare, have a second set of sheets on the bed with a pad in between and a second set of pajamas ready to go. If your child vomits, take him out of the crib and remove the dirty sheets, clean him up and change his pajamas. Then return him to the crib. Although this sounds terrible, it is necessary because children as young as 6 months can learn to vomit on demand. So if you help your child fall asleep after he vomits, then he may learn to vomit every night until he gets what he wants, which is you helping him fall asleep.

> *Although challenging, this treatment is very successful as long as you are consistent and follow through with all of the recommended steps. Keep in mind that you are doing this to help your child learn to sleep. The short-term benefit is that both you and your child will start sleeping better. The long-term benefits are numerous, including improved child and parent mood, improved parent–child interactions, and improved family functioning.*

HANDOUT 7

Dream Feed

The goal of a dream feed is to create a long stretch of uninterrupted sleep for both you and your child. Because of concerns related to your child's need to eat during the night, the dream feed will help you decide when she eats, rather than you having to wake multiple times during the night to feed her. The following provides guidance on how to implement the dream feed.

1. **Your child's dream feed should occur approximately two to three hours after she has fallen asleep at bedtime, and close to the time you usually go to bed.** For you, this dream feed should occur at _____.
2. **At that time, go in and gently rouse your child and feed her (nursing or bottle).** Then place her back in the crib (it is okay if she is asleep at this point).
3. **For all additional night wakings, respond consistently to your child but <u>do not</u> feed her.** For you, this response should be _____.
4. **When your child wakes for the final time in the morning (the time she usually wakes up to start the day), have a routine that is different than during the night.** For example, you can get her up, change her diaper and clothes, and take her in a different room before feeding her again.

   The dream feed is a helpful intervention for children who still need to eat during the night but who are waking multiple times or at unpredictable times to do so. By gently waking your child to eat before your own sleep onset, you can assure that additional feedings are not needed during the night.

HANDOUT 8

The Good Morning Light

The Good Morning Light is a simple way to teach your child the difference between night and day. As adults, we simply look at our clocks to tell us whether we should go back to sleep or get up. But young children do not have this ability. The following provides guidance on how to create and effectively use the Good Morning Light.

1. **Plug a night-light into a timer, the kind you would use to turn your lights on and off if you were on vacation, or to turn your holiday lights on and off.** Timers can be purchased at any hardware, home improvement, or large retail store.

If your child already uses a night-light

2. Set the timer so the light comes on about 30 minutes before your child's bedtime and goes off around the time your child is currently waking up in the morning to start the day. For you, the light should go on at _____ and off at _____.
3. During your bedtime routine and at bedtime, point at the light and say, "The light is on, it is sleeping time!"
4. If your child wakes during the night or before his current wake time, go in and point at the light and remind him, "The light is on, it is sleeping time!"
5. Once the light goes off in the morning, be ready to get up with your child. Point at the light and make a very big deal that the light is off and it is time to get up.

If your child does not use a night-light

2. Set the timer so the light comes on around the time your child is currently waking up in the morning to start the day. For you, the light should go on at _____.
3. During your bedtime routine and at bedtime point at the light and say, "The light is off, it is sleeping time!"
4. If your child wakes during the night or before his current wake time, go in and point at the light and remind him, "The light is off, it is sleeping time!"
5. Once the light goes on in the morning, be ready to get up with your child. Point at the light and make a very big deal that the light is on and it is time to get up.

After 1 to 2 weeks of pairing the light with your child's current waking time

6. Once your child understands that the light signals that it is morning time, you can move the timer so his wake time is 15 minutes later. You can continue to move the timer 15 minutes later every 5 to 7 days until the desired wake time is reached.
7. Once in place the Good Morning Light can also be used for naptime.

Important Things to Remember

- You must respond consistently to all night wakings for your child to understand that when the light changes, it is time to get up. For example, if you bring your child to your bed before the light changes, he will not look at the light to see if it is time to get up but will continue waking up hoping that eventually you'll take him to your bed.
- Make sure your child can see the light, otherwise he will not make the association between the light changing and waking up.
- At the same time, make sure your child cannot play with or change the timer.
- Once your child makes the association, do not change the time too quickly!! This can result in child frustration and prolonged crying.

> The Good Morning Light provides a quick and easy visual cue for your child to learn the difference between night and day. However, for it to really work, you need to have the light change at a time close to your child's current wake time. You also need to provide a consistent response to nighttime awakenings and not "rescue" your child before the light changing.

HANDOUT 9

Bedtime Chart

The Bedtime Chart will help you and your child have a consistent bedtime routine every night. If used consistently and with follow-through, it can also reduce the amount of bedtime protests and stalling you experience. The following provides guidance on how to create and effectively use a Bedtime Chart.

1. **Create a short, consistent bedtime routine that moves in one direction** (e.g., from the kitchen to the bathroom to the child's bedroom) **and ends in the child's sleeping environment.** For you, this bedtime routine will be _____
   _____.
2. **Find pictures that show every step of the routine.** This is something that you and your child can do together. Pictures for each activity on the chart (e.g., cup for a drink, toothbrush, toilet) can be taken with your camera, downloaded from the Internet, cut out from magazines, or simply drawn by your child.
3. **Put the pictures in order on a poster board or on individual pieces of heavy paper if making a book.**
4. **Every night, follow the steps of the chart in order.** Your chart can include a place for a sticker or check mark to show that each step is completed.

Important Things to Remember
- You can use a timer to help your child complete each step in an age-appropriate yet timely manner.
- If your child protests (which she will do the first few nights), be consistent and repeatedly refer to the chart ("The chart says it is now time to go potty" or "The chart says we've already read our two books tonight, so we'll have to save that book for tomorrow").

The Bedtime Chart provides a quick and easy visual reminder of what happens in the bedtime routine. This will ensure that your child has a consistent bedtime routine every night and that if there are two parents/caregivers, the routine does not change from night to night. If followed consistently, the bedtime chart will also reduce bedtime protests and stalling as your child can't argue with the chart or make requests of the chart the same way they would argue or make requests of you.

HANDOUT 10

Bedtime Fading

One reason your child may have difficulty falling asleep at night is due to his internal clock. Although you may have tried to have an early bedtime, your child rarely falls asleep before a certain time. *Bedtime fading* matches your child's bedtime with his natural sleep onset time in order to reduce bedtime problems. Once your child learns to fall asleep quickly at the designated time, then you can begin to gradually move his bedtime earlier. The following provides guidance on how to use bedtime fading with your child.

1. **Your child's new bedtime will be** _____. This means you should start his bedtime routine about 30 to 45 minutes before this, at _____.
2. **Your child's wake time on both weekdays and weekend days will be** _____. If he does not wake on his own, you will have to wake him at this time.
3. **In between his previous bedtime and this new bedtime, your child should engage in quiet activities that do not involve electronics.** This can include reading, drawing, or playing with dolls or LEGOs.
4. **After 5 to 7 nights of the child falling asleep quickly (under 30 minutes) and easily, you can begin to move his bedtime earlier by 15 minutes.**
5. **To reach the desired bedtime of** _____ **you can then move his bedtime earlier by 15 minutes every week** (or after 5 to 7 nights of him falling asleep quickly and easily).

Important Things to Remember

▪ Your child must have the same bedtime and wake time <u>every</u> night, both during the week and on weekends.
▪ Although it may seem strange to delay your child's bedtime, he is not really getting any less sleep than he is right now. Your child rarely (if ever) falls asleep before the new set bedtime, and this way he will learn to fall asleep faster at bedtime, reducing bedtime protests and struggles.
▪ **DO NOT** move his bedtime up too quickly! Gradual changes to bedtimes and wake times are not as noticeable to the body, with children adapting to the new time within about a week. However, rapid changes (e.g., 1 hour at a time) will be very noticeable and will make falling asleep harder for your child.

> *Some children cannot fall asleep early because of their natural internal clock. Bedtime fading addresses this issue by helping your child learn to fall asleep quickly at a set bedtime. Over time, you will be able to gradually move this bedtime earlier, reducing the bedtime struggles that often result from a child who is simply not tired at the designated bedtime.*

HANDOUT 11

Moving Parents Out

Many children have difficulty falling asleep without a parent in the room. To teach your child to fall asleep by himself, we need to gradually move you out of the room. The following provides guidance on how to move yourself out of the room at bedtime while not causing too much stress for your child.

1. **Have a consistent bedtime routine and a consistent bedtime in place.** For your child, this routine should include: _____ _____ and should end at _____ p.m.
2. **At the end of the routine, you should place your child in bed awake, and then stay with him until he is asleep.**
3. **Don't interact too much with your child.** This is not the time for questions or conversation. If your child tries to interact with you, have a consistent, simple response (e.g., "It is time to sleep now, I love you").
4. **After 3 to 5 nights of your child falling asleep relatively easily, you will move a little bit further away.** For some children this will be 1 to 2 feet every few nights. With other children, you can move first to the middle of the room (between the bed and the door), and then after a few more successful nights move to the doorway. The last move will be to the hallway outside the door (out of view of the child).
5. **When your child wakes during the night, you should respond immediately and consistently.** For your family, these responses should include _____ _____.

Important Things to Remember

- Your child may protest or try to interact with you more on the second night than the first night!
- If your child continues to try and interact with you, take a short break and return only when he agrees to lie quietly in bed.
- If your child gets out of bed and comes to you, simply return him to bed with minimal interaction, saying, "It's sleeping time, you need to stay in bed."

By gradually moving yourself away from your child at bedtime, he will learn to fall asleep without you there. Although it may take a little while to reach the goal of him falling asleep independently, you should see fewer "curtain calls" and bedtime protests, making bedtime less stressful for everyone in the house.

HANDOUT 12

Take a Break

We all have our favorite ways of falling asleep; for your child, that is falling asleep with you present. "Take a Break" is used to teach your child to fall asleep independently at bedtime with minimal protests. The following provides guidance on how to "Take a Break" with your child.

1. **Have a consistent bedtime routine and a consistent bedtime in place.** For your child this routine should include the following: _____
_____ and should end at _____ p.m.
2. **At the end of the routine, you should place your child in bed awake.** If you are not already consistently staying with your child in her bed at bedtime, for the first few nights, you should simply stay with her until she falls asleep. This will help to solidify her bedtime and ability to fall asleep at this time.
3. **After bedtime and sleep onset are consistent, stay with your child for 5 to 10 minutes (or less than half the time it takes her to fall asleep), then take a break!** Tell your child, "I'll be right back, Mommy has to use the potty" or "Daddy needs to brush his teeth, I'll be back shortly." For the first few nights, this break should only be 1 to 2 minutes (or less if you have a highly anxious child or a child who won't stay in bed alone for a long time).
4. **Return from your break and praise your child for staying in bed and trying to fall asleep.** Then remain with your child until she falls asleep.
5. **Each night, your break should get a little bit longer.** The goal is for your child to fall asleep while you are not in the room.
6. **Always return to check on your child after a certain amount of time.** If she is not asleep, stay with her until she falls asleep.
7. **If your child wakes during the night, you should respond immediately and consistently.** For your family, this response should be _____
_____.

Important Things to Remember
- As your break gets longer each night, be sure to set a timer to remind you to go back and check on your child.
- If your child gets out of bed before you return, return her to bed with minimal interaction, simply saying, "It's sleeping time, you need to stay in bed." The next night, you may need to shorten your break and then provide even more verbal praise for when the child does stay in bed as instructed.

Some children cannot fall asleep without a parent close by, whether in their bed or in their room. Take a Break is a gradual way to teach your child to fall asleep at bedtime without you present. Although it takes a little while to reach the goal of your child falling asleep independently, this approach reduces "curtain calls" and bedtime protests, making bedtime less stressful for everyone in the house.

HANDOUT 13

The Second Goodnight

Children rarely want to go to bed, preferring instead to stay up and play or simply spend time with parents. The result can be bedtime protests, stalling, or "curtain calls" (getting out of bed over and over to ask for something). The Second Goodnight is one way to teach your child to stay in bed and fall asleep independently with minimal protests. The following provides guidance on how to use the Second Goodnight with your child.

1. **Have a consistent bedtime routine and a consistent bedtime in place.** For your child, this routine should include the following: _____ and should end at _____ p.m.

2. **For each step of the bedtime routine, your child should earn a token for completing the task in a timely fashion.** Some examples of tokens are poker chips, tickets, or marbles placed in a jar. You will need to create some type of reward system where he can exchange tokens in the morning for a small age-appropriate prize (e.g., sticker, small toy, 15 extra minutes of screen time). One of the best rewards is not food or money but special time with a parent doing a favorite activity (e.g., bike ride, hitting baseballs, painting fingernails).

3. **Following a consistent bedtime routine and at a consistent time each night, your child should be placed in his own bed.**

4. **Once he is in bed, you should leave the room and return for a "second goodnight."** If your child is still lying quietly in bed, he earns a token.

5. **If your child calls out or gets out of bed, return him to bed with minimal interaction other than to remind him it is bedtime.** Then remove one token.

6. **The first few nights, you should return for multiple goodnight checks (e.g., every 5 minutes).** Each time, the child should be verbally praised and given another token. After the first few nights, the time in between goodnight checks should be increased each night.

7. **If your child wakes during the night, you should respond immediately and consistently.** For your family, this response should be _____ .

Important Things to Remember

▪ Although it may feel as if you are bribing your child for staying in bed, you are actually rewarding him for doing what you want. Over time, the need for rewards at bedtime will decrease as your child learns the skill of quickly and easily falling asleep at bedtime.

   Parental attention is very motivating to children, this is why they will make "curtain calls" or protest at bedtime. The Second Goodnight provides your child the desired attention, but in this case for the behavior that you want to see—him staying in bed and falling asleep. By regularly checking on your child and rewarding him for staying in bed, you are providing brief, frequent, and positive interactions that will reduce the stress of bedtime and help your child fall asleep easier.

HANDOUT 14

The Sleep Fairy

Children rarely want to go to bed, preferring instead to stay up and play or simply spend time with parents. The result can be bedtime protests, stalling, or "curtain calls" (getting out of bed over and over to ask for something). The Sleep Fairy is one way to encourage your child to stay in bed and fall asleep with minimal protests. The following provides guidance on how to use the Sleep Fairy with your child.

1. **Your child should be told that there is a Sleep Fairy who will come to visit her if she goes to bed when asked and falls asleep, leaving a small prize under her pillow.** Depending on the age of the child, prizes can include stickers, a penny, a small toy from the dollar store, or a couple of favorite treats (chocolate chips) in a bag.
2. **Following a consistent bedtime routine and bedtime, your child should be placed in bed.** She should be reminded that the Sleep Fairy will come to visit after she is asleep. Every night for 2 weeks, you should place a small prize under your child's pillow after she is asleep.
3. **After those initial 2 weeks, your child should be told that you don't know when the Sleep Fairy is going to come now because she has a lot of houses to visit.** You can leave a prize every second or third day initially and then on other random days to keep your child guessing.

   Children who are old enough to understand the Tooth Fairy often respond quickly to the Sleep Fairy, who rewards them for falling asleep. By receiving a prize every night for 2 weeks, your child learns to fall asleep at bedtime with fewer protests. After that, the use of a more irregular rewards schedule will help keep your child going to bed and falling asleep, as she is unsure if this is one of the nights the Sleep Fairy will come to visit.

HANDOUT 15

The Bedtime Pass

Children rarely want to go to bed, preferring instead to stay up and play or simply spend time with parents. The result can be bedtime protests, stalling, or "curtain calls" (getting out of bed over and over to ask for something). The Bedtime Pass is one way to teach your child to stay in bed and fall asleep independently with minimal protests. The following provides guidance on how to use the Bedtime Pass with your child.

1. **Have a consistent bedtime routine and a consistent bedtime in place.** For your child this routine should include the following: _____ and should end at _____ p.m.
2. **Following the bedtime routine, your child should be placed in his own bed and given a Bedtime Pass.** A Bedtime Pass is a notecard that he can decorate or some other type of tangible ticket or token. The first few nights, you may want to give your child two or three Bedtime Passes until he fully understands how the Bedtime Pass works.
3. **Your child should be reminded that if he calls out or gets out of bed, he will have to give up the Bedtime Pass.** Otherwise, if he keeps the pass, it can be exchanged in the morning for a small age-appropriate prize (e.g., sticker, small toy, 15 extra minutes of screen time). One of the best rewards is not food or money but special time with a parent doing a favorite activity (e.g., bike ride, painting fingernails, going to the playground).
4. **Once he is in bed, you should leave the room.** If your child calls out or gets up, you should respond to his request (e.g., another hug, a drink of water), return him to bed, and remove the Bedtime Pass.
5. **If your child calls out or gets up after he no longer has a Bedtime Pass, you should return him to bed with minimal interaction, ignoring any other requests.**

Important Things to Remember

- The Bedtime Pass can also be a Nighttime Pass for those children who wake you up in the middle of the night for an unnecessary reason.
- The rewards you and your child choose need to be motivating enough that he will want to hold on to his Bedtime Pass. Over time, the rewards may have to change to keep your child motivated. In addition, after the first week, you can require your child to earn more than one Bedtime Pass in order to earn a prize.
- When responding to your child, your interactions should be very brief, minimal, and boring. Otherwise the requests and curtain calls will continue as he is getting the attention he desires.

Parental attention is very motivating to children, this is why they will make "curtain calls" or protest at bedtime. The physical presence of the Bedtime Pass allows him to decide whether he would rather have immediate attention or a reward in the morning. That said, once the pass is gone, your child will quickly learn it is better to keep the pass, as he will not be getting your attention as desired.

HANDOUT 16

Flashlight Treasure Hunts

It is very common for young children to have a fear of the dark. Often, this can keep them from wanting to go to bed by themselves. The best way for anyone to learn to manage fears and worries is called *exposure with response prevention*. This means that the child is exposed to what she is afraid of (like the dark) but prevented from responding in the way she otherwise would to avoid her fear (like leaving the bedroom or calling out for you). The following provides guidance on how to help your child learn to face the fear using Flashlight Treasure Hunts, a very gradual and fun approach.

1. Without telling your child where it is, **hide a favorite toy in a simple location in the bedroom** that she can find quickly.
2. **Turn off the lights in the bedroom and have your child use a flashlight** to go into the bedroom and find the hidden toy.
3. **As she feels more comfortable and less scared, hide more toys** (3–5). This should then encourage your child to stay in the dark for a gradually longer period of time.
4. **Next, hide the toys in more difficult locations,** which again encourages her to stay in the dark room with the flashlight for a longer period of time.
   ▪ Your child should begin to **associate the darkened room with fun activities** rather than fear.
   ▪ Over time, your child should **begin to feel less afraid and more in control.**

Important Things to Remember
▪ It may be helpful in the beginning to reward your child with small prizes (e.g., stickers, tokens) for finding the hidden toy. For children who feel very afraid, this may give them the push to go into the dark room when they would otherwise feel too scared to do so.
▪ Your child may cope better with the fear by learning to say positive things while on the flashlight treasure hunt:
   ▪ I am brave.
   ▪ I am strong.
   ▪ It's just for a minute.
   ▪ Your child should say _____
   _____
   _____

Even children with the worst fear of the dark can learn to feel more comfortable in a dark bedroom, which can help them fall asleep better. As your child learns to face the fear, you may also see this confidence spread to other parts of her life. A child who learns to conquer a fear of the dark can learn to conquer many other fears and worries!

HANDOUT 17A

Parents Helping Their Children Overcome Fear of the Dark

Fear of the dark is one of the most common fears experienced by children. For some kids, however, this fear can be so powerful that they do not want to go to bed at bedtime or they get up from bed over and over again, asking parents to either stay with them or help them make sure there is nothing scary in their room. For children with severe fears that keep them from going to or staying in bed, a treatment called *exposure with response prevention* can be very helpful. This means that the child is exposed to his fear of the dark but is prevented from responding the way he otherwise would to avoid his fear (like leaving the bedroom or calling out for you). Over time, your child should start to feel confident that the dark room isn't such a bad place to be alone. The following provides guidance on how to use exposure with response prevention with your child.

1. **First, identify what your child is most afraid of.** This can be being in the room alone, being in the room in the dark, being in the room in the dark alone, and so on. Write down your child's specific fears here: _____
_____
_____

2. **Now think about these fears in order from what is the least scary to most scary** (called a *fear hierarchy*). For example, some children might say:
   1. Being in the room in the dark with mom and dad there.
   2. Being in the room alone with the light on.
   3. Being in the room alone with the bedroom light off but the hall light on.
   4. Being in the room alone with the bedroom light and the hall light off.
   ▪ Write down your child's fears in order from least to most scary here: _____
   _____
   _____
   _____

3. **Now think about ways to help your child learn to feel less scared with each step of the fear hierarchy.** Start with having your child do Step 1 of the fear. For the child in our example, this would be going into the bedroom in the dark with mom or dad there. For your child, Step 1 will be _____

4. **During the time that your child is doing Step 1, remind him to work on deep breathing and making positive, brave statements.** These positive statements can be things such as "I am brave"; "I am a big big boy"; and "I am safe." Your child's positive statements can be
_____
_____

5. **For deep breathing, remind your child of these steps.**
   ▪ Take in a big, slow breath through your nose.
   ▪ Feel the breath fill up your belly like a balloon.
   ▪ Count slowly to 5 while you breathe in.
   ▪ Slowly blow out your breath through your mouth like you are blowing out a candle.
   ▪ Count slowly to 5 while you breathe out.
   ▪ Repeat these steps while you are doing Step 1 of the fear hierarchy.
   ▪ Have your child rate his fear on the Fear Scale, below.
   ▪ Repeat Step 1 every day until your child's fear falls below a 4 on the scale.
   ▪ Once your child's fear falls below a 4, go on to Step 2, repeating all of the above steps.

(continued)

Important Points to Remember

- Most children with fears will ask you for reassurance over and over again. But providing this reassurance repeatedly will **increase** the likelihood that your child will stay afraid and think that you are needed to provide comfort.
- Instead, tell your child one time that he is safe, and then your only responses should be to encourage him to use deep breathing and repeat positive, brave statements. This will help your child start to gradually develop more confidence in battling those fears.

Even children with the worst fear of being alone in the dark can learn to feel more comfortable in a dark bedroom, which can help them fall asleep better. As your child learns to face the fear, you may also see this confidence spread to other parts of his life. A child who learns to conquer a fear of the dark can learn to conquer many other fears and worries!

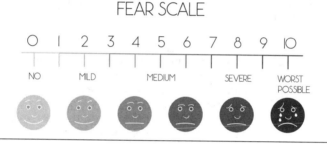

FEAR SCALE

HANDOUT 17B

Getting Rid of Fears

All kids feel scared from time to time. For some kids, it can be scary to go to bed at night alone in a room that is dark. But there are ways to feel brave and less scared when you are in a dark room. Your mom, dad, or another adult can help you do things to help yourself feel more brave.

1. Your mom or dad will help you **decide what you are most afraid of.**
2. Then they will help you **decide what is the LEAST scary.**
3. **Your mom or dad will help you do the least scary part.** This might be going into your bedroom with the light off but with your mom or dad there with you. This is called *facing your fear.*
4. **While you are facing your fear, there are things you can do to help yourself feel calm and brave.** This can be telling yourself good things and deep breathing. Good things to tell yourself can be, for example, "I am brave"; "I am a big big girl [or boy]"; and "I am safe." Write down some good things you can tell yourself here:_____

_____

5. **For deep breathing, remember these steps:**
   ▪ Take in a big, slow breath through your nose.
   ▪ Feel the breath fill up your belly like a balloon.
   ▪ Count slowly to 5 while you breathe in.
   ▪ Slowly blow out your breath through your mouth like you are blowing out a candle.
   ▪ Count slowly to 5 while you breathe out.
   ▪ Repeat at least 10 times.
6. **Tell your mom or dad how scared you feel by pointing to the face below that shows your fear:**

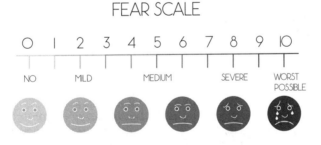

FEAR SCALE

7. **After you feel less scared with that fear, you will then go on to the next scary thing** (like being in your bedroom alone for 5 seconds with a flashlight) until you have faced your whole fear.

Remember: You might want to ask your mom or dad over and over if you are going to be okay or if you can stop facing your fear. They will tell you one time that you are okay, and then they will remind you to tell yourself good things and to breathe deeply. This helps you learn to face your fear and know that you are brave.

Learning to face your fears helps you know that you are growing up and that you can do things on your own, even if they are scary. You can do it!

HANDOUT 18

Worry Time

We all know that we need to be relaxed to fall asleep. Worrying at bedtime makes it hard to relax, which will then make it very difficult to fall asleep. Children who are "worriers" can spend most of their day and night worrying or asking parents to help them put aside their worries. Worry Time helps children understand that they can set aside time for their brain to worry and free up the rest of their day and bedtime for more helpful, relaxing thoughts. The following provides guidance on how to do Worry Time with your child.

1. **Set aside time each day for your child to worry.** Your child should worry ____ times per day for ____ minutes each.
2. **Together with your child, decide when this time should be** (although it should not be right before bedtime). For example, some children may choose to use the 15 minutes before dinner as their Worry Time. Your child's Worry Time will be _____

   _____
3. **Your child may choose to worry alone or with you there.**
4. **During Worry Time, your child can think, write down, or tell you about any and all worries.** You and/or your child may spend much of that time problem solving how to best address those worries.
5. **Any other time that your child begins to worry, give a reminder that this worry will need to wait for the next Worry Time.**

Important Things to Remember

▪ It may seem a little bit strange to a child who worries to be asked to "worry as much as you can." The purpose of Worry Time is to help your child learn to set aside worries during other times of the day. Once she learns to do that, your child learns to control the worrying better.
▪ After a short time (1–2 weeks), many children will begin to run out of worries during Worry Time. If you find that is the case, use the time to do something fun with your child: Play a game together, talk about your day, or go for a walk together. This can become special time between you and your child.
▪ Some children like to have a more concrete way to manage their worries. You can have your child write down the worries and place them in a box to "lock them away" for the rest of the day. Then, at the next Worry Time, your child can pull the worries back out of the box to see if they are still worried about it.

Worry Time can help your child learn to stop the worries throughout the day and at bedtime. By telling themselves, "I can worry about this later," children can be freed to have more positive, helpful thoughts. When children are able to stop worrying at bedtime, they will start to fall asleep much more easily.

HANDOUT 19

Think Like a Detective

Sometimes, kids find that they worry so much that they cannot make the worries stop. When that happens, worries can grow bigger and bigger until it is hard to tell whether these worries are about things that really might happen or about things that probably won't happen. You can help decide whether you should be worrying by thinking like a detective. Detectives look for clues to find out what the real solution is. When you are thinking like a detective, you can write down the answers to these questions or have your mom, dad, or other adult help you. Below is a sample chart you can use, showing an example about being worried about failing a test.

My worry	Is this true?	How likely is this to happen? (0–10; 0 = *not at all*; 5 = *it might happen*; 10 = *it definitely will happen*)	How can I stop this from happening?	How likely is that to work? (0–10; 0 = *not at all*; 5 = *it might work*; 10 = *it definitely will work*)
I am going to fail my test.	I don't really know yet because I haven't taken my test. No—this isn't true.	5	I can study for my test. I can ask my mom or dad to quiz me.	8

Now that you have thought like a detective, you can decide what a better, more helpful thought can be. In our example, we can think, "If I study hard for my test, I will probably make a good grade." For you, once you have thought like a detective and decided what you can do about your worry, write down a more helpful thought here:

_____

_____

_____

Remember that it takes practice to learn how to think like a detective. If you have thoughts that make you worried when you are trying to fall asleep (or go back to sleep), your body will not relax like it needs to in order to fall asleep. So, if you practice thinking like a detective during the day, it can help teach you to change the worries that are making it hard for you to sleep at night.

(continued)

HANDOUT 19 (*Continued*)

Think Like a Detective Practice Chart

My worry	Is this true?	How likely is this to happen? (0–10; 0 = *not at all*; 5 = *it might happen*; 10 = *it definitely will happen*)	How can I stop this from happening?	How likely is that to work? (0–10; 0 = *not at all*; 5 = *it might work*; 10 = *it definitely will work*)

HANDOUT 20

Monster Spray

For children who are afraid of monsters, ghosts, witches, or other imaginary creatures, "Monster Spray" can be just the trick to help them feel like they can get rid of those feared creatures!

- **Fill a spray bottle with water and put a label on it that says "Monster Spray"** (or "Ghost Spray," "Witch Spray," etc.).
- **You can tell your child that**
  - "Monsters are allergic to this spray and that they will sneeze if they come too close to it"; or
  - "Monster Spray protects you from monsters the same way that bug spray protects you from bugs;" or
  - You can be creative. If you can think of something that will help your child feel as if he can get rid of the feared creatures, you can change the Monster Spray instructions.
- **Let your child spray the Monster Spray around his room to "protect him from the monsters"** or anywhere that he believes the monster may hide (e.g., closet).
- **Repeat this every night before bed.**
- **You should eventually begin to see your child using the spray less and less** as he begins to believe that the monsters won't come back.

  Monster Spray can be a fun way to help your child feel safe and in control at bedtime (and during the night) by making sure that he can get rid of anything that causes fear.

HANDOUT 21

Helping Your Child Have More Helpful Thoughts

All of us worry from time to time, but children who have excessive worries at bedtime can have a very difficult time falling asleep. As hard as it may be to control worries during the day, when a child is alone at bedtime, worries can take on a life of their own. To help children learn to control worries at night, they first have to understand how to control worries during the day. They can then begin to use this skill at night. The following provides guidance on how you can help your child have more helpful thoughts.

1. **It is important to teach children to problem solve when experiencing worries** (but only during the day). Children should not spend time in their bed generating solutions to all of their worries. If they learn to worry at specific times of the day, and generate solutions to their problems, they can then remind themselves at bedtime that they have already worried and/or already thought of solutions. The Think Like a Detective and Worry Time exercises can assist you in helping your child deal with her worries during the day, helping her sleep better at night.

2. **It is natural to want to comfort your child when she is upset because of her worries.** When a child has a lot of worries, many parents find that they want to reassure their child that she is okay, that the worries are not real, and that she does not need to worry about those things. The more you reassure your child, however, the more she will seek you out for those reassurances. When that happens at bedtime, it may look as if your child is stalling by getting out of bed repeatedly.

3. To help your child develop confidence in her ability to manage these worries, it **is helpful to provide reassurance only once** and then turn to the skills she is using to help manage her worries (Worry Time, Thinking Like a Detective, problem solving, etc.). For example, you can remind your child, "You know how to think like a detective. How likely is this worry to happen? How can you stop it from happening?"

4. **As you provide less reassurance** and guide your child to use the skills she is learning to manage worry, **you will see your child gain confidence** in her ability to manage her own worries.

   Remember that most parents want to reassure their child that everything is going to be okay. Although this is a caring idea, it often serves to increase the child's dependence on the parent for providing comfort. Instead, by guiding your child to use the skills she is learning to manage worry, your child can begin to feel more self-confident. As this skill is built during the day, you will then see better sleep at night.

HANDOUT 22

Helping Your Child Be the Boss of Her Dreams

Many children have occasional nightmares. For children who have nightmares almost every night or several times a night, however, this can be very disruptive to the child's (and the parents') sleep. The following provides guidance on how to help your child be the boss of her dreams.

1. **Have your child describe a recent nightmare.** Ask for as many details as possible. What does your child see, hear, feel, smell, taste in the dream? What happens? Who is there?
2. **Have your child draw the dream** with as much detail as possible.
3. **Tell your child that she can learn to be the boss of her own dreams!** She can decide what she wants to dream.
4. **Have your child make up what she would rather dream about.** Again, what will happen in the new dream? What will your child see, hear, feel, smell, taste? Who will be there?
   ▪ Some children will want to have the beginning of the same bad dream but change the ending to be more positive. For some kids, this can mean having control over the bad part of the dream. For example, a child who is afraid of being eaten by monsters may decide to have a new dream where she shrinks the monster to the size of an ant and blows it away. Let your child be as creative as she likes.
5. **Have your child draw the new dream with as much detail as possible.**
6. **Your child may want to tear up the drawing of the scary dream** and hang the drawing of the new dream above her bed.
7. **Have your child tell you about the new, positive dream several times during the day,** always remembering to use as much detail as possible. This may be easier if she can look at her drawing to remind her of all of the pieces of the new dream.
8. **Once she can describe the dream easily to you, have her start talking about the new dream just before she goes to bed,** reminding her that she can be the boss of her dreams and tell her brain to dream about the new dream hanging over her bed.
9. **If your child wakes up during the night having a nightmare, provide brief comfort and then guide your child again in describing the new positive dream to you during the night.**

   If your child regularly practices describing new positive dreams during the day and before going to bed, in a short period of time she will have far fewer nightmares. Once your child learns to be the boss of her dreams, she can start to feel more confident in her ability to conquer fears.

HANDOUT 23

Stimulus Control

One of the reasons you have a hard time falling asleep and/or staying asleep is that your body has learned to spend a lot of time in bed not sleeping. So now your body becomes anxious or tense when you get in bed, which is not going to help you sleep! So the goal of Stimulus Control is to reteach your body and your brain that when you get into bed you should fall asleep. The primary rule of Stimulus Control is, **The bed is for sleep, and sleep is for the bed.** The following provides guidance on how to follow this rule and use Stimulus Control to help you sleep.

1. **Use your bed only for sleep.** You should try to avoid other activities, such as reading, watching TV, text messaging, using Facebook, surfing the Internet, talking on the phone, or doing homework, because then your brain doesn't learn that the bed is for sleep.
2. **Sleep should only occur in bed.** Try to avoid sleeping on the couch or in other places, because this can also get in the way of your brain making the connection between your bed and sleep.
3. **Keep a regular bedtime and wake-up time.** The more regular your schedule, the easier it will be for you to fall asleep. Keep your bedtime and wake time on weekends within 1 hour of what it is during the week. Also, avoid sleeping during the day while you are working on this.
   My bedtime will be _____.
   My wake-up time will be _____.
4. **Go to bed only when you are sleepy.** This is tough! It sometimes requires a balance of waiting until you are sleepy but also trying to stick with your regular schedule. If at first the time you can actually fall asleep is much later than the time you would like to fall asleep, go to bed at a time you can actually fall asleep within 15 to 30 minutes (this may be later than your regular bedtime). Once this is happening, move your bedtime 15 minutes earlier every few days. It is okay if you are sleepier than usual at first. This sleepiness will help to reset your schedule.
5. **When you are trying to sleep, if you are not asleep in 15 to 20 minutes, you should get out of bed and do something relaxing until you feel sleepy before getting back into bed.** This is the <u>MOST IMPORTANT</u> part of the process. It will keep you from spending too much time in bed tossing and turning instead of sleeping.
   ▪ Don't watch the clock. Just guess when 15 to 20 minutes have passed. Usually, this is the point where you start to worry that you will not fall asleep, or during the night, it is the point when you start counting how many hours you have left until your alarm goes off.
   ▪ For the first 2 to 3 weeks, you may be getting up quite a bit while your brain is retraining.
   ▪ Plan ahead of time what you are going to do during the time you are out of bed. What could you do during that time?

   _____
   _____
   _____

Following the rules of Stimulus Control is really hard and takes a lot of motivation and discipline to be successful. At first, you will feel as if your sleep is getting a little bit worse and not better. But remember, we are retraining your body to relearn healthy sleeping patterns, and just like any new skill, it takes practice to get really good at it. So if you are consistent and follow this plan every night, you will soon find yourself falling asleep faster and staying asleep through the night.

HANDOUT 24

Sleep Restriction

Although you may want to sleep a certain amount of time (e.g., 8 or 9 hours), right now your body is only producing a certain amount of sleep. So, even if you spend long periods of time in bed, your body will not sleep for that entire time, resulting in feelings of frustration and poor quality sleep. Sleep Restriction is used to more closely match the amount of time you spend in bed with the amount of sleep your body is producing. The following provides guidance on how to use Sleep Restriction to help you sleep.

1. **Limit your time in bed to** _____. This number is based on the information you provided about your average sleep duration (plus a little time to fall asleep). This means you should have a bedtime of _____ and a wake time of _____.
2. **Don't go to bed earlier than you are supposed to.** Although you may feel sleepy, if you go to bed too early your internal clock may not be ready to sleep and you may not have enough sleep pressure to help you fall asleep. Alternatively, you may go to bed early but then only sleep 1 to 2 hours and be up for the rest of the night. In other words, you are simply taking a late evening nap that interferes with your ability to get nighttime sleep.
3. **Go to bed only if you are sleepy (and not before your scheduled bedtime).** Again, if you are not sleepy, going to bed too early will only cause stress and frustration that you are not sleeping. By keeping a consistent bedtime and wake time you are also helping to set your internal clock, as well as building up sufficient sleep pressure to fall asleep.
4. **Wake up and get out of bed at the designated wake time.** Even if you haven't had the best night of sleep, it is really important that you stick to the set wake time of _____, **even on weekends.** Although challenging, it is really important to provide your internal clock with a consistent schedule. Also, if you sleep in, you may not have enough sleep pressure to help you fall asleep quickly at bedtime.
5. **If at all possible, no napping!** Unless you have activities that may be unsafe if you do not have a short nap, naps will interfere with your ability to fall asleep at night by reducing your sleep pressure.

Calculating Sleep Efficiency

The goal of sleep restriction is to have sleep efficiency of at least 85% before increasing the amount of time you spend in bed. *Sleep efficiency* is the proportion of time you spend sleeping compared with the amount of time you spend in bed. Specifically:

$$\text{Total Sleep Time / Time in Bed} \times 100$$

For example, if you went to bed at 11:00 p.m. and woke up at 7:00 a.m., your time in bed is 8 hours. But if it took you 1 hour to fall asleep and you were awake for 1 hour during the night, your total sleep time is only 6 hours.

$$6 / 8 \times 100 = 75\%$$

Until you have an 85% or higher sleep efficiency for at least a week, you should not go to bed any earlier or wake any later than the set times you've been given.

Although it may seem strange to hear that you should stay up later when your goal is to sleep more, until your body learns to sleep more efficiently you need to limit how much time you spend in bed. For the first few nights, it may feel as if you are sleeping less than before, but soon you should be falling asleep faster and waking less frequently or for shorter periods of time.

HANDOUT 25

Thought Record

The reason you use a Thought Record is to help you notice thoughts and beliefs that may make it harder for you to sleep. You will begin to learn how to identify and then change any thoughts or beliefs that make it hard for you to fall asleep or stay asleep. You learn this by writing down your thoughts and then coming up with other thoughts (or things you can say to yourself) to change that thought. Below is an example of how to fill out your Thought Record. It is important that you fill your Thought Record out every day. If you don't practice this skill during the day, it will be of no use to you at night!

Situation (date/time)	Automatic thoughts (what were you thinking?)	Feelings (rate intensity of each one from 0%–100%)	Other thoughts/ helpful coping statements	Feelings (rate intensity of each one from 0%–100%)
3/29, 1:30 p.m. sitting in class feeling tired	I'm never going to get through today I'm going to fail this class	Upset (100%) Worried (80%) Tired (100%)	I may not feel good, but somehow I always make it through the day. I've had insomnia for 2 years and have not gotten below a *B*	Upset (60%) Worried (20%) Tired (70%)
3/30, 2:00 a.m. lying in bed	I only have 4 hours before I have to get up; tomorrow will be miserable	Annoyed (100%) Upset (80%)	Even though I don't have much time to sleep, I always do okay. I don't even have to look at the clock. The last time I stayed awake this long, I still did fine the next day.	Annoyed (50%) Upset (60%)

HANDOUT 25 (Continued)

At first, it may feel strange to notice your thoughts and how they make you feel, but our body reacts to how we are feeling. When you are trying to fall asleep (or go back to sleep), if you have thoughts that make you stressed or worried, your body will not relax like it needs to do to fall asleep. Practicing with a Thought Record during the day will help teach you to identify and change thoughts that are making it hard for you to sleep.

Situation (date/time)	Automatic thoughts (what were you thinking?)	Feelings (rate intensity of each one from 0%–100%)	Other thoughts/helpful coping statements	Feelings (rate intensity of each one from 0%–100%)

HANDOUT 26

Bright Light Therapy

For people with a delayed circadian sleep–wake phase, it can be impossible to fall asleep at bedtime. It can be just as hard to wake up in the morning in time for school or work. Light in the morning is one of the best ways to make sure that the circadian rhythm is set to the correct time. Bright light therapy can teach your body to have a circadian rhythm that is matched with your school or work schedule. Here is how it works:

- **First, you need to wake up at about the same time every morning** (even on weekends!). For you this wake-up time should be _____.
- **Next, you need to have about the same bedtime every night.** This needs to be late enough that you can fall asleep in 30 minutes or less. It also needs to be early enough so that you get enough sleep at night. Your bedtime should be _____.
- **Every morning (7 days a week) when you wake up, you should sit about 12 to 18 inches from the light box** (or wear a light visor if you choose to buy a visor) for about 30 minutes each day.
- **If not using a visor, you may place the light box on a counter** while sitting in front of it. Light that comes from just above your eye level tends to work better on your internal clock.
- **Do not sit and stare at the light.** Instead, do something in front of the light (e.g., eat breakfast, read, watch TV, play a video game). Every once in a while, you may quickly glance toward the light box. <u>Do not look directly at the light.</u> This can give you headaches or eye problems.
- **Remember that the time you use the light is very important.** If you oversleep by more than 30 minutes in the morning or forget to use the light box, skip it for that day. Then start using your bright light therapy again the next day.
- **Once you are falling asleep pretty quickly, you should begin to move your bedtime and wake-up time by 15 minutes earlier every 2 to 5 days** (or however long it takes you to start falling asleep quickly at the new time).

Following the schedule and using light therapy every single day will make a huge difference to both your sleep and how you feel during the day! With regular use, light therapy should help you feel more awake in the morning. This can help you "get going" faster and do better at school or work in the morning. You should also start to feel sleepier closer to your new bedtime, making it easier to fall asleep faster. This will allow you to slowly move your bedtime earlier. In turn, you should get more sleep at night and still wake up in time for school or work in the morning.

HANDOUT 27

Chronotherapy

For people with a delayed circadian sleep–wake phase, it can be impossible to fall asleep at bedtime and equally difficult to wake up in the morning early enough for school or work. As you know, if you try to move your bedtime earlier, it can be hard to fall asleep, but if you go to bed later than you usually do, it is easier to fall asleep. This is because all humans have a circadian rhythm that is a little bit longer than 24 hours, unlike our clocks, which run on a strict 24-hour day. By taking advantage of this fact, we can move your bedtime and wake-up time later by a few hours each day. After about a week, you will be at the target bedtime and wake-up time that will enable you to get enough sleep but still wake up in time to go to school or work. The following provides guidance on how to use chronotherapy.

▪ Based on your sleep diary and report, you have been falling asleep most nights around _____. To ensure that you get enough sleep, this would mean that you should be waking up at _____.
▪ For the next _____ days, you should go to bed at _____ and wake up at _____.
▪ Then, you should go to bed and wake up 3 hours later each day until you get to your desired bedtime of _____ and wake-up time of _____.

Your sleep schedule should look like this.

	Bedtime	Wake-up time
Day 1		
Day 2		
Day 3		
Day 4		
Day 5		
Day 6		
Day 7		

Chronotherapy can work very quickly to move your bedtime and wake-up time to where they should be to help you wake up in time for school or work and still feel rested. Because of your delayed internal clock, it is really easy to go to bed later each night. This is good for chronotherapy but can be really bad if you are not consistent with following this schedule! Thus it is critical that you go to bed and wake up every day at the set times, and once you reach your target bedtime and wake time, consistency is key. Even staying up late one night and sleeping in the following morning can be enough to undo the changes you have made to your sleep schedule.

HANDOUT 28

Confusional Arousals, Sleep Terrors, and Sleepwalking

Confusional arousals, sleep terrors, sleep talking, and sleepwalking are all *disorders of arousal*, also known as *partial arousal parasomnias* (which literally means "partially awake and partially asleep"). Although your child may appear confused, distressed, or engage in behaviors as if he were awake, he is actually sleeping through these events. In addition, even though he may be saying things that are confusing or distressing, he is not dreaming or having a nightmare.

Information About Parasomnias
- Parasomnias usually occur in the first part of the night, as this is the time we get most of our deepest (or slow-wave) sleep.
- These events are typically benign and self-limiting. This means they are not a sign of underlying psychopathology or trauma but are rather a physiological occurrence that happens as your child transitions between sleep stages.
- The primary trigger for parasomnias is insufficient or poor-quality sleep. When people do not get enough sleep or their sleep is disrupted, they have more slow-wave sleep, and with more slow-wave sleep comes more parasomnias. So if your child is not getting enough sleep because of a late bedtime, early rise time, or a disruption to his sleep schedule, or if your child has a medical illness (e.g., asthma, ear infection) or sleep disorder (e.g., obstructive sleep apnea) that disrupts the quality of his sleep, he is at risk for having more frequent parasomnia events.

How to Manage Parasomnias
1. **Make sure your child is safe.** Although children with confusional arousal and sleep terrors may not get out of bed, those who sleepwalk are at risk for injuring themselves during the night. Here are some safety tips.
   - Make sure that doors and windows are locked. If a window is left open, ensure that it does not open wide enough for your child to climb out.
   - Use a bell or alarm to alert you if your child gets up. There are different types of bells or alarms that can be placed on your child's door. On the low-tech end, you can hang a cow bell or jingle bell on his doorknob to signal to you that he has left his room. On the high-tech end are wireless alarms that beep when the sensors are separated by an opened door or window.
   - Move things that are not in their normal places (e.g., toys in the hallway) that your child may trip over if he is sleepwalking.
   - Do not let your child sleep on a top bunk, and if you are concerned about him falling out of bed, move his mattress to the floor.
2. **Do not try to wake your child, as this will likely make the event last longer.** If your child is having a sleep terror, attend to him to ensure he is safe. If he is nonresponsive, let the sleep terror run its course. If your child is sleepwalking, simply guide him back to bed.
3. **Do not discuss the events in the morning.** Your child will not remember if he has a parasomnia event. However, if you discuss it with him the next day (e.g., "Do you know what you did last night?"), he may become fearful of having an event, which may delay sleep onset. This can result in your child not getting enough sleep and thus having even more parasomnia events.
4. **Have a consistent sleep schedule.** Parasomnias are more likely to occur when there is a schedule disruption, including a sleepover, late night because of a party or holiday, or when you go on vacation. Maintaining as close to a consistent sleep schedule as possible will reduce the likelihood of your child having a parasomnia event.

HANDOUT 28 *(Continued)*

5. **Try to increase your child's sleep duration.** For many children, simply getting a little more sleep each night is enough to decrease the frequency of parasomnias. You can either have your child go to bed 10 to 15 minutes earlier each night, or if you have to wake him in the morning, allow him an extra 10 to 15 minutes to sleep each morning. Although this does not seem like much, over 1 week an extra 15 minutes at bedtime or in the morning adds up to 1.75 hours of sleep!

6. **If your child is going to a sleepover or overnight camp, make sure the caregivers/staff are aware of his history of sleep terrors and sleepwalking so they are prepared to manage an event.**

Confusional arousals, sleep terrors, and sleepwalking are common events in childhood, especially in young children. Although these events are frightening for parents, children have no memories of these events, which are benign and self-limiting. To reduce the frequency of parasomnias, it is important to ensure your child has sufficient quality sleep each night, and when events occur, it is important to make sure your child is safe, and then try not to wake him or interfere with the event. Most children will naturally grow out of these events.

HANDOUT 29

Scheduled Awakenings for Disorders of Arousal (Parasomnias)

Confusional arousals, sleep terrors, sleep talking, and sleepwalking are different types of the same disorder. These events are also known as *partial arousal parasomnias* (which means "partially awake and partially asleep"). Your child may behave as if she is awake, or she may seem confused or upset. But she is actually sleeping through these events. Even though she may say things that do not make sense, she is not dreaming or having a nightmare.

Scheduled awakenings are used for children who have a lot of predictable parasomnia events. This means at least several times per week and around the same time each night. The following provides guidance on how to use scheduled awakenings with your child.

1. **For the next 2 weeks, keep track of your child's sleep patterns.** You should record her bedtime, wake time, and the timing of the parasomnia events.
2. **Once you see a consistent pattern of events, find the average time she has a sleep terror (or sleep walking) event and determine the amount of time between her falling asleep and the sleep terror event.** Scheduled awakenings should occur 15 to 30 minutes *before* she typically has her first event. So for example, if her average bedtime is 8:00 p.m. and her average sleep terror is at 9:30 p.m., the scheduled awakening time is between 9:00 and 9:15 p.m.
3. **At the designated time, go in and gently rouse your child** with a light touch or a soft verbal prompt.
4. **Once she arouses (i.e., opens her eyes, changes positions, and/or tells you that she is awake), allow her to return to sleep.**

Important Things to Remember

- If you cannot identify a consistent pattern for events, then you should not use scheduled awakenings.
- This is not a quick treatment! It usually takes 2 to 4 weeks of consistently waking her at the same time every night for the parasomnia events to subside.
- If the scheduled awakening time is after you usually go to bed, you will have to set an alarm clock to wake you at the same time each night. This will help you be consistent about arousing your child. (Although this feels like a disruption to your sleep, you will be waking up anyway when she has her event!)
- It is possible that you will trigger a sleep terror or sleep walking event in your child by using scheduled awakenings. If this happens, do not interfere with the event or try to wake her. Instead, move the scheduled awakening time earlier by 15 minutes.
- If you child has an event before the scheduled awakening time, move the time earlier by 15 minutes for subsequent nights.

Scheduled awakenings work well for children who have sleep terrors or sleep walking at the same time almost every night. However, this treatment can take 2 to 4 weeks, and you must be consistent every night for it to be effective.

HANDOUT 30

Dry Night Tracking Sheet

Sunday	Monday	Tuesday	Wednesday	Thursday	Friday	Saturday
Wet or Dry?	Wet or Dry?	Wet or Dry?	Wet or Dry?	Wet or Dry?	Wet or Dry?	Wet or Dry?
I woke up to my alarm.	I woke up to my alarm.	I woke up to my alarm.	I woke up to my alarm.	I woke up to my alarm.	I woke up to my alarm.	I woke up to my alarm.

 Color in on dry nights

 Color in on wet nights

 Color in if you wake up to your alarm

HANDOUT 31

Urine Alarm Training

Many children do not learn to sleep through the night without wetting the bed. Children wet the bed because they have not learned to wake up to the feeling of a full bladder. The best way to teach them to wake up to a full bladder is by using a urine alarm. When your child wears the alarm on his underwear, it will begin to sound and/or vibrate as soon as urine comes in contact with the sensor. This should then wake your child up each time his bladder is full. Over time, this should help your child understand: full bladder = wake up! The following provides guidance on how to use the urine alarm to help your child learn to wake up when his bladder is full.

1. **You can purchase a urine alarm from a number of online vendors.** You may try www.bedwettingstore.com or type "urine alarm" into an online search engine to see many different models of urine alarms.
2. **You can typically find alarm models with sound, vibration, or both.** Choose an alarm that seems best for your child's needs. Follow directions for the urine alarm included with the model you purchase.
3. **Your child should place the alarm sensor on his underwear** <u>before</u> bedtime.
4. **The alarm monitor must be turned on** to make sure that it will sound and/or vibrate when moisture from urine comes into contact with the sensor.
5. **If the alarm sounds and/or vibrates, your child should immediately get out of bed to finish urinating in the bathroom.**
6. **A tracking sheet (attached) should be maintained to record dry versus wet nights.**
7. It is also important to **help your child learn to change his pajamas and sheets** as independently as possible when he does have wetting accidents.
8. **Your child should also be responsible (as much as possible) for placing dirty pajamas and sheets in the washer.**
9. **Once your child has remained dry throughout the night for 14 nights, you can stop using the alarm.**

   Using a urine alarm is the best way to help your child to learn to stop wetting the bed. It is important to keep in mind, though, that this can be a time-consuming process. Some children have a very hard time waking up to the alarm. If this is the case, you may want to purchase an alarm that has a separate monitor to place in your room. Then, you can wake your child up to finish urinating in the bathroom. It is also important to know that some children will start wetting the bed again after they have stopped. If this happens, use the urine alarm again, following all of the above steps, and your child should stop wetting the bed again.

HANDOUT 32

Full-Spectrum Treatment for Bedwetting

When children wet the bed, using a urine alarm is the best way to help them learn to wake up to a full bladder. However, many children will begin wetting the bed again even after they have used the urine alarm. Adding some extra steps to this process can help make sure that your child does not start wetting the bed again. The following will provide you guidance on using a full-spectrum treatment for bedwetting.

1. Follow the instructions included in the Urine Alarm Training handout.
2. The next step is *retention control training*, which helps your child learn to control the muscles around her bladder. To do so, she should tighten and release her urinary muscles over and over again while urinating. This should help your child understand the muscle control required to postpone urination when her bladder is full.
3. The next step is to postpone urination when your child feels that her bladder is full.
   - First, your child should wait 1 minute to urinate when she feels that her bladder is full.
   - The next day, your child should wait 5 minutes before urinating.
   - Your child should wait 10 minutes the next day, adding 5 minutes each day until your child is able to wait 45 minutes between the time her bladder feels full and she urinates.
4. The next step of the process of teaching your child to hold urine when her bladder is full is called **overlearning.** For overlearning to occur, your child should drink extra liquids before bed so that she will have more chances to have a full bladder during sleep.
5. Overlearning should be started when your child has had 14 completely dry nights in a row.
6. Your child should drink _____ ounces of water 1 hour before bedtime.
7. Before going to bed, your child should urinate and then place the urine alarm on her underwear.
8. Your child should continue to drink water an hour before bed every night until she has had another 14 completely dry nights in a row.
9. Once your child has done this, you can stop having her drink extra water and using the alarm.

   Full-spectrum treatment can be time consuming and difficult to complete. It is impor-tant to keep in mind, though, that this makes it far more likely that your child will truly learn to wake up to a full bladder and be able to wait before urinating when her bladder is full. Both of these skills will help your child learn to stay dry for the whole night.

HANDOUT 33

Task Analysis Chart

The purpose of a task analysis chart is to help your child learn to become more comfortable with his positive airway pressure (PAP) equipment. Because many kids find PAP to be uncomfortable, this is done very gradually. The task analysis chart lists each of the steps that need to be practiced at home. **It is important that you do not move too quickly from step to step, or skip steps.** For your child, the steps should be as outlined below.

	Task	Start with ___ seconds	Move to next step when he can do _____ seconds/minutes
Step 1			
Step 2			
Step 3			
Step 4			
Step 5			
Step 6			
Step 7			
Step 8			

Important Things to Remember
- It is important to provide your child with a lot of praise when he is doing the step correctly. However, it is even more important that you ignore any unwanted behaviors (crying, hitting, saying no) and do not give your child negative attention ("Why can't you just put it on!").
- Using a timer can be helpful so that it is not you telling your child when the step is over, but rather the neutral timer. In addition, the timer can provide some distraction for children when they are asked to be the timekeeper.
- Pair each step with something enjoyable (e.g., video game, favorite TV show). However, if your child removes the mask or turns off the machine before time is up, immediately remove the fun activity.
- If your child removes his mask, immediately place it back on and hold it there gently until the time goal is reached.
- Provide a small reward when your child successfully completes each step.

> *Helping your child learn to adapt to PAP therapy can be incredibly challenging! However, with consistent practicing and lots of patience, your child can develop the tolerance needed for this important therapy. For most children, if you take the time to help them become more comfortable wearing PAP, they will be more likely to keep wearing it over time, with significant benefits to their health, development, learning, and behavior.*

References

Achermann, P., & Borbély, A. A. (2010). Sleep homeostasis and models of sleep regulation. In M. Kryger, T. Roth, & W. Dement (Eds.), *Principles and practices of sleep medicine* (5th ed., pp. 431–444). Philadelphia, PA: Elsevier.

Adolescent Sleep Working Group, Committee on Adolescence, & Council on School Health. (2014). School start times for adolescents. *Pediatrics, 134,* 642–649. http://dx.doi.org/10.1542/peds.2014-1697

American Academy of Sleep Medicine. (2005). *International classification of sleep disorders: Diagnostic and coding manual* (2nd ed.). Darien, IL: Author.

American Academy of Sleep Medicine. (2014). *International classification of sleep disorders: Diagnostic and coding manual* (3rd ed.). Darien, IL: Author.

American Psychiatric Association. (1994). *Diagnostic and statistical manual of mental disorders* (4th ed.). Washington, DC: Author.

American Psychiatric Association. (2013). *Diagnostic and statistical manual of mental disorders* (5th ed.). Arlington, VA: Author.

Anders, T. F., Halpern, L. F., & Hua, J. (1992). Sleeping through the night: A developmental perspective. *Pediatrics, 90,* 554–560.

Arendt, J., & Skene, D. J. (2005). Melatonin as a chronobiotic. *Sleep Medicine Reviews, 9,* 25–39. http://dx.doi.org/10.1016/j.smrv.2004.05.002

Asarnow, L. D., McGlinchey, E., & Harvey, A. G. (2014). The effects of bedtime and sleep duration on academic and emotional outcomes in a nationally representative sample of adolescents. *Journal of Adolescent Health, 54,* 350–356. http://dx.doi.org/10.1016/j.jadohealth.2013.09.004

Ashbaugh, R., & Peck, S. M. (1998). Treatment of sleep problems in a toddler: A replication of the faded bedtime with response cost protocol. *Journal of Applied Behavior Analysis, 31,* 127–129. http://dx.doi.org/10.1901/jaba.1998.31-127

Azrin, N. H., Sneed, T. J., & Foxx, R. M. (1974). Dry-bed training: Rapid elimination of childhood enuresis. *Behaviour Research and Therapy, 12,* 147–156. http://dx.doi.org/10.1016/0005-7967(74)90111-9

Azrin, N. H., & Thienes, P. M. (1978). Rapid elimination of enuresis by intensive learning without a conditioning apparatus. *Behavior Therapy, 9,* 342–354. http://dx.doi.org/10.1016/S0005-7894(78)80077-X

Babcock, D. A. (2011). Evaluating sleep and sleep disorders in the pediatric primary care setting. *Pediatric Clinics of North America, 58,* 543–554. http://dx.doi.org/10.1016/j.pcl.2011.03.001

Beebe, D. W. (2011). Cognitive, behavioral, and functional consequences of inadequate sleep in children and adolescents. *Pediatric Clinics of North America, 58,* 649–665. http://dx.doi.org/10.1016/j.pcl.2011.03.002

Beebe, D. W., Rose, D., & Amin, R. (2010). Attention, learning, and arousal of experimentally sleep-restricted adolescents in a simulated classroom. *Journal of Adolescent Health, 47,* 523–525. http://dx.doi.org/10.1016/j.jadohealth.2010.03.005

Beebe, D. W., Simon, S., Summer, S., Hemmer, S., Strotman, D., & Dolan, L. M. (2013). Dietary intake following experimentally restricted sleep in adolescents. *Sleep, 36,* 827–834.

Bhushan, B., Maddalozzo, J., Sheldon, S. H., Haymond, S., Rychlik, K., Lales, G. C., & Billings, K. R. (2014). Metabolic alterations in children with obstructive sleep apnea. *International Journal of Pediatric Otorhinolaryngology, 78,* 854–859. http://dx.doi.org/10.1016/j.ijporl.2014.02.028

Blunden, S. (2011). Behavioural treatments to encourage solo sleeping in pre-school children: An alternative to controlled crying. *Journal of Child Health Care, 15,* 107–117. http://dx.doi.org/10.1177/1367493510397623

Bootzin, R. R. (1972). Stimulus control treatment for insomnia. In *Proceedings, 80th Annual Convention of the American Psychological Association,* pp. 395–396.

Bootzin, R. R., & Stevens, S. J. (2005). Adolescents, substance abuse, and the treatment of insomnia and daytime sleepiness. *Clinical Psychology Review, 25,* 629–644. http://dx.doi.org/10.1016/j.cpr.2005.04.007

Borbély, A. A. (1982). A two-process model of sleep regulation. *Human Neurobiology, 1,* 195–204.

Borkovec, T. D., Wilkinson, L., Folensbee, R., & Lerman, C. (1983). Stimulus control applications to the treatment of worry. *Behaviour Research and Therapy, 21,* 247–251. http://dx.doi.org/10.1016/0005-7967(83)90206-1

Burke, R. V., Kuhn, B. R., & Peterson, J. L. (2004). Brief report: A "storybook" ending to children's bedtime problems—The use of a rewarding social story to reduce bedtime resistance and frequent night waking. *Journal of Pediatric Psychology, 29,* 389–396.

Buysse, D. J., Germain, A., Moul, D. E., Franzen, P. L., Brar, L. K., Fletcher, M. E., . . . Monk, T. H. (2011). Efficacy of brief behavioral treatment for chronic insomnia in older adults. *Archives of Internal Medicine, 171,* 887–895. http://dx.doi.org/10.1001/archinternmed.2010.535

Carney, C. E., Buysse, D. J., Ancoli-Israel, S., Edinger, J. D., Krystal, A. D., Lichstein, K. L., & Morin, C. M. (2012). The consensus sleep diary: Standardizing prospective sleep self-monitoring. *Sleep, 35,* 287–302.

Carskadon, M. A. (2011). Sleep in adolescents: The perfect storm. *Pediatric Clinics of North America, 58,* 637–647. http://dx.doi.org/10.1016/j.pcl.2011.03.003

Carskadon, M. A., Acebo, C., Richardson, G. S., Tate, B. A., & Seifer, R. (1997). An approach to studying circadian rhythms of adolescent humans. *Journal of Biological Rhythms, 12,* 278–289. http://dx.doi.org/10.1177/074873049701200309

Carskadon, M. A., & Dement, W. C. (2010). Normal human sleep: An overview. In M. Kryger, T. Roth, & W. C. Dement (Eds.), *Principles and practices of sleep medicine* (5th ed., pp. 16–26). Philadelphia, PA: Elsevier.

Chesson, A. L., Jr., Littner, M., Davila, D., Anderson, W. M., Grigg-Damberger, M., Hartse, K., . . . Wise, M. (1999). Practice parameters for the use of light therapy in the treatment of sleep disorders. An American Academy of Sleep Medicine Report, Standards of Practice Committee of the American Academy of Sleep Medicine. *Sleep, 22,* 641–660.

Cirelli, C., & Tononi, G. (2008). Is sleep essential? *PLoS Biology, 6,* e216. http://dx.doi.org/10.1371/journal.pbio.0060216

Cohen, S., Doyle, W. J., Alper, C. M., Janicki-Deverts, D., & Turner, R. B. (2009). Sleep habits and susceptibility to the common cold. *Archives of Internal Medicine, 169,* 62–67. http://dx.doi.org/10.1001/archinternmed.2008.505

Crabtree, V., & Williams, N. A. (2009). Normal sleep in children and adolescents. *Child and Adolescent Psychiatric Clinics of North America, 18,* 799–811. http://dx.doi.org/10.1016/j.chc.2009.04.013

Crosby, B., LeBourgeois, M. K., & Harsh, J. (2005). Racial differences in reported napping and nocturnal sleep in 2- to 8-year-old children. *Pediatrics, 115,* 225–232. http://dx.doi.org/10.1542/peds.2004-0815D

Crowley, S. J., Acebo, C., & Carskadon, M. A. (2007). Sleep, circadian rhythms, and delayed phase in adolescence. *Sleep Medicine, 8,* 602–612. http://dx.doi.org/10.1016/j.sleep.2006.12.002

Davis, J. L., & Wright, D. C. (2007). Randomized clinical trial for treatment of chronic nightmares in trauma-exposed adults. *Journal of Traumatic Stress, 20*, 123–133. http://dx.doi.org/10.1002/jts.20199

de Bruin, E. J., Oort, F. J., Bögels, S. M., & Meijer, A. M. (2014). Efficacy of Internet- and group-administered cognitive behavioral therapy for insomnia in adolescents: A pilot study. *Behavioral Sleep Medicine, 12*, 235–254. http://dx.doi.org/10.1080/15402002.2013.784703

de Carvalho, L. B., do Prado, L. B., Ferreira, V. R., da Rocha Figueiredo, M. B., Jung, A., de Morais, J. F., & do Prado, G. F. (2013). Symptoms of sleep disorders and objective academic performance. *Sleep Medicine, 14*, 872–876. http://dx.doi.org/10.1016/j.sleep.2013.05.011

Dewald-Kaufmann, J. F., Oort, F. J., & Meijer, A. M. (2013). The effects of sleep extension and sleep hygiene advice on sleep and depressive symptoms in adolescents: A randomized controlled trial. *Journal of Child Psychology and Psychiatry, 55*, 273–283.

Dodson, E. R., & Zee, P. C. (2010). Therapeutics for circadian rhythm sleep disorders. *Sleep Medicine Clinics, 5*, 701–715. http://dx.doi.org/10.1016/j.jsmc.2010.08.001

Durmer, J. S., & Quraishi, G. H. (2011). Restless legs syndrome, periodic leg movements, and periodic limb movement disorder in children. *Pediatric Clinics of North America, 58*, 591–620. http://dx.doi.org/10.1016/j.pcl.2011.03.005

Edinger, J. D., & Sampson, W. S. (2003). A primary care "friendly" cognitive behavioral insomnia therapy. *Sleep, 26*, 177–182.

Flint, J., Kothare, S. V., Zihlif, M., Suarez, E., Adams, R., Legido, A., & De Luca, F. (2007). Association between inadequate sleep and insulin resistance in obese children. *The Journal of Pediatrics, 150*, 364–369. http://dx.doi.org/10.1016/j.jpeds.2006.08.063

Frank, M. G. (2006). The mystery of sleep function: Current perspectives and future directions. *Reviews in the Neurosciences, 17*, 375–392. http://dx.doi.org/10.1515/revneuro.2006.17.4.375

Frank, N. C., Spirito, A., Stark, L., & Owens-Stively, J. (1997). The use of scheduled awakenings to eliminate childhood sleepwalking. *Journal of Pediatric Psychology, 22*, 345–353. http://dx.doi.org/10.1093/jpepsy/22.3.345

Freeman, K. A. (2006). Treating bedtime resistance with the bedtime pass: A systematic replication and component analysis with 3-year-olds. *Journal of Applied Behavior Analysis, 39*, 423–428. http://dx.doi.org/10.1901/jaba.2006.34-05

Friman, P. C., Hoff, K. E., Schnoes, C., Freeman, K. A., Woods, D. W., & Blum, N. (1999). The bedtime pass: An approach to bedtime crying and leaving the room. *Archives of Pediatrics & Adolescent Medicine, 153*, 1027–1029. http://dx.doi.org/10.1001/archpedi.153.10.1027

Galland, B. C., Taylor, B. J., Elder, D. E., & Herbison, P. (2012). Normal sleep patterns in infants and children: A systematic review of observational studies. *Sleep Medicine Reviews, 16,* 213–222. http://dx.doi.org/10.1016/j.smrv.2011.06.001

Gangwisch, J. E., Malaspina, D., Babiss, L. A., Opler, M. G., Posner, K., Shen, S., . . . Ginsberg, H. N. (2010). Short sleep duration as a risk factor for hypercholesterolemia: Analyses of the National Longitudinal Study of Adolescent Health. *Sleep, 33,* 956–961.

Glazener, C. M., Evans, J. H., & Peto, R. E. (2005). Alarm interventions for nocturnal enuresis in children. *Cochrane Database of Systematic Reviews,* CD002911.

Gordon, J., King, N., Gullone, E., Muris, P., & Ollendick, T. H. (2007a). Nighttime fears of children and adolescents: Frequency, content, severity, harm expectations, disclosure, and coping behaviours. *Behaviour Research and Therapy, 45,* 2464–2472. http://dx.doi.org/10.1016/j.brat.2007.03.013

Gordon, J., King, N. J., Gullone, E., Muris, P., & Ollendick, T. H. (2007b). Treatment of children's nighttime fears: The need for a modern randomised controlled trial. *Clinical Psychology Review, 27,* 98–113. http://dx.doi.org/10.1016/j.cpr.2006.07.002

Gregory, A. M., & Sadeh, A. (2012). Sleep, emotional, and behavioral difficulties in children and adolescents. *Sleep Medicine Reviews, 16,* 129–136. http://dx.doi.org/10.1016/j.smrv.2011.03.007

Gruber, R., Cassoff, J., Frenette, S., Wiebe, S., & Carrier, J. (2012). Impact of sleep extension and restriction on children's emotional lability and impulsivity. *Pediatrics, 130,* e1155–e1161. http://dx.doi.org/10.1542/peds.2012-0564

Gruber, R., Michaelsen, S., Bergmame, L., Frenette, S., Bruni, O., Fontil, L., & Carrier, J. (2012). Short sleep duration is associated with teacher-reported inattention and cognitive problems in healthy school-aged children. *Nature and Science of Sleep, 4,* 33–40. http://dx.doi.org/10.2147/NSS.S24607

Harford, K. L., Jambhekar, S., Com, G., Pruss, K., Kabour, M., Jones, K., & Ward, W. L. (2013). Behaviorally based adherence program for pediatric patients treated with positive airway pressure. *Clinical Child Psychology and Psychiatry, 18,* 151–163. http://dx.doi.org/10.1177/1359104511431662

Hart, C. N., Carskadon, M. A., Considine, R. V., Fava, J. L., Lawton, J., Raynor, H. A., . . . Wing, R. (2013). Changes in children's sleep duration on food intake, weight, and leptin. *Pediatrics, 132,* e1473–e1480. http://dx.doi.org/10.1542/peds.2013-1274

Hiscock, H., Bayer, J. K., Hampton, A., Ukoumunne, O. C., & Wake, M. (2008). Long-term mother and child mental health effects of a population-based infant sleep intervention: Cluster-randomized, controlled trial. *Pediatrics, 122,* e621–e627. http://dx.doi.org/10.1542/peds.2007-3783

Hjalmas, K., Arnold, T., Bower, W., Caione, P., Chiozza, L. M., von Gontard, A., . . . Yeung, C. K. (2004). Nocturnal enuresis: An international evidence based management strategy. *The Journal of Urology, 171,* 2545–2561. http://dx.doi.org/10.1097/01.ju.0000111504.85822.b2

Honaker, S. M., & Meltzer, L. J. (2014). Bedtime problems and night wakings in young children: An update of the evidence. *Paediatric Respiratory Reviews, 15,* 333–339.

Houts, A. C. (1996). Behavioral treatment of enuresis. *Clinical Psychologist, 49,* 5–6.

Houts, A. C., Peterson, J. K., & Whelan, J. P. (1986). Prevention of relapse in full spectrum home training for primary enuresis: A components analysis. *Behavior Therapy, 17,* 462–469. http://dx.doi.org/10.1016/S0005-7894(86)80075-2

Iber, C., Ancoli-Israel, S., Chesson, A. L., Jr., & Quan, S. F., & American Academy of Sleep Medicine. (2007). *The AASM manual for the scoring of sleep and associated events.* Westchester, IL: American Academy of Sleep Medicine.

Iglowstein, I., Jenni, O. G., Molinari, L., & Largo, R. H. (2003). Sleep duration from infancy to adolescence: Reference values and generational trends. *Pediatrics, 111,* 302–307. http://dx.doi.org/10.1542/peds.111.2.302

Ivanenko, A., Crabtree, V. M., & Gozal, D. (2004). Sleep in children with psychiatric disorders. *Pediatric Clinics of North America, 51,* 51–68. http://dx.doi.org/10.1016/S0031-3955(03)00181-0

Jacobs, G. D., Pace-Schott, E. F., Stickgold, R., & Otto, M. W. (2004). Cognitive behavior therapy and pharmacotherapy for insomnia: A randomized controlled trial and direct comparison. *Archives of Internal Medicine, 164,* 1888–1896. http://dx.doi.org/10.1001/archinte.164.17.1888

Javaheri, S., Storfer-Isser, A., Rosen, C. L., & Redline, S. (2011). Association of short and long sleep durations with insulin sensitivity in adolescents. *The Journal of Pediatrics, 158,* 617–623. http://dx.doi.org/10.1016/j.jpeds.2010.09.080

Jellesma, F. C., Verkuil, B., & Brosschot, J. F. (2009). Postponing worrisome thoughts in children: The effects of a postponement intervention on perseverative thoughts, emotions and somatic complaints. *Social Science & Medicine, 69,* 278–284. http://dx.doi.org/10.1016/j.socscimed.2009.04.031

Jenni, O. G., & Carskadon, M. A. (2005). Normal human sleep at different ages: Infants to adolescents. In Sleep Research Society (Ed.), *SRS basics of sleep guide* (pp. 11–19). Westchester, IL: Sleep Research Society.

Jenni, O. G., Deboer, T., & Achermann, P. (2006). Development of the 24-h rest–activity pattern in human infants. *Infant Behavior and Development, 29,* 143–152. http://dx.doi.org/10.1016/j.infbeh.2005.11.001

Konofal, E., Lecendreux, M., & Cortese, S. (2010). Sleep and ADHD. *Sleep Medicine, 11,* 652–658. http://dx.doi.org/10.1016/j.sleep.2010.02.012

Koontz, K. L., Slifer, K. J., Cataldo, M. D., & Marcus, C. L. (2003). Improving pediatric compliance with positive airway pressure therapy: The impact of behavioral intervention. *Sleep, 26,* 1010–1015.

Krakow, B., Sandoval, D., Schrader, R., Keuhne, B., McBride, L., Yau, C. L., & Tandberg, D. (2001). Treatment of chronic nightmares in adjudicated adolescent girls in a residential facility. *Journal of Adolescent Health, 29,* 94–100. http://dx.doi.org/10.1016/S1054-139X(00)00195-6

Krakow, B., & Zadra, A. (2006). Clinical management of chronic nightmares: Imagery rehearsal therapy. *Behavioral Sleep Medicine, 4,* 45–70. http://dx.doi.org/10.1207/s15402010bsm0401_4

Kuhn, B. R. (2011). The excuse-me drill: A behavioral protocol to promote independent sleep initiation skills and reduce bedtime problems in young children. In M. Perlis, M. Aloia, & B. R. Kuhn (Eds.), *Behavioral treatments for sleep disorders* (pp. 299–309). Burlington, MA: Academic Press. http://dx.doi.org/10.1016/B978-0-12-381522-4.00031-6

Kurth, S., Ringli, M., LeBourgeois, M. K., Geiger, A., Buchmann, A., Jenni, O. G., & Huber, R. (2012). Mapping the electrophysiological marker of sleep depth reveals skill maturation in children and adolescents. *NeuroImage, 63,* 959–965. http://dx.doi.org/10.1016/j.neuroimage.2012.03.053

Kushnir, J., & Sadeh, A. (2012). Assessment of brief interventions for nighttime fears in preschool children. *European Journal of Pediatrics, 171,* 67–75. http://dx.doi.org/10.1007/s00431-011-1488-4

Lack, L. C., & Wright, H. R. (2007). Clinical management of delayed sleep phase disorder. *Behavioral Sleep Medicine, 5,* 57–76. http://dx.doi.org/10.1080/15402000709336726

Lam, P., Hiscock, H., & Wake, M. (2003). Outcomes of infant sleep problems: A longitudinal study of sleep, behavior, and maternal well-being. *Pediatrics, 111,* e203–e207. http://dx.doi.org/10.1542/peds.111.3.e203

Lask, B. (1988). Novel and nontoxic treatment for night terrors. *BMJ, 297,* 592. http://dx.doi.org/10.1136/bmj.297.6648.592

Lask, B. (1993). Sleep disorders. "Working treatment" best for night terrors. *BMJ (Clinical Research Ed.), 306,* 1477. http://dx.doi.org/10.1136/bmj.306.6890.1477

LeBourgeois, M. K., Carskadon, M. A., Akacem, L. D., Simpkin, C. T., Wright, K. P., Jr., Achermann, P., & Jenni, O. G. (2013). Circadian phase and its relationship to nighttime sleep in toddlers. *Journal of Biological Rhythms, 28,* 322–331. http://dx.doi.org/10.1177/0748730413506543

LeBourgeois, M. K., Wright, K. P., Jr., LeBourgeois, H. B., & Jenni, O. G. (2013). Dissonance between parent-selected bedtimes and young children's circadian physiology influences nighttime settling difficulties. *Mind, Brain, and Education, 7,* 234–242. http://dx.doi.org/10.1111/mbe.12032

Lee, K. A., Landis, C., Chasens, E. R., Dowling, G., Merritt, S., Parker, K. P., . . . Weaver, T. E. (2004). Sleep and chronobiology: Recommendations for nursing education. *Nursing Outlook, 52,* 126–133. http://dx.doi.org/10.1016/j.outlook.2003.12.002

Lewandowski, A. S., Toliver-Sokol, M., & Palermo, T. M. (2011). Evidence-based review of subjective pediatric sleep measures. *Journal of Pediatric Psychology, 36,* 780–793. http://dx.doi.org/10.1093/jpepsy/jsq119

Lewandowski, A. S., Ward, T. M., & Palermo, T. M. (2011). Sleep problems in children and adolescents with common medical conditions. *Pediatric Clinics of North America, 58,* 699–713. http://dx.doi.org/10.1016/j.pcl.2011.03.012

Li, S. X., Yu, M. W., Lam, S. P., Zhang, J., Li, A. M., Lai, K. Y., & Wing, Y. K. (2011). Frequent nightmares in children: Familial aggregation and associations with parent-reported behavioral and mood problems. *Sleep, 34,* 487–493.

Liu, X. (2004). Sleep and adolescent suicidal behavior. *Sleep, 27,* 1351–1358.

Longstreth, W. T., Jr., Koepsell, T. D., Ton, T. G., Hendrickson, A. F., & van Belle, G. (2007). The epidemiology of narcolepsy. *Sleep, 30,* 13–26.

Lumeng, J. C., & Chervin, R. D. (2008). Epidemiology of pediatric obstructive sleep apnea. *Proceedings of the American Thoracic Society, 5,* 242–252. http://dx.doi.org/10.1513/pats.200708-135MG

Ma, C., Zhou, Y., Zhou, W., & Huang, C. (2014). Evaluation of the effect of motivational interviewing counselling on hypertension care. *Patient Education and Counseling, 95,* 231–237. http://dx.doi.org/10.1016/j.pec.2014.01.011

Marcus, C. L., Brooks, L. J., Draper, K. A., Gozal, D., Halbower, A. C., Jones, J., . . . American Academy of Pediatrics. (2012). Diagnosis and management of childhood obstructive sleep apnea syndrome. *Pediatrics, 130,* 576–584. http://dx.doi.org/10.1542/peds.2012-1671

Mason, T. B. A., II, & Pack, A. I. (2007). Pediatric parasomnias. *Sleep, 30,* 141–151.

Meltzer, L. J., Avis, K. T., Biggs, S., Reynolds, A. C., Crabtree, V. M., & Bevans, K. B. (2013). The Children's Report of Sleep Patterns (CRSP): A self-report measure of sleep for school-aged children. *Journal of Clinical Sleep Medicine, 9,* 235–245.

Meltzer, L. J., & Mindell, J. A. (2014). Systematic review and meta-analysis of behavioral interventions for pediatric insomnia. *Journal of Pediatric Psychology, 39,* 932–948. http://dx.doi.org/10.1093/jpepsy/jsu041

Meltzer, L. J., Montgomery-Downs, H. E., Insana, S. P., & Walsh, C. M. (2012). Use of actigraphy for assessment in pediatric sleep research. *Sleep Medicine Reviews, 16,* 463–475. http://dx.doi.org/10.1016/j.smrv.2011.10.002

Meltzer, L. J., Phillips, C., & Mindell, J. A. (2009). Clinical psychology training in sleep and sleep disorders. *Journal of Clinical Psychology, 65,* 305–318.

Meltzer, L. J., Walsh, C. M., Traylor, J., & Westin, A. M. (2012). Direct comparison of two new actigraphs and polysomnography in children and adolescents. *Sleep, 35*, 159–166.

Mignot, E. (2008). Why we sleep: The temporal organization of recovery. *PLoS Biology, 6*, e106.

Miller, W. R., & Rollnick, S. (2013). *Glossary of motivational interviewing terms*. Retrieved from http://www.motivationalinterviewing.org/sites/default/files/glossary_of_mi_terms-1.pdf

Mindell, J. A., Bartle, A., Ahn, Y., Ramamurthy, M. B., Huong, H. T., Kohyama, J., . . . Goh, D. Y. (2013). Sleep education in pediatric residency programs: A cross-cultural look. *BMC Research Notes, 6*, 130. http://dx.doi.org/10.1186/1756-0500-6-130

Mindell, J. A., Kuhn, B., Lewin, D. S., Meltzer, L. J., & Sadeh, A. (2006). Behavioral treatment of bedtime problems and night wakings in infants and young children. *Sleep, 29*, 1263–1276.

Mindell, J. A., Meltzer, L. J., Carskadon, M. A., & Chervin, R. D. (2009). Developmental aspects of sleep hygiene: Findings from the 2004 National Sleep Foundation Sleep in America Poll. *Sleep Medicine, 10*, 771–779. http://dx.doi.org/10.1016/j.sleep.2008.07.016

Mindell, J. A., & Owens, J. A. (2010). *A clinical guide to pediatric sleep: Diagnosis and management of sleep problems* (2nd ed.). Philadelphia, PA: Lippincott Williams & Wilkins.

Mindell, J. A., Owens, J. A., Alves, R., Bruni, O., Goh, D. Y. T., Hiscock, H., . . . Sadeh, A. (2011). Give children and adolescents the gift of a good night's sleep: A call to action. *Sleep Medicine, 12*, 203–204.

Mindell, J. A., Telofski, L. S., Wiegand, B., & Kurtz, E. S. (2009). A nightly bedtime routine: Impact on sleep in young children and maternal mood. *Sleep, 32*, 599–606.

Mohri, I., Kato-Nishimura, K., Kagitani-Shimono, K., Kimura-Ohba, S., Ozono, K., Tachibana, N., & Taniike, M. (2012). Evaluation of oral iron treatment in pediatric restless legs syndrome (RLS). *Sleep Medicine, 13*, 429–432. http://dx.doi.org/10.1016/j.sleep.2011.12.009

Moore, B. A., Friman, P. C., Fruzzetti, A. E., & MacAleese, K. (2007). Brief report: Evaluating the Bedtime Pass Program for child resistance to bedtime—A randomized, controlled trial. *Journal of Pediatric Psychology, 32*, 283–287. http://dx.doi.org/10.1093/jpepsy/jsl025

Moore, M., & Meltzer, L. J. (2008). The sleepy adolescent: Causes and consequences of sleepiness in teens. *Paediatric Respiratory Reviews, 9*, 114–121. http://dx.doi.org/10.1016/j.prrv.2008.01.001

Moore, T., & Ucko, L. E. (1957). Night waking in early infancy. I. *Archives of Disease in Childhood, 32*, 333–342. http://dx.doi.org/10.1136/adc.32.164.333

Morgenthaler, T., Kramer, M., Alessi, C., Friedman, L., Boehlecke, B., Brown, T., . . . American Academy of Sleep Medicine. (2006). Practice parameters for the psychological and behavioral treatment of insomnia: An update. An American Academy of Sleep Medicine report. *Sleep, 29*, 1415–1419.

Morgenthaler, T. I., Owens, J., Alessi, C., Boehlecke, B., Brown, T. M., Coleman, J., Jr., . . . American Academy of Sleep Medicine. (2006). Practice parameters for behavioral treatment of bedtime problems and night wakings in infants and young children: An American Academy of Sleep Medicine report. *Sleep, 29*, 1277–1281.

Morin, C. M., Bootzin, R. R., Buysse, D. J., Edinger, J. D., Espie, C. A., & Lichstein, K. L. (2006). Psychological and behavioral treatment of insomnia: Update of the recent evidence (1998–2004). *Sleep, 29*, 1398–1414.

Morin, C. M., Culbert, J. P., & Schwartz, S. M. (1994). Nonpharmacological interventions for insomnia: A meta-analysis of treatment efficacy. *The American Journal of Psychiatry, 151*, 1172–1180.

Morin, C. M., Vallières, A., Guay, B., Ivers, H., Savard, J., Mérette, C., . . . Baillargeon, L. (2009). Cognitive behavioral therapy, singly and combined with medication, for persistent insomnia: A randomized controlled trial. *JAMA, 301*, 2005–2015. http://dx.doi.org/10.1001/jama.2009.682

Morin, C. M., Vallières, A., & Ivers, H. (2007). Dysfunctional beliefs and attitudes about sleep (DBAS): Validation of a brief version (DBAS-16). *Sleep, 30*, 1547–1554.

Mowrer, O. H. (1938). Apparatus for the study and treatment of enuresis. *The American Journal of Psychology, 51*, 163–166. http://dx.doi.org/10.2307/1416427

Naar-King, S., & Suarez, M. (2010). *Motivational interviewing with adolescents and young adults.* New York, NY: Guilford Press.

National Institutes of Health. (2005). National Institutes of Health State of the Science Conference statement on manifestations and management of chronic insomnia in adults, June 13–15, 2005. *Sleep, 28*, 1049–1057.

National Sleep Foundation. (2004). *Sleep in America poll.* Retrieved from http://www.sleepfoundation.org

National Sleep Foundation. (2011). *Sleep in America poll.* Retrieved from http://www.sleepfoundation.org

O'Brien, L. M. (2009). The neurocognitive effects of sleep disruption in children and adolescents. *Child and Adolescent Psychiatric Clinics of North America, 18*, 813–823. http://dx.doi.org/10.1016/j.chc.2009.04.008

Okawa, M., Uchiyama, M., Ozaki, S., Shibui, K., & Ichikawa, H. (1998). Circadian rhythm sleep disorders in adolescents: Clinical trials of combined treatments based on chronobiology. *Psychiatry and Clinical Neurosciences, 52*, 483–490. http://dx.doi.org/10.1046/j.1440-1819.1998.00449.x

Olson, A. L., Gaffney, C. A., Lee, P. W., & Starr, P. (2008). Changing adolescent health behaviors: The healthy teens counseling approach.

American Journal of Preventive Medicine, 35, 359–364. http://dx.doi.org/10.1016/j.amepre.2008.08.014

Owens, J., Adolescent Sleep Working Group, & Committee on Adolescence. (2014). Insufficient sleep in adolescents and young adults: An update on causes and consequences. *Pediatrics, 134,* e921–e932. http://dx.doi.org/10.1542/peds.2014-1696

Owens, J. A. (2005). Epidemiology of sleep disorders during childhood. In S. H. Sheldon, R. Ferber, & M. H. Kryger (Eds.), *Principles and practices of pediatric sleep medicine* (pp. 27–33). Philadelphia, PA: Elsevier Saunders.

Owens, J. A., Spirito, A., McGuinn, M., & Nobile, C. (2000). Sleep habits and sleep disturbance in elementary school-aged children. *Journal of Developmental and Behavioral Pediatrics, 21,* 27–36. http://dx.doi.org/10.1097/00004703-200002000-00005

Paavonen, E. J., Aronen, E. T., Moilanen, I., Piha, J., Räsänen, E., Tamminen, T., & Almqvist, F. (2000). Sleep problems of school-aged children: A complementary view. *Acta Paediatrica, 89,* 223–228. http://dx.doi.org/10.1111/j.1651-2227.2000.tb01220.x

Paine, S., & Gradisar, M. (2011). A randomised controlled trial of cognitive-behaviour therapy for behavioural insomnia of childhood in school-aged children. *Behavioral Research and Therapy, 49,* 379–388. http://dx.doi.org/10.1016/j.brat.2011.03.008

Piazza, C. C., & Fisher, W. W. (1991). Bedtime fading in the treatment of pediatric insomnia. *Journal of Behavior Therapy and Experimental Psychiatry, 22,* 53–56. http://dx.doi.org/10.1016/0005-7916(91)90034-3

Piazza, C. C., Fisher, W. W., & Sherer, M. (1997). Treatment of multiple sleep problems in children with developmental disabilities: Faded bedtime with response cost versus bedtime scheduling. *Developmental Medicine & Child Neurology, 39,* 414–418.

Picchietti, D., Allen, R. P., Walters, A. S., Davidson, J. E., Myers, A., & Ferini-Strambi, L. (2007). Restless legs syndrome: Prevalence and impact in children and adolescents—The Peds REST study. *Pediatrics, 120,* 253–266. http://dx.doi.org/10.1542/peds.2006-2767

Picchietti, D. L., Arbuckle, R. A., Abetz, L., Durmer, J. S., Ivanenko, A., Owens, J. A., . . . Walters, A. S. (2011). Pediatric restless legs syndrome: Analysis of symptom descriptions and drawings. *Journal of Child Neurology, 26,* 1365–1376. http://dx.doi.org/10.1177/0883073811405852

Picchietti, D. L., Bruni, O., de Weerd, A., Durmer, J. S., Kotagal, S., Owens, J. A., . . . The International Restless Legs Syndrome Study Group. (2013). Pediatric restless legs syndrome diagnostic criteria: An update by the International Restless Legs Syndrome Study Group. *Sleep Medicine, 14,* 1253–1259. http://dx.doi.org/10.1016/j.sleep.2013.08.778

Picchietti, D. L., England, S. J., Walters, A. S., Willis, K., & Verrico, T. (1998). Periodic limb movement disorder and restless legs syndrome in children with attention-deficit hyperactivity disorder. *Journal of Child Neurology, 13*, 588–594. http://dx.doi.org/10.1177/088307389801301202

Picchietti, D. L., Underwood, D. J., Farris, W. A., Walters, A. S., Shah, M. M., Dahl, R. E., . . . Hening, W. A. (1999). Further studies on periodic limb movement disorder and restless legs syndrome in children with attention-deficit hyperactivity disorder. *Movement Disorders, 14*, 1000–1007. http://dx.doi.org/10.1002/1531-8257(199911)14:6<1000::AID-MDS1014>3.0.CO;2-P

Pincus, D. B., Weiner, C. L., & Friedman, A. G. (2012). Differential efficacy of home monitoring and cognitive-behavioral treatment for decreasing children's maladaptive nighttime fears. *Child & Family Behavior Therapy, 34*, 1–19. http://dx.doi.org/10.1080/07317107.2012.654426

Price, A. M., Wake, M., Ukoumunne, O. C., & Hiscock, H. (2012). Five-year follow-up of harms and benefits of behavioral infant sleep intervention: Randomized trial. *Pediatrics, 130*, 643–651. http://dx.doi.org/10.1542/peds.2011-3467

Prochaska, J. O., & DiClemente, C. C. (1992). Stages of change in the modification of problem behaviors. *Progress in Behavior Modification, 28*, 183–218.

Rains, J. C. (1995). Treatment of obstructive sleep apnea in pediatric patients. Behavioral intervention for compliance with nasal continuous positive airway pressure. *Clinical Pediatrics, 34*, 535–541. http://dx.doi.org/10.1177/000992228950340100 5

Reid, M. J., Walter, A. L., & O'Leary, S. G. (1999). Treatment of young children's bedtime refusal and nighttime wakings: A comparison of "standard" and graduated ignoring procedures. *Journal of Abnormal Child Psychology, 27*, 5–16. http://dx.doi.org/10.1023/A:1022606206076

Revell, V. L., Burgess, H. J., Gazda, C. J., Smith, M. R., Fogg, L. F., & Eastman, C. I. (2006). Advancing human circadian rhythms with afternoon melatonin and morning intermittent bright light. *The Journal of Clinical Endocrinology and Metabolism, 91*, 54–59. http://dx.doi.org/10.1210/jc.2005-1009

Reynolds, A. M., & Malow, B. A. (2011). Sleep and autism spectrum disorders. *Pediatric Clinics of North America, 58*, 685–698. http://dx.doi.org/10.1016/j.pcl.2011.03.009

Rollnick, S., Miller, W. R., & Butler, C. C. (2008). *Motivational interviewing in health care: Helping patients change behavior.* New York, NY: Guilford Press.

Rosen, R., Mahowald, M., Chesson, A., Doghramji, K., Goldberg, R., Moline, M., . . . Dement, W. (1998). The Taskforce 2000 survey on medical education in sleep and sleep disorders. *Sleep, 21*, 235–238.

Rosen, R., & Zozula, R. (2000). Education and training in the field of sleep medicine. *Current Opinion in Pulmonary Medicine, 6*, 512–518. http://dx.doi.org/10.1097/00063198-200011000-00009

Sadeh, A. (2011a). The role and validity of actigraphy in sleep medicine: An update. *Sleep Medicine Reviews, 15*, 259–267. http://dx.doi.org/10.1016/j.smrv.2010.10.001

Sadeh, A. (2011b). Sleep assessment methods. In M. El-Sheikh (Ed.), *Sleep and development: Familial and socio-cultural considerations* (pp. 355–371). New York, NY: Oxford University Press. http://dx.doi.org/10.1093/acprof:oso/9780195395754.003.0015

Sadeh, A., Gruber, R., & Raviv, A. (2003). The effects of sleep restriction and extension on school-age children: What a difference an hour makes. *Child Development, 74*, 444–455. http://dx.doi.org/10.1111/1467-8624.7402008

Sadeh, A., Raviv, A., & Gruber, R. (2000). Sleep patterns and sleep disruptions in school-age children. *Developmental Psychology, 36*, 291–301. http://dx.doi.org/10.1037/0012-1649.36.3.291

Scher, A. (2005). Crawling in and out of sleep. *Infant and Child Development, 14*, 491–500. http://dx.doi.org/10.1002/icd.427

Scher, A., & Cohen, D. (2005). Locomotion and nightwaking. *Child: Care, Health and Development, 31*, 685–691. http://dx.doi.org/10.1111/j.1365-2214.2005.00557.x

Schlarb, A. A., Liddle, C. C., & Hautzinger, M. (2011). JuSt—A multimodal program for treatment of insomnia in adolescents: A pilot study. *Nature and Science of Sleep, 3*, 13–20.

Schmid, S. M., Hallschmid, M., & Schultes, B. (2014). The metabolic burden of sleep loss. *Lancet Diabetes and Endocrinology, 2*, e12.

Schumacher, J. A., Coffey, S. F., Stasiewicz, P. R., Murphy, C. M., Leonard, K. E., & Fals-Stewart, W. (2011). Development of a brief motivational enhancement intervention for intimate partner violence in alcohol treatment Settings. *Journal of Aggression, Maltreatment & Trauma, 20*, 103–127. http://dx.doi.org/10.1080/10926771.2011.546749

Section 504 of the Rehabilitation Act of 1973, 34 C.F.R. Part 104.

Simard, V., & Nielsen, T. (2009). Adaptation of imagery rehearsal therapy for nightmares in children: A brief report. *Psychotherapy: Theory, Research, Practice, Training, 46*, 492–497. http://dx.doi.org/10.1037/a0017945

Simard, V., Nielsen, T. A., Tremblay, R. E., Boivin, M., & Montplaisir, J. Y. (2008). Longitudinal study of bad dreams in preschool-aged children: Prevalence, demographic correlates, risk and protective factors. *Sleep, 31*, 62–70.

Sivertsen, B., Omvik, S., Pallesen, S., Bjorvatn, B., Havik, O. E., Kvale, G., . . . Nordhus, I. H. (2006). Cognitive behavioral therapy vs. zopiclone for treatment of chronic primary insomnia in older adults: A randomized controlled trial. *JAMA, 295*, 2851–2858. http://dx.doi.org/10.1001/jama.295.24.2851

Slifer, K. J., Kruglak, D., Benore, E., Bellipanni, K., Falk, L., Halbower, A. C., . . . Beck, M. (2007). Behavioral training for increasing preschool children's adherence with positive airway pressure: A preliminary study. *Behavioral Sleep Medicine, 5,* 147–175. http://dx.doi.org/10.1080/15402000701190671

So, K., Adamson, T. M., & Horne, R. S. (2007). The use of actigraphy for assessment of the development of sleep/wake patterns in infants during the first 12 months of life. *Journal of Sleep Research, 16,* 181–187. http://dx.doi.org/10.1111/j.1365-2869.2007.00582.x

Spielman, A., & Glovinsky, P. (1991). The varied nature of insomnia. In P. J. Hauri (Ed.), *Case studies in insomnia* (pp. 1–15). New York, NY: Plenum Press.

Spruyt, K., & Gozal, D. (2011). Pediatric sleep questionnaires as diagnostic or epidemiological tools: A review of currently available instruments. *Sleep Medicine Reviews, 15,* 19–32. http://dx.doi.org/10.1016/j.smrv.2010.07.005

Task Force on Sudden Infant Death Syndrome. (2011). SIDS and other sleep-related infant deaths: Expansion of recommendations for a safe infant sleeping environment. *Pediatrics, 128,* 1030–1039. http://dx.doi.org/10.1542/peds.2011-2284

Troxel, W. M., Germain, A., & Buysse, D. J. (2012). Clinical management of insomnia with brief behavioral treatment (BBTI). *Behavioral Sleep Medicine, 10,* 266–279. http://dx.doi.org/10.1080/15402002.2011.607200

Viorritto, E. N., Kureshi, S. A., & Owens, J. A. (2012). Narcolepsy in the pediatric population. *Current Neurology and Neuroscience Reports, 12,* 175–181. http://dx.doi.org/10.1007/s11910-011-0246-3

Wahlstrom, K., Dretzke, B., Gordon, M., Peterson, K., Edwards, K., & Gdula, J. (2014). *Examining the impact of later school start times on the health and academic performance of high school students: A multisite study.* St. Paul: Center for Applied Research and Educational Improvement, University of Minnesota.

Walton, M. A., Chermack, S. T., Shope, J. T., Bingham, C. R., Zimmerman, M. A., Blow, F. C., & Cunningham, R. M. (2010). Effects of a brief intervention for reducing violence and alcohol misuse among adolescents: A randomized controlled trial. *JAMA, 304,* 527–535. http://dx.doi.org/10.1001/jama.2010.1066

Weitzman, E. D., Czeisler, C. A., Coleman, R. M., Spielman, A. J., Zimmerman, J. C., Dement, W., . . . Pollak, C. P. (1981). Delayed sleep phase syndrome. A chronobiological disorder with sleep-onset insomnia. *Archives of General Psychiatry, 38,* 737–746. http://dx.doi.org/10.1001/archpsyc.1981.01780320017001

Wever, R. A. (1984). Properties of human sleep–wake cycles: Parameters of internally synchronized free-running rhythms. *Sleep, 7,* 27–51.

Wittmann, M., Dinich, J., Merrow, M., & Roenneberg, T. (2006). Social jetlag: Misalignment of biological and social time. *Chronobiology International, 23*, 497–509. http://dx.doi.org/10.1080/07420520500545979

Wolf, R. B., Kassim, A. A., Goodpaster, R. L., & DeBaun, M. R. (2014). Nocturnal enuresis in sickle cell disease. *Expert Review of Hematology, 7*, 245–254. http://dx.doi.org/10.1586/17474086.2014.892412

Wolfson, A. R., & Carskadon, M. A. (1998). Sleep schedules and daytime functioning in adolescents. *Child Development, 69*, 875–887. http://dx.doi.org/10.1111/j.1467-8624.1998.tb06149.x

Wood, B., Rea, M. S., Plitnick, B., & Figueiro, M. G. (2013). Light level and duration of exposure determine the impact of self-luminous tablets on melatonin suppression. *Applied Ergonomics, 44*, 237–240. http://dx.doi.org/10.1016/j.apergo.2012.07.008

Wyatt, J. K. (2011). Circadian rhythm sleep disorders. *Pediatric Clinics of North America, 58*, 621–635. http://dx.doi.org/10.1016/j.pcl.2011.03.014

Index

About the Authors

Lisa J. Meltzer, PhD, CBSM, is an associate professor of pediatrics at National Jewish Health. She received her doctorate in clinical and health psychology from the University of Florida, and she completed her clinical internship and postdoctoral fellowship at the Children's Hospital of Philadelphia. She was selected as a Pickwick Postdoctoral Fellow in Sleep Research by the National Sleep Foundation, studying sleep patterns in parents of children with chronic illnesses. Dr. Meltzer is board certified in behavioral sleep medicine by the American Board of Sleep Medicine, and she directs both the Pediatric Behavioral Sleep Clinic and the Actigraphy Program at National Jewish Health. She also has a funded program of research examining sleep in children with chronic illnesses and their parents, the impact of deficient sleep on health outcomes in adolescents with asthma, as well as the development and validation of objective and subjective measures of pediatric sleep.

Valerie McLaughlin Crabtree, PhD, CBSM, is an assistant faculty member in the Department of Psychology at St. Jude Children's Research Hospital. She received her doctorate in counseling psychology from the University of Southern Mississippi and completed her internship and postdoctoral fellowship at the University of Louisville School of

Medicine. Dr. Crabtree is board certified in behavioral sleep medicine by the American Board of Sleep Medicine and directs the psychology clinic and psychology training programs at St. Jude. Her clinical work and research are focused on sleep in children and adolescents with cancer.